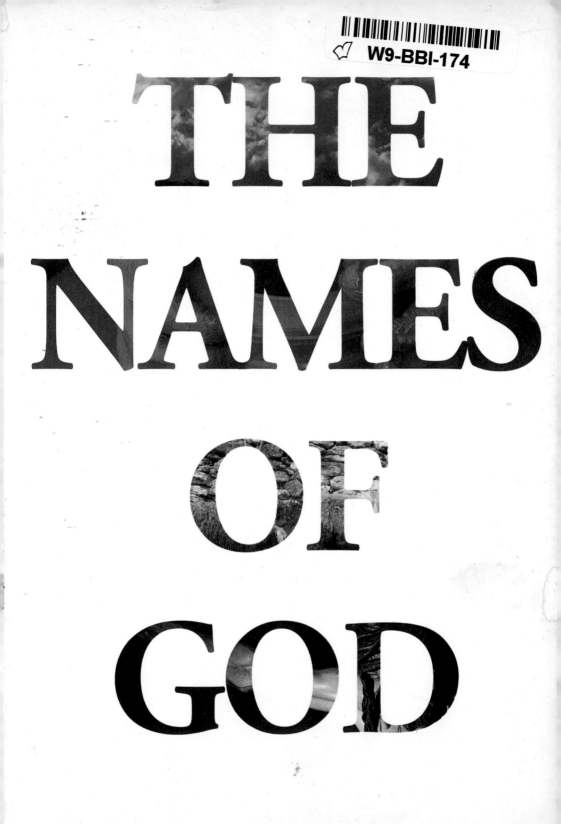

THE NAMES OF GOD

THE NAMES OF GOD

GEORGE W. KNIGHT

BARBOUR
PUBLISHING

© 2009 by George W. Knight

ISBN 978-1-60260-343-1

Published by Barbour Publishing, Inc., P.O. Box 719, Uhrichsville, Ohio 44683, www.barbourbooks.com

Our mission is to publish and distribute inspirational products offering exceptional value and biblical encouragement to the masses.

 Member of the
Evangelical Christian
Publishers Association

Printed in the United States of America.

PART 1 Names of God the Father

CONTENTS

PART 2 Names of God the Son

CONTENTS

CONTENTS

PART 3 Names of God the Holy Spirit

A Book of Names

A friend recently asked me what project I was working on. When I told him I was writing a book on the divine names in the Bible—those of the Father, the Son, and the Holy Spirit—he said, "That's great, but I wonder how you will ever fill up a book with just those three names."

Like my friend, many people are surprised to learn that there are many names assigned to God the Father, God the Son, and God the Holy Spirit in the Bible. I have covered only the major ones here in this book—and the number still comes to more than 250. The three Persons of the Trinity are so exalted in Their glory that it takes multiple names to describe who They are and the work They perform in the world.

Writing this book opened my eyes to a new and exciting way to study God's Word. I had studied the Bible in all the traditional ways—by focusing with intensity on each book, by exploring major subjects and themes, and by examining the lives of Bible personalities. But I had not spent as much time concentrating on the divine names contained in scripture. When I did, it changed some of my preconceived ideas, enriched my theological understanding, and gave me a new appreciation for the awesome God we serve. My prayer is that this book will guide you to the same experience.

I also discovered that many of the divine names in the Bible have been immortalized in the great old hymns of the church. Often when I was musing over a name, the words of a hymn that incorporated that name would come to mind. For example, Martin Luther's "A Mighty Fortress Is Our God" fits the prophet Jeremiah's description of God as our Fortress (see Jeremiah 16:19 and *Fortress* in part 1, Names of God the Father). This connection between names and hymns was so natural that I decided to use words from some of these hymns as sidebars alongside the corresponding names throughout the book. This added feature may bring back some fond memories of the great Christian hymns we used to sing more often than we do today.

The book falls naturally into three sections: names of God the Father, God the Son, and God the Holy Spirit. The names in each section are arranged alphabetically. At the back of the book, you will find a handy scripture index, arranged from Genesis through Revelation, that will help you find the Bible passages where these names occur.

In compiling the names for this book, I used the familiar King James Version of the Bible. But alternate names from four modern translations—the Holman Christian Standard Bible, the New American Standard Bible, the New International Version, and the New Revised Standard Version—are also included and cross-referenced to the KJV names.

You may be surprised at how these modern translations follow the KJV rendering in many places. But your understanding will be enriched by their different translations of other names. For example, the KJV's *Daysman* as a name for Jesus is rendered as *Umpire* by the NASB and the NRSV, and as *Someone to Arbitrate* by the NIV. Thus, the idea suggested by this name is that Jesus serves like a referee or impartial judge who speaks to God the Father on our behalf.

My thanks to Paul Muckley of Barbour Publishing for challenging me to write this book. The discipline it required made me a better person. It stretched my mental faculties further than I thought they could go. And it deepened my commitment to our Savior Jesus Christ, who was exalted by God the Father and "given. . .a name which is above every name" (Philippians 2:9).

George W. Knight
Nashville

PART 1

Names of God the Father

The Bible declares that God is a unique, one-of-a-kind being. No idea, object, or person is comparable to Him. His various names show that He is at work in the world and in the lives of Christians.

As the Creator, God brought the world into being. Before anything existed, He was. He is all-powerful, stronger than any force in the universe. He never changes, and He is present everywhere at one and the same time. Because there is no place where God is not, He knows everything about us. It is impossible for humans to hide their thoughts and actions from Him.

God has certain moral attributes that define His character. He is holy, righteous, loving, and wise. All these truths about Him are illustrated by the following seventy-three names assigned to Him in the Bible.

ABBA, FATHER

> And he said, **Abba, Father**, all things are possible unto thee; take away this cup from me: nevertheless not what I will, but what thou wilt.
>
> MARK 14:36

This is the name by which Jesus the Son addressed God the Father in His agonizing prayer in the Garden of Gethsemane. *Abba* is an Aramaic word of affection for "father," similar in meaning to *Papa* in English.

The Jews generally avoided such affectionate terms for God. They thought of Him as an exalted and larger-than-life being who demanded respect. He was to be spoken of in hushed reverence, rather than addressed as if He were a member of the family.

A child's love of their father can mirror Christians' love for God the Father.

But it was appropriate for Jesus to address the Father as "Abba." As God's Son, Jesus knew Him more intimately than anyone has ever known God. Jesus Himself declared, "As the Father knoweth me, even so know I the Father" (John 10:15).

Through Jesus' death on the cross, He made it possible for us to know God as a loving, forgiving Father. The apostle Paul declares, "Because ye are sons, God hath sent forth the Spirit of his Son into your hearts, crying, Abba, Father" (Galatians 4:6).

ALMIGHTY GOD

> And when Abram was ninety years old and nine, the LORD appeared to Abram, and said unto him, I am the **Almighty God**; walk before me, and be thou perfect [NIV: blameless].
>
> GENESIS 17:1

God had already promised Abraham that He would make his descendants a great nation and give them a land of their own (see Genesis 12:1–3; 13:15–17). But Abraham had no son through whom this promise could be fulfilled. The Lord, by identifying Himself as the Almighty God in this verse, declared to Abraham that He had the power to make this happen.

The Hebrew words behind this compound name also express the idea of plenty. Some interpreters suggest that they may be rendered as "the All-Sufficient One" or "the All-Bountiful One." God not only has the power to bless His people, but He will also do so abundantly. The apostle Paul put it like this: God is "able to do exceeding abundantly above all that we ask or think" (Ephesians 3:20).

Other titles of God that express the same idea as Almighty God are Lord Almighty (2 Corinthians 6:18), Lord God Almighty (Revelation 15:3), Lord God Omnipotent (Revelation 19:6), Mighty God (Jeremiah 32:18), Mighty One of Israel (Isaiah 1:24), Mighty One of Jacob (Isaiah 49:26), and Most Mighty (Psalm 45:3).

ANCIENT OF DAYS

This name of God is used only by the prophet Daniel (see Daniel 7:13, 22). He had a vision of four world empires that rose to great power and prominence, only to eventually fall and crumble into insignificance.

In contrast to the short shelf life of these world powers is One who has always existed and always will. Daniel's use of the imagery of old age to describe God suggests His eternalness. Unlike humans and worldly affairs, the Ancient of Days is not limited by time. Everything around us changes, but He remains the same. The only real security we have in this world is to place our trust in the Ancient of Days.

King of Old, a title used by the psalmist (see Psalm 74:12), expresses basically the same idea about God as Ancient of Days.

> I beheld till the thrones were cast down, and the **Ancient of days** did sit, whose garment was white as snow, and the hair of his head like the pure wool: his throne was like the fiery flame, and his wheels as burning fire.
> DANIEL 7:9
> [NRSV: **Ancient One**]

Praise for the Ancient of Days

In his hymn "Immortal, Invisible," Walter Chalmers Smith expresses exuberant praise for the Lord as the Ancient of Days.

Immortal, invisible, God only wise,
In light inaccessible hid from our eyes,
Most blessed, most glorious, the Ancient of Days,
Almighty, victorious, Thy great name we praise.

BEAUTIFUL CROWN. See *Crown of Glory/ Diadem of Beauty.*

BEAUTIFUL WREATH. See *Crown of Glory/ Diadem of Beauty.*

BUCKLER

A buckler was a small shield that warriors wore on their arms. It was a defensive weapon that protected them from the thrusts of swords and spears in hand-to-hand combat. To the psalmist, the Lord was like a buckler because He shielded him from the harsh words and savage attacks of his enemies.

According to the writer of Proverbs, God is also "a buckler to them that walk uprightly" (Proverbs 2:7). God promises protection for His people if we trust in Him and follow His commands.

As for God, his way is perfect: the word of the LORD is tried: he is a **buckler** to all those that trust in him.
PSALM 18:30
[NASB, NIV, NRSV: **shield**]

Assyrian bronze shield from the eighth century BC. It was easy for people in Bible times to understand God as a "buckler" or shield since they were used to seeing them worn by the armies of the day.

CONSUMING FIRE

God is often associated with fire in the Bible. Sometimes fire symbolizes His guidance and protection. For example, He spoke to Moses from a burning bush (see Exodus 3:2). He guided the Israelites through the wilderness at night by a pillar of fire (see Exodus 13:21).

Wherefore we receiving a kingdom which cannot be moved, let us have grace, whereby we may serve God acceptably with reverence and godly fear: For our God is a **consuming fire**.
HEBREWS 12:28–29

But this verse from the book of Hebrews shows that fire is also a symbol of God's wrath. To those who are disrespectful or disobedient, He is a searing flame of judgment. Every person must decide for himself whether the Lord will be a guiding light or a consuming fire in his life.

CREATOR

The prophet Isaiah was amazed that the people of Judah had rejected the one true God and were worshipping false gods instead. The Creator God had brought the universe into being by the power of His word (Hebrews 11:3). These pagan idols were weak and puny by comparison.

From the first chapter of the Bible, we learn several important truths about God's creation of the world and its inhabitants. (1) He created the world from nothing; He is the ultimate cause of all that exists. (2) The Creation was accomplished in orderly fashion, in six successive days. This means that God has placed order and design into the universe. (3) Man is the crown of God's creation. (4) The Lord has given us the responsibility to take care of His world.

As Isaiah reminded the people of his nation, only the one-and-only Creator God is worthy of our loyalty and worship.

Hast thou not known? hast thou not heard, that. . . the **Creator** of the ends of the earth fainteth not, neither is weary? there is no searching of his understanding [NIV: his understanding no one can fathom].
ISAIAH 40:28

The expanse of all creation reveals the power of our Creator.

CREATOR OF ISRAEL

> I am the LORD, your Holy One, the **creator of Israel**, your King.
> ISAIAH 43:15
> [NIV: **Israel's Creator**]

Through the prophet Isaiah, the Lord made it clear why the nation of Israel existed. They had been created by God Himself to serve as His agents of redemption to the rest of the world. This had been revealed centuries before Isaiah's time when the Lord told Abraham, "I will make of thee a great nation. . .and in thee shall all families of the earth be blessed" (Genesis 12:2–3).

But over and over again, the Israelites forgot the reason for their existence. They tended to think they deserved God's special blessing because of their cultural traditions and moral superiority. They had to be reminded constantly of the purpose of the One who was the Creator of Israel.

God, through His Son Jesus Christ, is still in the business of creating a special kingdom of people for Himself. It's known as the church. But our purpose is not to celebrate our favored status as believers. We should be about the task of helping others come to know Jesus as Lord and Savior.

Other "Israel" Names of the Creator of Israel

- God of Israel (Matthew 15:31)
- Holy One of Israel (Psalm 78:41)
- Hope of Israel (Jeremiah 14:7–8)
- Judge of Israel (Micah 5:1)
- Light of Israel (Isaiah 10:17)
- Lord God of Israel (1 Kings 8:23)
- Redeemer of Israel (Isaiah 49:7)
- Rock of Israel (2 Samuel 23:3)
- Stone of Israel (Genesis 49:24)
- Strength of Israel (1 Samuel 15:29)

CROWN OF GLORY/DIADEM OF BEAUTY

Isaiah 28 contains a prediction that Israel's sin will cause it to be overrun by an enemy nation. But God has a special "residue," or remnant, of people who will avoid His judgment because of their faithfulness to Him. God will be a Crown of Glory to these obedient ones. They will share in His character—His holiness, righteousness, and justice.

God will also reward this obedient remnant by giving

them a *Diadem of Beauty*. A diadem was a band around the head of a king that symbolized his royal authority. We as Christians wear a diadem of sorts—our salvation. This shows to the world that we belong to the Lord and that He has commissioned us to serve as His witnesses in the world.

This copper crown, over 5,000 years old, was discovered near the Dead Sea. It represented religious or royal authority in its day.

In that day shall the Lord of hosts be for a **crown of glory**, and for a **diadem of beauty**, unto the residue [NASB, NIV: remnant] of his people.
Isaiah 28:5
[NASB: **beautiful crown/glorious diadem**; NIV: **glorious crown/beautiful wreath**; NRSV: **garland of glory/diadem of beauty**]

DELIVERER

Deliverer is a name for God that was used often by David, as he does in this psalm. Perhaps it was one of his favorite divine names (see Psalms 18:2; 40:17; 2 Samuel 22:2) because he had experienced God as Deliverer many times throughout his life.

For example, David escaped several attempts by King Saul to kill him (see 1 Samuel 18:10–11; 19:11–12; 23:24–28). Before facing Goliath, the Philistine giant, this shepherd boy who later became the king of Israel declared, "The Lord that delivered me out of the paw of the lion, and out of the paw of the bear, he will deliver me out of the hand of this

But I am poor and needy: make haste unto me [NIV: come quickly to me], O God: thou art my help and my **deliverer**; O Lord, make no tarrying [NIV: do not delay].
Psalm 70:5

Philistine" (1 Samuel 17:37). David prevailed over the giant because of his faith in the divine Deliverer.

God may not choose to deliver us from every danger in this life. But He has provided ultimate deliverance from sin and death through the death of His Son for all who believe.

DIADEM OF BEAUTY. See *Crown of Glory/Diadem of Beauty.*

DWELLING PLACE

This psalm may be the oldest in the entire book of Psalms, because it is attributed to Moses (see title above this psalm), who led the Israelites during their years of wandering in the wilderness. This was a time, before they settled in Canaan, when they did not have permanent houses. They lived in tents, which they moved from place to place (see Numbers 9:17; Joshua 3:14).

In spite of their spartan living arrangements, they still thought of God as their ultimate Dwelling Place. His presence followed them wherever they moved, and His faithfulness continued from one generation to the next.

God is still a Dwelling Place for His people. Whether we live in a mobile home or a mansion, we find in Him all the joys and comforts of home.

> Lord, thou hast been our **dwelling place** in [NIV: throughout] all generations.
> PSALM 90:1

Modern-day Bedouins' nomadic lifestyle recalls the experience of the Israelites in the wilderness.

EL-ROI. See *God Who Sees.*

ETERNAL GOD. See *Everlasting God.*

EVERLASTING GOD

Abraham had moved from place to place for several years in the land of Canaan, the territory that God had promised to his descendants (see Genesis 12:1–5). Finally, he decided to make a site known as Beersheba the center of the territory where he would graze his flocks and herds. There he dug a well and planted a grove of trees to mark the site as his settling-down place.

At Beersheba, it was appropriate that Abraham call on

the name of the Everlasting God, the One without beginning and end, who would never cease to be. He would guide Abraham into the future and fulfill His promise that Abraham's offspring would eventually populate this entire region.

God kept His promise, but it took a while. It was more than five centuries after Abraham's time before the Israelites conquered this land and made it their own. We should remember that the Everlasting God does not watch the clock like we humans do.

EVERLASTING KING. See *King Eternal, Immortal, Invisible.*

And Abraham planted a grove in Beersheba, and called there on the name of the LORD, the **everlasting God**.
GENESIS 21:33
[NIV: **Eternal God**]

A grove of tamarisk trees in modern-day Beersheba—perhaps like Abraham saw when settling this area of the Negev.

> But now, O LORD,
> thou art our **father**;
> we are the clay,
> and thou our potter;
> and we all are the
> work of thy hand.
> ISAIAH 64:8

FATHER

In this verse, the prophet Isaiah declares that God has a role in shaping His people, just as earthly fathers participate in the creative process of bringing children into the world.

This is one of the few places in the Old Testament where God is referred to as *Father* (see also Deuteronomy 32:6; Psalm 89:26; Isaiah 63:16; Malachi 2:10). By contrast, *Father* as a name for God occurs often in the New Testament, particularly on the lips of Jesus (e.g., Matthew 26:39; Luke 23:34; John 17:1).

People of Old Testament times generally did not think of God in fatherly terms. To them, He was an all-powerful being who stood above and beyond the relationships and events of everyday life. It took Jesus to show us that God is a loving Father: "For God so loved the world, that he gave his only begotten Son, that whosoever believeth in him should not perish, but have everlasting life" (John 3:16).

FATHER OF COMPASSION. See *Father of Mercies.*

FATHER OF GLORY

> That the God of our
> Lord Jesus Christ, the
> **Father of glory**,
> may give unto you
> the spirit of wisdom
> and revelation in the
> knowledge of him.
> EPHESIANS 1:17

Ephesians 1 is the only place in the Bible where God is called the Father of Glory. The apostle Paul used this name in his assurance to the believers at Ephesus that he was praying to the Father on their behalf.

The word *glory* appears many times throughout the Bible, usually in reference to God's splendor, moral beauty, and perfection. At times, His glory was revealed visibly, as

Beautiful sunsets such as this one over the mountains of Edom reveal the splendor of God's creation.

in the tabernacle and temple after they were built (see Exodus 40:34; 1 Kings 8:11). The prophet Isaiah declares of the Lord, "The whole earth is full of his glory" (Isaiah 6:3). Or, to put it another way, the beauty and majesty of the physical world gives evidence of God's presence in His creation.

God the Father is also referred to in the Old Testament as the Crown of Glory (see Isaiah 28:5). In his long speech before his persecutors, Stephen in New Testament times also referred to Him as the God of Glory (see Acts 7:2).

Other Manifestations of God's Glory
- To Moses, on Mount Sinai, when God revealed His plan for the tabernacle (Exodus 24:16–17)
- To the world at the coming of the Messiah (Isaiah 40:4–5; 60:1)
- To the prophet Ezekiel, as he ministered among Jewish exiles in Babylon (Ezekiel 3:22–23)
- To the shepherds at the announcement of the birth of Jesus (Luke 2:9)

FATHER OF LIGHTS

With this name of God, James probably had in mind the creation account in the book of Genesis. On the fourth day, God created the sun, moon, and stars and "set them in the firmament of the heaven to give light upon the earth" (Genesis 1:17).

The people of many ancient cultures thought of the heavenly bodies as gods. But James declared that they were created things, brought into being by the one true God of the universe. Only the Father of Lights is worthy of worship.

This God who created the light-giving bodies of the heavens is also dependable and trustworthy. As the NIV translates it, God "does not change like shifting shadows." His presence is an unwavering light that guides His people throughout this life and beyond.

> Every good gift and every perfect gift is from above, and cometh down from the **Father of lights**, with whom is no variableness, neither shadow of turning [NIV: who does not change like shifting shadows].
> JAMES 1:17
> [NIV: **Father of the heavenly lights**]

FATHER OF MERCIES

Father of Mercies is another of the apostle Paul's names for God that appears in only one verse in the Bible (see also Father of Glory). In this case, he used *Father of Mercies* in his prayer for the believers in the church he founded at Corinth.

God is the Father of Mercies because He has mercy on

Blessed be God,
even the Father of
our Lord Jesus Christ,
the **Father of
mercies**, and the
God of all comfort.
2 CORINTHIANS 1:3
[NIV: **Father of
compassion**]

His people. If He withheld His mercy and grace, and gave
us exactly what we deserved, we would be destitute and lost,
hopelessly trapped by our sin and rebellion. But His love and
patience won't let us go. He keeps calling us back into His
presence by extending His mercy and forgiveness.

Because God is the originator—or Father—of Mercies,
He expects His people to show this attribute of His character
to others. Jesus declared, "Be ye therefore merciful, as your
Father also is merciful" (Luke 6:36).

FATHER OF OUR LORD JESUS CHRIST

This name of God used by the apostle Paul draws attention
to the miraculous birth of Jesus the Son. Jesus did not have a
human father, but was miraculously conceived in the womb
of Mary by God the Father, acting through the Holy Spirit
(see Luke 1:34–35).

We give thanks to
God and the **Father
of our Lord Jesus
Christ**, praying
always for you.
COLOSSIANS 1:3

Jesus was sent by God to fulfill the Father's work of
redemption in the world. When He was only twelve years
old, Jesus stated that this was His divine mission (see Luke
2:48–49). His declaration from the cross, "It is finished"
(John 19:30), shows that He accomplished the purpose for
which He was sent—our salvation.

God Shows He Is Pleased with His Son

- "And there came a voice from heaven, saying, Thou art my beloved Son, in whom I am well pleased" (Mark 1:11).
- "And the Holy Ghost descended in a bodily shape like a dove upon him, and a voice came from heaven, which said, Thou art my beloved Son; in thee I am well pleased" (Luke 3:22).
- "For it pleased the Father that in him should all fulness dwell" (Colossians 1:19).
- "For he received from God the Father honour and glory, when there came such a voice to him from the excellent glory, This is my beloved Son, in whom I am well pleased" (2 Peter 1:17).

FATHER OF OUR SPIRITS. See *Father of Spirits.*

FATHER OF SPIRITS

This is one of those places in the Bible where the addition
of one word makes all the difference in its meaning. Rather
than "Father of spirits," the NIV renders this name of God as

"Father of Our Spirits." This rendering makes it clear that the writer of Hebrews was contrasting physical fathers ("fathers of our flesh") with God as our Father in a spiritual sense.

Earthly fathers discipline their children and teach them right from wrong and respect for others. God, our spiritual Father, teaches us to obey Him as the ultimate authority, to follow His commands, and to present our lives as living sacrifices for His honor and glory. The next verse in the NIV puts it like this: "Our fathers disciplined us for a little while as they thought best; but God disciplines us for our good, that we may share in his holiness" (Hebrews 12:10 NIV).

FATHER OF HEAVENLY LIGHTS. See *Father of Lights.*

FIRE. See *Consuming Fire; Wall of Fire.*

FORTRESS

A fortress was any heavily guarded or fortified place that provided protection from enemy attacks. In Bible times, a defensive wall around a city, with its reinforced towers and gates, was considered the ultimate fortress.

In this verse, Jeremiah portrays the Lord as his Fortress. The prophet's unpopular message that Judah would fall to its enemies subjected him to ridicule, imprisonment, and

> We have had fathers of our flesh [NIV: human fathers] which corrected us, and we gave them reverence [NIV: respected them]: shall we not much rather be in subjection unto [NIV: submit to] the **Father of spirits**, and live?
> HEBREWS 12:9
> [NIV: **Father of our spirits**]

> O LORD, my strength and my **fortress**, and my refuge in the day of affliction [NIV: distress].
> JEREMIAH 16:19
> [NASB, NRSV: **stronghold**]

The fortress ruins of Arad in southern Israel provide us with a visual image of what the prophet might have thought of when he wrote that the Lord was his fortress (Jeremiah 16:19).

charges of treason. At the beginning of Jeremiah's ministry, God promised that He would make him "a defenced city, and an iron pillar, and brasen walls against the whole land" (Jeremiah 1:18). The Lord had made good on His promise.

Like Jeremiah, all of us need a fortress at times. This advice from Peter can help us hang in there when troubles seem to fall from the sky like the spring rain: "Cast all your anxiety on him because he cares for you" (1 Peter 5:7 NIV).

Martin Luther's Fortress

The hymn "A Mighty Fortress Is Our God" was written by Martin Luther during the turbulent years of the Protestant Reformation in the 1500s. His faith in God in spite of the threats against his life have inspired generations of Christians.

A mighty fortress is our God,
A bulwark never failing;
Our helper He, amid the flood
Of mortal ills prevailing.
Let goods and kindred go,
This mortal life also;
The body they may kill:
God's truth abideth still,
His kingdom is forever.

For my people have committed two evils; they have forsaken me the **fountain of living waters**, and hewed them out cisterns [NIV: dug their own cisterns], broken cisterns, that can hold no water.
JEREMIAH 2:13
[NIV: **spring of living water**]

FOUNTAIN OF LIVING WATERS

This name of God appears in Jeremiah's prophecy in connection with the Lord's condemnation of the people of Judah for their idolatry (see also Jeremiah 17:13). God found it hard to believe that they had rejected the waters of a flowing spring (that is, worship of the one true God) and instead chose to drink stagnant water from a broken cistern (by worshipping the untrustworthy and powerless gods of surrounding pagan nations).

This situation is not unique to Jeremiah's time. When we allow anything besides God to take first place in our lives, it's like drinking contaminated water from a muddy pond. God wants only the best for us. He gives water in abundance from "the fountain of the water of life" to all who will come and drink (Revelation 21:6).

The flowing waters at En Gedi near the Dead Sea. The Lord provides the waters of life even in wilderness areas.

GARLAND OF GLORY. See *Crown of Glory/ Diadem of Beauty.*

GLORIOUS CROWN. See *Crown of Glory/ Diadem of Beauty.*

GLORIOUS DIADEM. See *Crown of Glory/ Diadem of Beauty.*

GOD MOST HIGH. See *Most High God.*

GOD MY SAVIOUR. See *God of My Salvation.*

GOD OF ABRAHAM, ISAAC, AND JACOB

God used this name for Himself when He called Moses to lead the Israelites out of slavery in Egypt. The Lord assured Moses that He had promised the land of Canaan to Abraham and his descendants many years before. He had not changed; He was the same God who would finally lead the Israelites to

The LORD God of your fathers, the **God of Abraham,** the God of **Isaac,** and the God of **Jacob**, hath sent me unto you: this is my name for ever, and this is my memorial unto all generations.
EXODUS 3:15

take this land and make it their own.

This promise had originally been made to Abraham, then renewed with Abraham's son Isaac, and then renewed again with Isaac's son Jacob. In Moses' time, this promise had been all but forgotten. The Israelites had been in Egypt for more than four hundred years, suffering as slaves for part of that time (see Exodus 12:40).

The message of this divine name is that God keeps His promises. Their fulfillment may take a while, but God will make good on what He says He will do for His people.

GOD OF ALL COMFORT

The context of this verse makes it clear that when the apostle Paul spoke of the Lord as the God of All Comfort, he was thinking of the sufferings that believers endure. We as Christians are often ridiculed by the world for our beliefs and the stands we take. But our persecution should not lead us to despair. God's comforting presence will enable us to remain joyful and optimistic in spite of our hurt (see James 1:2).

Because we know and feel God's comfort, we are expected to channel this comfort to others. Paul declares in the next verse of this passage that we should "comfort them which are in any trouble, by the comfort wherewith we ourselves are comforted of God" (2 Corinthians 1:4).

GOD OF ALL CONSOLATION. See *God of All Comfort*.

GOD OF GLORY. See *Father of Glory*.

GOD OF GODS

King Nebuchadnezzar of Babylon had a disturbing dream about a huge statue. None of his pagan priests or magicians could interpret the dream. But the Hebrew prophet Daniel told him what the dream meant, after declaring that it would be revealed to him by the one true God.

The pagan king was so impressed by this interpretation of his dream that he declared Daniel's God to be the God of gods—or the God above all the other deities in the kingdom of Babylon. This was a shocking admission, because the Babylonians had a god for every need and purpose—war, fertility, science, literature, etc. This type of worship was typical

---

Blessed be God, even the Father of our Lord Jesus Christ, the Father of mercies, and the **God of all comfort**.
2 CORINTHIANS 1:3
[NRSV: **God of all consolation**]

The king answered unto Daniel, and said, Of a truth [NIV: Surely] it is, that your God is a **God of gods**, and a Lord of kings, and a revealer of secrets [NIV: mysteries], seeing thou couldest reveal this secret [NIV: mystery].
DANIEL 2:47

of all the pagan nations during Bible times.

As Christians, we know that God is capable of mighty acts. But sometimes He amazes even unbelievers with His awesome deeds.

GOD OF HEAVEN

This verse describes Nehemiah's reaction when he heard disturbing news about the Jewish exiles who had returned to their homeland. The Persian king had allowed the people to return to rebuild the city of Jerusalem. But the work was at a standstill, and the Jews were being persecuted by their enemies.

Nehemiah's name for God in this verse—God of Heaven—appears several times in his book (see Nehemiah 1:5; 2:4, 20) as well as in the book of Ezra (see Ezra 5:12; 6:9–10; 7:21, 23). These two books describe the bleak conditions of God's people after the Exile. They had lived for almost seventy years as captives of the pagan nations of Babylon and Persia. They had to start life all over again when they were finally allowed to return to their homeland.

Perhaps the Israelites had a hard time seeing God at work in their midst during these turbulent times. But Ezra and Nehemiah assured them that God was still in His heaven and had not forsaken His people.

When you feel lonely and forgotten, try addressing a prayer to the God of Heaven—the One who has an unobstructed view of everything that is happening on the earth. This should assure you that He is watching over you.

And it came to pass, when I heard these words, that I sat down and wept, and mourned certain days, and fasted, and prayed before the **God of heaven**.
Nehemiah 1:4

This historical record known as the Cyrus cylinder describes the decree of the Persian king, Cyrus (539 BC), who granted the Jewish exiles permission to return to their homeland.

GOD OF ISRAEL. See *Creator of Israel.*

GOD OF JACOB. See *Mighty One of Jacob.*

GOD OF MY SALVATION

This passage from the little-known prophet Habakkuk is one of the most beautiful in the Bible. It is filled with agricultural imagery from the prophet's time, including crop failures and the loss of livestock. But Habakkuk's faith allowed him to see beyond the troubles of the moment to the deeper reality that the God of Salvation was in charge. He would not let him down.

Rephrased in modern terms, Habakkuk's sentiments might read something like this: "Although the grocery money is gone, energy prices are going through the ceiling, my mortgage payment just jumped by four hundred dollars a month, and I don't know where the next meal is coming from, I will rejoice in the Lord and continue to trust in the God of My Salvation."

> Although the fig tree shall not blossom, neither shall fruit be in the vines; the labour of the olive shall fail, and the fields shall yield no meat; the flock shall be cut off from the fold, and there shall be no herd in the stalls: Yet I will rejoice in the Lord, I will joy in the **God of my salvation**.
> HABAKKUK 3:17–18
> [NIV: **God my Savior**]

Our Faithful God

God's faithfulness to His people is celebrated in the hymn "Great Is Thy Faithfulness," written by Thomas O. Chisholm.

> Great is Thy faithfulness, O God my Father;
> There is no shadow of turning with thee;
> Thou changest not, Thy compassions, they fail not;
> As thou hast been, Thou forever wilt be.
> Great is Thy faithfulness! Great is Thy faithfulness!
> Morning by morning new mercies I see;
> All I have needed Thy hand hath provided;
> Great is Thy faithfulness, Lord, unto me!

GOD OF PEACE

The author of the epistle to the Hebrews brought his book to a close with a request for the blessings of the God of Peace to rest upon His people. This is one of the most beautiful benedictions in the Bible.

Some people think of peace as the absence of conflict. But peace according to the New Testament is the inner tranquillity of those who have placed their trust in Jesus Christ and have been reconciled to God because their sins have been forgiven.

The Lord is the God of Peace because He sent His own Son to make it possible for us to experience this sense of well-being. This is how the apostle Paul expresses it: "Therefore being justified by faith, we have peace with God through our Lord Jesus Christ" (Romans 5:1).

GOD OF THE WHOLE EARTH

This name of God from the prophet Isaiah emphasizes His unlimited jurisdiction. There is no place on earth where His authority is limited. This idea is just the opposite of the view of most pagan nations of Bible times. They believed their gods were local or regional in scope. These deities existed to serve their needs and protect them from their enemies, so their authority as gods did not extend beyond national borders.

This is why Naaman, a Syrian military commander, wanted to carry dirt from Israel back to his country after he was healed by the prophet Elisha in Israelite territory (see 2 Kings 5:17). He thought this miracle-working God was a regional god whose power he could transfer to his own people.

The Lord's presence doesn't have to be carried back and forth from one country to another. He already exists in every place—the supreme God over all the world. The psalmist declares, "The earth is the Lord's, and the fulness thereof; the world, and they that dwell therein" (Psalm 24:1).

A "household" idol from modern-day Iraq, dating back to at least 1600 BC.

> Now the **God of peace**, that brought again from the dead our Lord Jesus. . . through the blood of the everlasting covenant, make you perfect in every good work [NIV: equip you with everything good] to do his will, working in you that which is wellpleasing in his sight, through Jesus Christ; to whom be glory for ever and ever. Amen.
> HEBREWS 13:20–21

> For thy Maker is thine husband; the LORD of hosts is his name; and thy Redeemer the Holy One of Israel; The **God of the whole earth** shall he be called.
> ISAIAH 54:5

Other Earth-Related Names of God the Father
- Judge of All the Earth (Genesis 18:25)
- King over All the Earth (Psalm 47:2)
- Lord of All the Earth (Joshua 3:13)
- Lord of the Whole Earth (Micah 4:13)
- Most High over All the Earth (Psalm 83:18)
- Possessor of Heaven and Earth (Genesis 14:19)

GOD THE FATHER. See *Abba, Father; Father.*

GOD WHO SEES

Sarah's servant, Hagar, called God by this name when the angel of the Lord appeared to her in the wilderness. After conceiving a child by Abraham, she had been driven away by Sarah, Abraham's wife. The Lord assured Hagar that He was aware of her plight, and He would bless her and others through the life of her unborn child.

After Hagar gave birth to a son, she named him Ishmael, meaning "God hears." Hagar's experience shows us that the Lord is not a distant and detached God who refuses to get involved in our lives. He sees our needs, hears our prayers, and comes to our aid in our times of trouble.

And she called the name of the LORD that spake unto her, **Thou God seest me**: for she said, Have I also here looked after him [NIV: I have now seen the One] that seeth me?
GENESIS 16:13
[NRSV: **El-roi**]

Hagar encountered the Lord somewhere in the wilderness of Paran, pictured here. Despite such a vast expanse, the Lord sees us wherever we are.

GOVERNOR

The word *governor* appears often in the Bible as a designation for a ruler over a nation or a section of a nation. For example, Joseph was made a governor in Egypt (see Genesis 42:6), and Nehemiah held a similar position for a time in the nation of Judah (see Nehemiah 12:26).

But Psalm 22 is the only place in the Old Testament where this title is applied to God. Earthly rulers sometimes abuse their authority, but the Lord rules over the nations and

His people with righteousness and justice (see Nehemiah 9:32–33; Exodus 9:27).

In the New Testament, Jesus is also described as a Governor (Matthew 2:6). He is the perfect ruler who governs the spiritual kingdom to which all believers belong—the church.

GUIDE EVEN TO THE END. See *Guide unto Death*.

GUIDE FOREVER. See *Guide unto Death*.

GUIDE UNTO DEATH

The unknown author of this psalm made the same declaration that David did when he wrote the Twenty-third Psalm. God will abide with us and continue to lead us, even through the experience of death itself. As David expresses it, "Yea, though I walk through the valley of the shadow of death, I will fear no evil: for thou art with me" (Psalm 23:4).

The prophet Jeremiah spoke of God as "the guide of my youth" (Jeremiah 3:4). It is comforting to know that whether our life is just beginning or coming to an end, we can trust God as our never-failing Guide.

HIDING PLACE

This name of God appears in a psalm that is attributed to David. During his early years, David had to flee for his life because the jealous King Saul was trying to kill him. Once, he hid in a cave; he later wrote about this experience in one of his psalms (see 1 Samuel 22:1; Psalm 142).

> For the kingdom is the LORD's: and he is the **governor** among the nations. PSALM 22:28

> For this God is our God for ever and ever: he will be our **guide** even **unto death**. PSALM 48:14 [NRSV: **guide forever**; NIV: **guide even to the end**]

> Thou art my **hiding place**; thou shalt preserve [NIV: protect] me from trouble; thou shalt compass me about [NIV: surround me] with songs of deliverance. PSALM 32:7

David found hiding places from King Saul in the caves near En Gedi. David understood that while the terrain provided a physical hiding place, the Lord was the One who really kept him hidden from danger.

The problem with a physical hiding place is that it can't last forever. David eventually had to come out of his cave for food and water. But he found the Lord to be his ultimate Hiding Place. There's no safer place to be than under the protective hand of a loving, benevolent God.

HIGH TOWER. See *Strong Tower.*

HOLY ONE

> I am the LORD, your **Holy One**, the creator of Israel, your King.
> ISAIAH 43:15

This name of God, spoken by the Lord Himself, shows one of His most distinctive attributes—His holiness. The Hebrew word behind "holy" expresses the idea of separation. Thus God is separated from or exalted above all earthly things. We as humans are limited in our abilities and are subject to sin and death. But God is totally different and separate in His nature. He is perfect in His moral excellence.

The holiness of God is one of the major themes of the prophet Isaiah. At the beginning of his ministry, Isaiah had a vision of God in the temple. He was sitting on His throne, and winged seraphim (angelic messengers) were singing His praises: "Holy, holy, holy, is the LORD of hosts: the whole earth is full of his glory" (Isaiah 6:3).

This vision of the Holy One made Isaiah aware of his sin and unworthiness. But God seared his lips with a hot coal carried by one of the seraphim. This symbolized God's purging of the prophet's sin (see Isaiah 6:5). God's holiness and our sin are just as pronounced as they were in Isaiah's time; His forgiveness is still our only hope.

In addition to calling God the Holy One, Isaiah also refers to Him several times as the Holy One of Israel (see Isaiah 1:4; 12:6; 60:9) and the Holy One of Jacob (see Isaiah 29:23).

Holy to the Third Degree

The repetition of the word *holy* in Isaiah 6:3 is reflected in the hymn "Holy, Holy, Holy," by Reginald Heber. The threefold repetition emphasizes this attribute of God's character.

Holy, holy, holy! tho' the darkness hide Thee,
Tho' the eye of sinful man Thy glory may not see;
Only Thou art holy; there is none beside Thee;
Perfect in power, in love, and purity.

HOLY ONE OF ISRAEL. See *Creator of Israel*; *Holy One*.

HOLY ONE OF JACOB. See *Holy One*; *Mighty One of Jacob*.

HOPE OF ISRAEL. See *Creator of Israel*.

HORN OF MY SALVATION

David wrote this psalm to express his praise to God for saving him from "all his enemies, and from the hand of Saul" (Psalm 18 NIV). In David's time, the horn of an animal was a symbol of strength. To lift one's horn in arrogance like an ox or a goat was to show pride and power (see Psalm 75:4–5). Thus, God had been a Horn of Salvation on David's behalf by delivering him from those who were trying to kill him.

This imagery from the Old Testament was picked up in the New Testament and applied to Jesus in a spiritual sense. Zacharias, the father of John the Baptist, declared that God, through His Son, had "raised up an horn of salvation for us in the house of his servant David" (Luke 1:69).

> The LORD is my rock, and my fortress, and my deliverer; my God, my strength, in whom I will trust; my buckler, and the **horn of my salvation**, and my high tower.
> PSALM 18:2

The majestic horns of the Ibex could have been an inspiration to David as he wrote Psalm 18.

HUSBAND

This name of God appears in connection with the prophet Jeremiah's description of the new covenant that God will make with His people. He had led them out of Egypt and through the wilderness like a loving husband cares for his family. But He would provide even more abundantly for His own by sending the Messiah, who would save them from their sins.

The role of a husband involves more than providing for the physical needs of his family. He should also be an encourager, a listener, an emotional support, and a protector for his wife and children. God as a loving Husband provides all of these things in abundance for His people.

> Behold, the days come, saith the LORD, that I will make a new covenant with the house of Israel, and with the house of Judah: Not according to the covenant that I made with their fathers in the day that I took them by the hand to bring them out of the land of Egypt; which my covenant they brake [NIV: broke], although I was an **husband** unto them, saith the LORD.
> JEREMIAH 31:31–32

I AM THAT I AM

And God said unto Moses, **I AM THAT I AM**: and he said, Thus shalt thou say unto the children of Israel [NIV: Israelites], I AM hath sent me unto you.
EXODUS 3:14
[NASB, NIV, NRSV: **I AM WHO I AM**]

When God appeared to Moses in a burning bush, Moses wanted to know who was sending him back to Egypt to lead the Israelites out of slavery. He may have been puzzled by the Lord's reply that I Am That I Am was behind this plan.

This name for God is a form of the verb "to be" in the Hebrew language. It expresses His self-existence and the unchangeableness of His character. He transcends the past, the present, and the future. We might express the meaning of this name like this: He has always been, He is, and He will always be.

This is the only place in the Bible where this name appears. But *Jehovah* or *Yahweh*, generally rendered as *Lord*, is a closely related name that also comes from the Hebrew form of "to be." This name appears hundreds of times throughout the Old Testament. In most translations of the Bible, it appears with a large capital *L* and smaller capital letters like this: LORD.

The great I Am never changes; he will never leave us or forsake us. The hymn writer Henry F. Lyte expressed this truth in the form of a prayer:

Change and decay in all around I see:
O Thou who changest not, abide with me!

Jebel Caterina—one of many mountains in the Sinai region thought to be associated with Mount Horeb. The Lord revealed Himself to Moses as "I AM" at Mount Horeb in this region of the Sinai Mountains.

I AM WHO I AM. See *I Am That I Am.*

ISRAEL'S CREATOR. See *Creator of Israel.*

JAH

Jah (pronounced *Yah*) is a shortened form of the Hebrew title *Jehovah* (see below), which is rendered as "Lord" in most English translations of the Bible. This is the only place where *Jah* appears in the King James Version of the Bible.

The word also appears as part of several compound biblical names. For example, the name Abijah means "whose father is Jehovah." The word *alleluiah* [NIV: *hallelujah*] means "praise the Lord" (see Revelation 19:1).

> Sing unto God, sing praises to his name: extol him that rideth upon the heavens [NIV: rides on the clouds] by his name **JAH**, and rejoice before him.
> PSALM 68:4
> [NASB, NIV, NRSV: **the LORD**]

JEHOVAH

With these words, the Lord reassured Moses that He would stand with him and give him the strength and power to lead the Israelites out of Egyptian slavery. He had already given Moses this promise at the burning bush (see Exodus 3:2, 12), but Moses needed encouragement after Pharaoh rejected his first request to release the Israelites.

God declared to Moses that He was prepared to perform miracles for His people that they had never seen before. As Jehovah, He was the infinite and self-existent God who caused everything to happen and to whom all things must eventually be traced. He would not fail in His determination to bring freedom to His people.

When God makes a promise, it's as good as done.

See also *I Am That I Am.*

> And I appeared unto Abraham, unto Isaac, and unto Jacob, by the name of God Almighty, but by my name **JEHOVAH** was I not known to them.
> EXODUS 6:3
> [NASB, NIV, NRSV: **the LORD**]

Guidance from Jehovah

In his hymn "Guide Me, O Thou Great Jehovah," Peter Williams asked God to provide for him, just as He had cared for the Israelites in the wilderness.

> Guide me, O Thou great Jehovah,
> Pilgrim through this barren land;
> I am weak, but Thou art mighty;
> Hold me with Thy powerful hand.

JEHOVAH-JIREH

And Abraham called the name of that place **Jehovah-jireh**: as it is said to this day, In the mount [NIV: mountain] of the LORD it shall be seen.
GENESIS 22:14
[NASB, NIV, NRSV: **The LORD Will Provide**]

Abraham called God by this name and assigned it to the site where God had told him to sacrifice his son, Isaac, as a burnt offering to the Lord. This was God's way of testing Abraham's faith and obedience.

When Abraham raised a knife to take Isaac's life, God stopped him. Then Abraham noticed a ram that had been trapped in a nearby thicket. He offered this ram as a sacrifice instead of Isaac. It was clear to him that God had provided the ram for this purpose—thus the name The Lord Will Provide, as rendered by modern translations.

God still delights in providing for His people. Whatever our needs, He will meet them through His love and grace.

Byzantine relief from Asia Minor depicting Abraham's willingness to sacrifice his son Isaac. This artistic representation helped people remember how the Lord provided a substitute ram for Abraham.

JEHOVAH-NISSI

And Moses built an altar, and called the name of it **Jehovah-nissi.**
EXODUS 17:15
[NASB, NIV, NRSV: **The LORD is my Banner**]

Moses gave this name to an altar that he built in the wilderness near Rephidim. The altar memorialized an Israelite victory over the Amalekites because of God's miraculous intervention on their behalf. Most modern translations render these two Hebrew words as The LORD Is My Banner.

In Bible times, armies fought under a banner or battle flag that identified their tribe or nation. *Jehovah-nissi* was Moses' way of saying that the Israelites in the wilderness did not need such a flag. The Lord was the banner under which they fought, and He had given the victory.

In a messianic passage in the book of Isaiah, the prophet looks forward to the coming of the Messiah, whom he describes as an *Ensign*, or battle flag (see Isaiah 11:10).

JEHOVAH-SHALOM

God gave Gideon the task of delivering His people from Midianite raiders who were destroying their crops and stealing their livestock. He assured Gideon of His presence and guidance by burning up a sacrificial offering that Gideon had placed on an altar.

This display frightened Gideon. But God showed him that His intentions were peaceful and that Gideon had nothing to fear. With this assurance, Gideon gave God a special name—translated as The Lord Is Peace by modern translations—and also applied this name to the altar he had built.

"Peace to you and your house" was a common greeting of Bible times, just as we greet people today with "Good morning" or "How are you?" With this divine name, Gideon expressed his confidence that God intended to bless him and to strengthen him for the task to which he had been called.

God extends this same promise to His people today. The psalmist declares, "The LORD will give strength unto his people; the LORD will bless his people with peace" (Psalm 29:11).

> And the LORD said unto him, Peace be unto thee; fear not: thou shalt not die. Then Gideon built an altar there unto the LORD, and called it **Jehovah-shalom**. JUDGES 6:23–24 [NASB, NIV, NRSV: **The LORD Is Peace**]

JUDGE

The clear teaching of this verse is that some people are worthy of positions of leadership and authority while others are not. God as Judge has the ability to tell the difference and to elevate one and demote the other.

Right and wrong, good and evil, often get so intermingled in this world that even the most discerning people can't tell the difference. But God is the ultimate dispenser of justice. He has the insight to separate the true from the false. He can be trusted to sort things out, reward the deserving, and punish the pretenders.

The Bible is filled with accounts of God's actions as Judge. For example, King Ahab of Israel and his wicked queen, Jezebel, cheated, lied, and enlisted false witnesses to have Naboth killed so they could take his vineyard (see 1 Kings 21:1–16). No earthly judge or civil court had the

> But God is the **judge**: he putteth down one [NIV: brings one down], and setteth up [NIV: exalts] another. PSALM 75:7

resolve or courage to bring this powerful couple to trial. But God had the last word in the matter.

King Ahab was killed by a stray arrow from an enemy soldier (see 1 Kings 22:34–40). Jezebel was tossed to her death from a window when Jehu took over the kingship (2 Kings 9:30–37). These events didn't happen immediately, but God's justice eventually prevailed—and it always does.

JUDGE OF ALL. See *Judge of All the Earth*.

JUDGE OF ALL THE EARTH

This name of God was spoken by Abraham when he talked with the Lord about His decision to destroy the city of Sodom because of its wickedness. Abraham believed that God was just in all His actions. Surely the Judge of All the Earth would not destroy the righteous people of Sodom along with the wicked.

God did follow through on His plan to destroy the city. But He sent an angel to warn the only righteous people in Sodom—Lot and his family—to flee before His judgment fell (see Genesis 19:1, 15–17). This proved that the Lord is fair and equitable in His work in the world as the righteous dispenser of justice.

Two related titles of God that express this same idea are Judge of the Earth (see Psalm 94:2) and Judge of All (see Hebrews 12:23).

> That be far from thee to do after this manner [NIV: Far be it from you to do such a thing], to slay the righteous with the wicked. . . . Shall not the **Judge of all the earth** do right?
> GENESIS 18:25

Remains of the city wall of Bab edh-Dhra, thought to be the ancient city of Sodom. The scant remains of where this sinful city once stood are a reminder of God as Judge over all evil on the earth.

JUDGE OF ISRAEL. See *Creator of Israel.*

JUDGE OF THE EARTH. See *Judge of All the Earth.*

JUST ONE. See *Most Upright.*

KEEPER

This is the only place in the Bible where God is referred to as our Keeper. This name refers to His protection, provision, and watchfulness. The NIV translates the phrase as "The LORD watches over you."

No matter where we are or what we are doing, God has His watchful eye on us. This is both comforting and disturbing. As the writer of Proverbs said, "The eyes of the LORD are in every place, beholding the evil and the good" (Proverbs 15:3).

> The LORD is thy **keeper**: the LORD is thy shade upon thy right hand.
> PSALM 121:5

KING

Samuel spoke these words to the leaders of Israel when they requested that he appoint a central political figure to rule over them. It was clear to Samuel that they were choosing poorly—turning away from God as their ruler and King to place their confidence in an earthly king.

The Lord is spoken of as King many times throughout the Bible. Kings of ancient times had unlimited authority. They were answerable to no one, and their word was considered the law of the land. When they died, their sons had the right to succeed them. Thus their influence and power were passed on from generation to generation.

But above all these political kings stands the ultimate King, the ruler of the universe. He alone is worthy of our worship and unquestioning obedience.

> And when ye saw that Nahash the king of the children of Ammon came against you, ye said unto me, Nay; but a king shall reign over us: when the LORD your God was your **king**.
> 1 SAMUEL 12:12

Bow Down Before the King
- "The LORD is King for ever and ever" (Psalm 10:16).
- "For the LORD. . .is a great King over all the earth" (Psalm 47:2).
- "Make a joyful noise before the LORD, the King" (Psalm 98:6).
- "Let the children of Zion be joyful in their King" (Psalm 149:2).
- "Then said I, Woe is me! for I am undone; because I am a man of unclean lips, and I dwell in the midst of a people of unclean lips: for mine eyes have seen the King, the LORD of hosts" (Isaiah 6:5).

KING ETERNAL, IMMORTAL, INVISIBLE

Now unto the **King eternal, immortal, invisible**, the only wise God, be honour and glory for ever and ever. Amen.
1 TIMOTHY 1:17
[NRSV: **King of the ages, immortal, invisible**]

This benediction from the apostle Paul in his first epistle to Timothy is the only place in the Bible where God is called by this name. The adjectives *eternal*, *immortal*, and *invisible* express three of His characteristics, or attributes.

God is eternal because He has always existed and He always will. Unlike man, who is mortal, God is not subject to sickness and death. And He is invisible, because He is a spiritual being who exists everywhere at the same time (see John 4:24).

The prophet Jeremiah also referred to God as the Everlasting King (Jeremiah 10:10). Both he and Paul were familiar with earthly kings who ruled for a few years and then were succeeded by other members of the royal family. Even the long reign of fifty-five years achieved by King Manasseh of Judah (see 2 Kings 21:1) is like the blink of an eye when compared to God's eternal kingship over the nations of the world.

KING OF GLORY

Lift up your heads, O ye gates; and be ye lift [NIV: lifted] up, ye everlasting doors; and the **King of glory** shall come in. Who is this **King of glory**? The LORD strong and mighty, the LORD mighty in battle. Lift up your heads, O ye gates; even lift them up, ye everlasting doors; and the **King of glory** shall come in. Who is this **King of glory**? The LORD of hosts, he is the **King of glory**.
PSALM 24:7–10

This is the only place in the Bible where God is called the King of Glory, and the name appears five times in these four verses. The title of the psalm ascribes authorship to David.

The exuberant joy of Psalm 24 leads some interpreters to speculate that it may have been sung when the ark of the covenant was moved to the city of Jerusalem in David's time. On this occasion, David "danced before the LORD" as trumpets sounded and the people shouted with joy (2 Samuel 6:14–15).

Two choirs, singing responsively, may have accompanied the ark. One choir sang, "Who is this King of glory?" And the other choir responded by identifying Him as Yahweh, the strong and mighty God of the Israelites.

As the King of Glory, God is worthy of our praise. The psalmist declares, "Not unto us, O LORD, not unto us, but unto thy name give glory" (Psalm 115:1).

KING OF OLD. See *Ancient of Days.*

KING OF JACOB. See *Mighty One of Jacob.*

David danced with joy before the Lord—the King of Glory—when the Ark of the Covenant (as modeled in this replica) was moved to Jerusalem.

KING OF THE AGES, IMMORTAL, INVISIBLE. See *King Eternal, Immortal, Invisible.*

KING OVER ALL THE EARTH. See *God of the Whole Earth.*

LAWGIVER

God revealed His Ten Commandments to Moses (see Exodus 20:1–17), a moral code to guide the behavior of His people. These laws are a good example of God's role as Lawgiver. God is sovereign over His creation, and He is the source of truth, righteousness, and holiness. He has the right to make the laws and set the standards by which people should live.

Many people have a strictly negative view of God's laws. They think of them only in binding and restrictive terms. But these laws are actually given for our benefit. Following God the Lawgiver's directives and commands is the key to joy and contentment in this life. The psalmist focuses on this positive side of God's laws when he declares, "You are good, and what you do is good; teach me your decrees" (Psalm 119:68 NIV).

For the LORD is our judge, the LORD is our **lawgiver**, the LORD is our king; he will save us.
ISAIAH 33:22
[NRSV: **ruler**]

LIGHT

> The LORD is my **light** and my salvation; whom shall I fear? the LORD is the strength of my life; of whom shall I be afraid?
> PSALM 27:1

When God created the world, the first thing He brought into being was light (see Genesis 1:3–5). His glory or presence is often compared to the light (see Psalm 104:1–2). He led His people in the wilderness during the Exodus with the light from a pillar of fire (see Exodus 13:21). Perhaps the psalmist had all these things in mind when he referred to the Lord as his Light.

As the Light, God is still a guide for His people. He gives us wisdom and insight to help us make good decisions. In our moments of darkness and discouragement, He gives us hope. He lights up our lives constantly with His love and grace.

God's written Word, the Bible, also shows that Light is an appropriate name for Him. He inspired it by divine revelation many centuries ago. Then He worked throughout history to preserve it and pass it down to our generation. His eternal Word still shines like a beacon in a dark and sinful world. As Christians, we can declare with the psalmist, "Thy word is a lamp unto my feet, and a light unto my path" (Psalm 119:105).

The psalmist also refers to God as the Sun (Psalm 84:11), comparing Him to the brightest light in the universe.

Guided by the Lord's Light

- "Come ye, and let us walk in the light of the LORD" (Isaiah 2:5).
- "The sun shall be no more thy light by day. . .but the LORD shall be unto thee an everlasting light" (Isaiah 60:19).
- "When I sit in darkness, the LORD shall be a light unto me" (Micah 7:8).

LIGHT OF ISRAEL

> And the **light of Israel** shall be for a fire, and his Holy One for a flame: and it shall burn and devour his thorns and his briers in one day.
> ISAIAH 10:17

This name of God was used by the prophet Isaiah in connection with his prophecy about the nation of Assyria. The Assyrians overran the nation of Israel (the northern kingdom) about 722 BC. Isaiah predicted that Assyria would eventually be punished by the Lord for their mistreatment of His people. God—the Light of Israel—would become a blazing fire that would consume this pagan nation. This prophecy was fulfilled about a century after Isaiah's time, when Assyria fell to the Babylonians.

These images of light and fire show two different sides of

God's nature. It is always better to experience the light of His love than the fire of His wrath.

LIVING GOD

King Darius of Persia called the Lord by this name when he came to see if Daniel had survived the night he spent among the lions. Even a pagan king recognized that it would take the Living God to deliver Daniel from this den of ferocious animals, which had been turned into an execution chamber.

God is referred to as the Living God several times throughout the Bible (see Joshua 3:10; 1 Samuel 17:26; Jeremiah 10:10; Hebrews 10:31). This title contrasts the one true God—the One who actually exists—with pagan idols that are lifeless counterfeits.

Unlike pagan deities, the Living God is capable of acting on behalf of His people. Just as He saved Daniel from the lions, He hears our prayers and stands beside us in our time of need.

And the king spake and said. . .O Daniel, servant of the **living God**, is thy God, whom thou servest continually, able to deliver thee from the lions?
DANIEL 6:20

This Lion statue, near the ruins of ancient Babylon, is a reminder of Daniel, the lion's den, and king Darius's proclamation of "The Living God."

LIVING WATERS. See *Fountain of Living Waters.*

LORD. See *I Am That I Am.*

LORD ALMIGHTY. See *Almighty God; Lord of Hosts.*

LORD GOD ALMIGHTY. See *Almighty God; Lord of Hosts.*

LORD GOD OF ISRAEL

Zacharias, the father of John the Baptist, used this name for God when he broke out in praise at the news that the Messiah would soon be born. Just as the Lord had blessed His people in the past, He was now getting ready to fulfill His promise to send a great Deliverer.

But the Messiah was more than a gift to Israel alone. Through Him the entire world would be blessed. We as Christians proclaim this truth every year at Christmas when we sing this familiar hymn by Isaac Watts:

Joy to the world! The Lord is come;
Let earth receive her King;
Let every heart prepare Him room,
And heaven and nature sing.

LORD GOD OMNIPOTENT. See *Almighty God.*

LORD IS MY BANNER. See *Jehovah-nissi.*

LORD IS PEACE. See *Jehovah-shalom.*

LORD OF ALL THE EARTH. See *God of the Whole Earth.*

LORD OF HOSTS

Zechariah 8 could be called the "Lord of Hosts" chapter of the Bible, because this divine name appears eighteen times in the chapter. Actually, this name is one of the more popular in the entire Bible. It appears about 250 times, particularly in the prophets and the Psalms.

The compound Hebrew word behind this name is *Yahweh-sabaoth,* "Lord of Hosts." *Sabaoth* means "armies"

Blessed be the **Lord God of Israel**; for he hath visited and redeemed his people.
LUKE 1:68

Yea, many people and strong nations shall come to seek the **LORD of hosts** in Jerusalem, and to pray before the LORD.
ZECHARIAH 8:22
[NIV: **LORD Almighty**]

or "hosts." Thus, one meaning of the name is that God is superior to any human army, no matter its number. The Lord often led His people to victory over a superior military force (see, for example, Judges 7:12–25).

Another possible meaning of Lord of Hosts is that God exercises control over all the hosts of heaven—or the heavenly bodies—including the sun, moon, and stars. The psalmist declares, "Praise ye him, all his hosts. Praise ye him, sun and moon: praise him, all ye stars of light" (Psalm 148:2–3).

In the King James Version, the title *Lord of Sabaoth* appears twice (see Romans 9:29; James 5:4). These are rendered as "Lord of Hosts" by modern translations.

LORD OF SABAOTH. See *Lord of Hosts.*

LORD OF THE WHOLE EARTH. See *God of the Whole Earth.*

LORD OUR RIGHTEOUSNESS

These words of the Lord were delivered to His people through the prophet Jeremiah. God would punish His people for their sin and idolatry by allowing the Babylonians to overrun the nation of Judah. But He would preserve a remnant of His people, who would remain faithful to Him. He would bless them, allow them to return to their homeland, and give them a special name—the Lord Our Righteousness.

This name of God emphasizes two of the more important truths of the Bible: (1) God demands righteousness of His people, and (2) we are not able to meet this demand on

> In his days Judah shall be saved, and Israel shall dwell safely: and this is his name whereby he shall be called, THE LORD OUR RIGHTEOUSNESS.
> JEREMIAH 23:6

Depending on the Lord Our Righteousness
- "Hear me when I call, O God of my righteousness" (Psalm 4:1).
- "The LORD. . .shall judge the world with righteousness, and the people with his truth" (Psalm 96:13).
- "I the LORD speak righteousness, I declare things that are right" (Isaiah 45:19).
- "This is the heritage of the servants of the LORD, and their righteousness is of me, saith the LORD" (Isaiah 54:17).

our own. We must look to Him as the Lord Our Righteousness to provide for us what we cannot attain no matter how hard we try.

The ultimate fulfillment of this verse did not occur until several centuries after Jeremiah's time. God sent His own Son into the world to pay the price for our sin, so that we could become justified, or righteous, in His sight. This is strictly a gift of His grace, not something we deserve because we measure up to His demands. The apostle Paul expresses it like this: "For he [God] hath made him [Jesus] to be sin for us, who knew no sin; that we might be made the righteousness of God in him" (2 Corinthians 5:21).

LORD WHO HEALS

This is the only place in the Bible where God is called the Lord Who Heals. The Lord used this name to describe Himself after He healed the bitter waters at Marah in the wilderness, making it safe for the Israelites to drink.

The healing power of God is often demonstrated in the Old Testament. For example, He healed Miriam of her leprosy (see Numbers 12:10–16). He healed King Hezekiah of Judah of a mysterious illness (see 2 Kings 20:1–10). He healed people in the wilderness after they were bitten by poisonous snakes (see Numbers 21:5–9).

God is also portrayed in the Old Testament as the healer of the ultimate sickness—sin. The psalmist prays, "LORD, be merciful unto me: heal my soul; for I have sinned against thee" (Psalm 41:4).

> And [God] said, If thou wilt diligently hearken [NIV: listen carefully] to the voice of the LORD thy God. . .I will put none of these diseases upon thee, which I have brought upon the Egyptians: for I am the **LORD that healeth** thee.
> EXODUS 15:26
> [NASB: **LORD your healer**]

LORD WHO MAKES YOU HOLY. See *Lord Who Sanctifies.*

LORD WHO SANCTIFIES

God reminded the Israelites, through Moses, that the Sabbath was a special day that had been set apart, or sanctified, by Him (see Genesis 2:3). His people were to honor this day by resting from their labors and praising Him through acts of worship.

Just as God set apart the seventh day of the week as a memorial to Himself, so He also sanctified the Israelites as a nation devoted to Him. As the Lord

This well, from the area with the bitter waters of Marah, is associated with the Springs of Moses where the Lord healed the "bitter waters."

Who Sanctifies, He has the right to demand loyalty and commitment from His people. When He sets us apart for His special use, He also empowers us with the strength and ability to serve as His witnesses in the world.

LORD WILL PROVIDE. See *Jehovah-jireh*.

LORD YOUR HEALER. See *Lord Who Heals*.

MAJESTY IN THE HEAVENS. See *Majesty on High*.

Speak thou also unto the children of Israel, saying, Verily my sabbaths ye shall keep: for it is a sign between me and you throughout your generations; that ye may know that I am the **LORD that doth sanctify you**. EXODUS 31:13 [NIV: **LORD who makes you holy**]

Fresco of Jesus in His "Majesty on High." Church of the Ascension, Mount of Olives.

MAJESTY ON HIGH

This powerful verse from the book of Hebrews refers to Jesus' ascension into heaven. After His resurrection, He spent forty days among His followers. Then He was "taken up" into heaven and "a cloud received him out of their sight" (Acts 1:9). Now in heaven, He is seated at the right hand of God His Father (see Ephesians 1:20; Colossians 3:1; 1 Peter 3:22)—or, as the writer of Hebrews puts it, next to the Majesty on High.

Who being the brightness of his glory. . .when he had by himself purged our sins, sat down on the right hand of the **Majesty on high**. HEBREWS 1:3 [NIV: **Majesty in heaven**]

This name of God is a poetic way of referring to His power and glory. He is incomparable in His excellence, magnificence, and splendor. This name appears only here in the Bible. The book of Hebrews also speaks of God as the Majesty in the heavens (Hebrews 8:1).

God's Majesty in the Psalms

- "The voice of the LORD is powerful; the voice of the LORD is full of majesty" (Psalm 29:4).
- "Honour and majesty are before him: strength and beauty are in his sanctuary" (Psalm 96:6).
- "O LORD my God, thou art very great; thou art clothed with honour and majesty" (Psalm 104:1).
- "To make known to the sons of men his mighty acts, and the glorious majesty of his kingdom" (Psalm 145:12).

Shall mortal man be more just [NIV: Can a mortal be more righteous] than God? shall a man be more pure than his **maker**?
JOB 4:17

MAKER

This name of God was spoken by Eliphaz the Temanite, one of Job's three friends who came to counsel him in his affliction. Job had accused God of causing His suffering when he, Job, had done nothing wrong. To Eliphaz, a mere mortal such as Job had no right to question the actions of his Maker, the immortal One who did not have to explain His actions to anyone.

God's role as our Maker is similar to His acts as our Creator and Provider (see *Creator*). The psalmist declares, "Know ye that the LORD he is God: it is he that hath made us, and not we ourselves; we are his people, and the sheep of his pasture" (Psalm 100:3).

A craftsman chisels designs into wood. Though he is "making" a piece of art, he's using existing materials. Only God could "make" from nothing.

MIGHT. See *Song*.

MIGHTY GOD. See *Almighty God*.

MIGHTY ONE OF ISRAEL. See *Almighty God*.

MIGHTY ONE OF JACOB

This name of God appears only twice in the Bible, both times in the book of Isaiah (see also Isaiah 60:16). In these two verses, "Jacob" is a poetic way of referring to the nation of Israel. The descendants of Jacob's twelve sons developed into the twelve tribes of Israel. Jacob himself was also known as "Israel," a name given to him by the Lord after his struggle with God at Peniel (see Genesis 32:28; 35:10).

Three similar names for God that appear in the Old Testament are God of Jacob (2 Samuel 23:1; Psalm 75:9), Holy One of Jacob (Isaiah 29:23), and King of Jacob (Isaiah 41:21).

> And all flesh [NIV: all mankind] shall know that I the LORD am thy Saviour and thy Redeemer, the **mighty One of Jacob**.
> ISAIAH 49:26

MOST HIGH

This name of God appears in a psalm that David wrote after he was delivered from King Saul and others who were trying to kill him (see 2 Samuel 22:1; 1 Samuel 20:1; Psalm 18). David compares God's ability to save to the power that is unleashed during a severe thunderstorm. The rolling thunder is like God's voice from heaven.

The book of Psalms refers frequently to God as the Most High (see Psalms 9:2; 73:11; 107:11). The prophet Daniel also used this name (see Daniel 4:24; 7:18). In his long speech in the New Testament, just before his death, the martyr Stephen declares that "the most High dwelleth not in temples made with hands" (Acts 7:48).

There is nothing in this world greater than the Most High. He deserves our deepest loyalty and most fervent praise.

> The LORD thundered from heaven, and the **Most High** resounded.
> 2 SAMUEL 22:14 NIV

Our Vision of the Most High

An ancient Irish hymn titled "Be Thou My Vision" declares that God as the Most High should be the inspiration of our lives.

> Be thou my vision, O Lord of my heart;
> Naught be all else to me, save that Thou art:
> Thou my best thought, by day or by night,
> Walking or sleeping, Thy presence my light.

And Melchizedek king of Salem brought forth bread and wine: and he was the priest of the **most high God**. And he blessed him, and said, Blessed be Abram of the **most high God**, possessor of heaven and earth.

GENESIS 14:18–19 [NIV: **God Most High**]

MOST HIGH GOD

Both Abraham and Melchizedek worshipped and served the same God—the Most High God—the One in whose name Melchizedek blessed Abraham. This God had given Abraham victory over a coalition of Canaanite kings (Genesis 14:1–24). To express his thanks to God, Abraham gave Melchizedek a tithe of all his goods.

"Most High God" is a name for the one true God. He is superior to all the false gods that were worshipped by the pagan peoples of Abraham's time. They had a god for every need and purpose—a god of war, fertility, love, rain, science, literature, truth, etc. But Melchizedek and Abraham worshipped only one God. He was the supreme God of creation, who stood above all these "lesser gods" in power and authority.

A lot has changed since the days of Melchizedek and Abraham. But the temptation to worship the "lesser gods" of the world rather than the one true God of the universe has not. Money, fame, and power are the new gods of our age. But the first of God's Ten Commandments still stands: "Thou shalt have no other gods before me" (Exodus 20:3).

MOST HIGH OVER ALL THE EARTH. See *God of the Whole Earth.*

MOST MIGHTY. See *Almighty God.*

This Babylonian idol, dating as far back as 2000 BC, was believed to be responsible for omens. Ancient people often had gods for limited purposes—as opposed to the "Most High God" who has authority over everything.

MOST UPRIGHT

This is the only place in the Bible where this name of God appears. Isaiah's point is that even the most righteous and upright people are as nothing in comparison to the holiness of God.

Even Christians who try to walk the path of righteousness are capable of slipping into sin at any time. But God is not capable of error or wrongdoing. He is the Most Upright, the one consistent standard by which all human behavior is judged. Isaiah considers this dramatic contrast between the Lord's righteousness and our sin, then declares, "All our righteousnesses are as filthy rags. . .and our iniquities, like the wind, have taken us away" (Isaiah 64:6).

But that is not the end of the story. In spite of our unworthiness, God comes to our rescue through the sacrificial death of His Son: "For by grace are ye saved through faith; and that not of yourselves: it is the gift of God: not of works, lest any man should boast" (Ephesians 2:8–9).

> The way of the just is uprightness: thou, **most upright**, dost weigh the path of the just [NIV: make the way of the righteous smooth].
> ISAIAH 26:7
> [NASB, NIV: **Upright One**; NRSV: **Just One**]

PORTION

The word *portion* appears often in the Bible in connection with inheritance rights. For example, each of the twelve tribes of Israel received a portion of the land of Canaan as an inheritance that the Lord had promised (see Joshua 19:9). By law, the firstborn son in a family received a double portion of his father's estate as an inheritance (see Deuteronomy 21:17). In Jesus' parable of the prodigal son, the youngest son asks his father for his portion, or share, of the estate ahead of time (see Luke 15:12).

The psalmist probably had this inheritance imagery in mind when he called God his Portion. The Lord was his spiritual heritage, passed down to him by godly people of past generations. Unlike an earthly inheritance that can be squandered, this is an inheritance that will last forever.

But comparing God to a legacy from the past has its limits. Truths about God can be passed on from generation to generation, but personal faith cannot. Parents can and should teach their offspring about God, but it is up to each child to accept this heritage through his own personal choice.

Two other names of God the Father that describe Him as a portion are Portion in the Land of the Living (Psalm 142:5) and Portion of Mine Inheritance (Psalm 16:5).

> Thou art my **portion**, O LORD: I have said that I would keep thy words.
> PSALM 119:57

PORTION IN THE LAND OF THE LIVING. See *Portion*.

PORTION OF MINE INHERITANCE.
See *Portion*.

POSSESSOR OF HEAVEN AND EARTH. See *God of the Whole Earth*.

POTTER

But now, O LORD, thou art our father; we are the clay, and thou our **potter**; and we all are the work of thy hand.
ISAIAH 64:8

The prophet Isaiah longed for the wayward people of Judah to subject themselves to God. If they became pliable clay in the Lord's hands, they would be shaped into beautiful vessels who would glorify His name.

God as the master Potter is a graphic image that appears often throughout the Bible. For example, while the prophet Jeremiah looked on, a potter ruined a vase he was working on and had to start over again with the same lump of clay. Jeremiah compared the nation of Judah to this pottery reshaping process. Shape up, he declared, or you will be reshaped by the Lord's discipline.

The hymn writer George C. Stebbins expresses this truth in a positive way:

Have thine own way, Lord! Have thine own way!
Thou art the Potter, I am the clay.
Mold me and make me after thy will,
While I am waiting, yielded and still.

REDEEMER

This name of God is a reflection of the Old Testament concept of the kinsman redeemer. In the close-knit families and clans of Bible times, the nearest relative of a family member in trouble was expected to come to that person's rescue.

Ancient Egyptian clay figurine of a potter working his potter's wheel.

For example, if a person lost his property as a debtor, his kinsman redeemer was responsible for buying back the property and restoring it to his family member. This is exactly what happened in the book of Ruth. Boaz, a kinsman of Naomi's deceased husband, Elimelech, bought back the property Elimelech had lost and restored it to Naomi (see Ruth 4:1–11).

The prophet Isaiah declares that God is the ultimate Redeemer who will come to the rescue of His people. We can rest assured that no trouble we experience is so deep that it is beyond His reach. Job had this assurance. From out of his suffering, he declared, "I know that my redeemer liveth, and that he shall stand at the latter day upon the earth" (Job 19:25).

In another passage in his book, the prophet Isaiah also refers to the Lord as "the Redeemer of Israel" (Isaiah 49:7).

REDEEMER OF ISRAEL. See *Redeemer.*

REFUGE

Moses called God by this name as the Israelites were getting ready to enter the Promised Land. He reminded the people to follow the Lord as they populated the land, because He alone was a dependable source of refuge and protection.

After they settled in Canaan, the Israelites designated

> In a little wrath [NIV: a surge of anger] I hid my face from thee for a moment; but with everlasting kindness will I have mercy on thee, saith the LORD thy **Redeemer**.
> ISAIAH 54:8

> The eternal God is thy **refuge**, and underneath are the everlasting arms.
> DEUTERONOMY 33:27 [NASB: **dwelling place**]

Remains of ancient Shechem (Tell Balata). Shechem was one of the six cities of refuge described in the books of Numbers and Joshua.

certain population centers as cities of refuge (see Numbers 35:6–7; Joshua 20:7–9). An Israelite who killed another person accidentally could flee to one of these cities to escape the dead man's family who were seeking revenge. The killer's safety was guaranteed by the elders of the city while the circumstances surrounding the homicide were under investigation.

With God as our refuge, we have nothing to fear from those who seek to do us harm. Even in death, there is no safer place to be than in the arms of the everlasting God.

Another name of God that expresses basically the same idea as Refuge is Shelter (Psalm 61:3). See also *Dwelling Place*.

Safe in the Arms of the Lord

The phrase *everlasting arms* in Deuteronomy 33:27 has been immortalized in the hymn "Leaning on the Everlasting Arms," by Elisha A. Hoffman. Generations of Christians have been inspired by this grand old hymn.

What a fellowship, what a joy divine,
Leaning on the everlasting arms;
What a blessedness, what a peace is mine,
Leaning on the everlasting arms.
Leaning, leaning,
Safe and secure from all alarms;
Leaning, leaning,
Leaning on the everlasting arms.

ROCK

There is none holy as the LORD: for there is none beside thee: neither is there any **rock** like our God.
1 SAMUEL 2:2

This verse is part of Hannah's prayer of dedication when she brought her son, Samuel, to Eli the priest. God had answered her prayer for a son, and she followed through on her promise to devote him to the Lord. She had found the Lord to be the Rock, the strong and dependable One who answers the prayers of His people.

The word *rock*, when used of God, refers not to a small stone but to a massive outcropping, such as that on a mountainside. These huge formations are common throughout the land of Israel. These types of rocks remain fixed in place from one generation to the next, just as God is the eternal, unmovable One who is not subject to the ravages of time.

Other names of God the Father that describe Him as the Rock or the Stone are Rock of Israel (2 Samuel 23:3), Rock of My Refuge (Psalm 94:22), Rock of My Salvation (2 Samuel 22:47), and Rock of My Strength (Psalm 62:7).

Rock facade at Caesarea Philippi associated with Jesus' proclamation that the kingdom of evil would not overpower those belonging to God's Kingdom (Matthew 16:13–18).

ROCK OF ISRAEL. See *Rock*.

ROCK OF MY REFUGE. See *Rock*.

ROCK OF MY SALVATION. See *Rock*.

ROCK OF MY STRENGTH. See *Rock*.

SALVATION. See *God of My Salvation; Horn of Salvation*.

SAVIOUR

And there is no God else beside me [NIV: no God apart from me]; a just God and a **Saviour**; there is none beside me [NIV: none but me].
ISAIAH 45:21

These words from the Lord were delivered to the Israelites through the prophet Isaiah. God reminded the people that He, as their Savior, was the only true God. He demanded their loyalty and obedience.

The word *savior* refers to one who rescues or delivers others from danger. When used of God in the Old Testament, it usually refers to physical deliverance. The supreme example of this was God's rescue of the Israelites from Egyptian slavery through the Exodus. Acting as a Savior, or Deliverer, He sent plagues against the Egyptians until Pharaoh gave in and let God's people leave the country.

Not until the New Testament does God's role as Savior reach its full flower. He sent His Son Jesus as a spiritual Savior to deliver us from our bondage to sin.

Giza pyramids and Sphinx. When the Lord rescued the Israelites from the mighty hand of Pharaoh during the time of Moses, the pyramids in Egypt were no longer in use.

SHADE

This unusual name for God was probably inspired by the hot, dry climate of the land of Israel. To the psalmist, God was his figurative Shade under whom he could rest from the oppressive heat during the hottest part of the day.

In this verse, he also describes God as his cooling-off

place "upon [his] right hand." The right hand was considered the place of favor and honor. Thus, to experience the Lord as his Shade on the right was to be doubly refreshed and blessed.

Are you overworked, overheated, frustrated, confused, or confounded? Maybe it's time you took a refreshing break by sitting down under the ultimate Shade.

The LORD is thy keeper: the LORD is thy **shade** upon thy right hand.
PSALM 121:5

Like Elijah, who slept under a broom tree, people today still seek relief from the heat in the hot, dry climate of Israel.

SHELTER. See *Refuge.*

SHEPHERD

This name of God is one of the favorites of Bible students, perhaps because it occurs in one of the more familiar passages in God's Word—the Twenty-third Psalm. This psalm has been called the "Shepherd Psalm" because of its beautiful description of the Lord as the Shepherd of His people.

David wrote this psalm in his latter years, as he reflected on the Lord and how He had led him throughout his life. Like a shepherd who leads his sheep to green pastures and peaceful streams for food and water, the Lord had supplied David's needs. From David's humble beginnings as a shepherd boy, to the throne of Israel, God had walked with him and blessed him with more than he deserved. David was confident that God would continue to sustain him, even as he walked "through the valley of the shadow of death" (Psalm 23:4).

Like David, we all need the divine Shepherd, who will guide us throughout this life and beyond. What a blessing it is to count ourselves as "the sheep of his pasture" (Psalm 100:3).

Another name of God that uses shepherd imagery is Shepherd of Israel (Psalm 80:1)

The LORD is my **shepherd**; I shall not want [NIV: I shall not be in want].
PSALM 23:1

A shepherd caring for his sheep. Such an image would have been common to people of Bible times.

SHEPHERD OF ISRAEL. See *Shepherd.*

SHIELD

This verse is from one of the psalms of David, in which he prays for protection from his enemies. He uses military terminology to characterize God as his Shield who will surround him and absorb the blows of those who are on the attack.

The Hebrew word behind *shield* in this verse refers to the large, full-body shield that warriors crouched behind. This protected them from arrows being shot by archers from a distance. Another type of shield was the buckler, which was worn on the arm to protect soldiers in hand-to-hand combat (see *Buckler*).

As our Shield, God provides maximum protection. He literally surrounds us with His watchful care.

For thou, Lord, wilt bless the righteous; with favour wilt thou compass [NIV: surround] him as with a **shield**.
PSALM 5:12

SONG

The twelfth chapter of Isaiah is one of the shortest in his book. But it is unapologetically joyful as the prophet thinks about the Lord whom he serves. In addition to this verse, which describes God as his Song, every one of its verses expresses this theme of praise and celebration (see sidebar).

God's people have a lot to sing about. He has provided for our salvation through His Son. He sustains us every day with His love and grace. He has promised us eternal life with Him in heaven after we depart this earthly life. He, as our Song, deserves to be praised with our songs of joy.

> Behold, God is my salvation; I will trust, and not be afraid: for the Lord JEHOVAH is my strength and my **song**; he also is become my salvation.
> ISAIAH 12:2
> [NRSV: **might**]

Egyptian statuette of a person playing the lyre.

Other Verses of Isaiah 12

- "O LORD, I will praise thee" (verse 1)
- "With joy shall ye draw water out of the wells of salvation" (verse 3)
- "Praise the LORD" (verse 4)
- "Sing unto the LORD" (verse 5)
- "Cry out and shout" (verse 6)

SPRING OF LIVING WATER. See *Fountain of Living Waters.*

STONE OF ISRAEL. See *Creator of Israel.*

STRENGTH

This verse is part of the passage of scripture known as the Song of Moses (Exodus 15:1–19). Moses led the Israelites to sing this song of praise to the Lord after He rescued them from the pursuing army of Pharaoh at the Red Sea.

The people had witnessed the awesome power of the Lord as He divided the waters of the sea to give them safe passage. Even before this event, the Lord had plagued the Egyptians again and again until Pharaoh allowed the Israelites to leave the country. No wonder Moses referred to this wonder-working God as his Strength.

> The LORD is my **strength** and song, and he is become my salvation. . .my father's God, and I will exalt him.
> EXODUS 15:2

There is no shortage of power in the God we serve. And He invites us to partake of His strength in our times of need.

Claiming the Promises of God's Strength

- "But they that wait upon the LORD shall renew their strength; they shall mount up with wings as eagles; they shall run, and not be weary; and they shall walk, and not faint" (Isaiah 40:31).
- "The LORD God is my strength, and he will make my feet like hinds' feet, and he will make me to walk upon mine high places" (Habakkuk 3:19).
- "God is our refuge and strength, a very present help in trouble" (Psalm 46:1).

STRENGTH OF ISRAEL. See *Creator of Israel*.

STRONGHOLD. See *Fortress*.

STRONG TOWER

The name of the LORD is a **strong tower**: the righteous runneth into it, and is safe.
PROVERBS 18:10

In ancient cities, towers were massive stone structures built above the defensive perimeter walls. From these elevated positions, defenders could shoot arrows or hurl stones on the enemy forces outside. These towers also served as a final line of defense if the invading army should succeed in breaking through the walls or battering down the city gates.

Towers from an Israelite fortress at Arad may have inspired the proverb writer's description of God as a "strong tower."

The author of this proverb compares the Lord to one of these defensive towers. His righteous followers can seek safety and security in Him as the Strong Tower.

This imagery also appears in the Psalms, where God is referred to as a High Tower (see Psalms 18:2; 144:2).

SUN. See *Light*.

TOWER. See *Strong Tower*.

UPRIGHT ONE. See *Most Upright*.

WALL OF FIRE

This name of God appears only here in the Bible. The prophet Zechariah uses it to describe God's protection of the city of Jerusalem after the Exile. The city's defensive walls had been destroyed by the Babylonians several decades before. This meant that the Jewish exiles who returned to Jerusalem were in a precarious position. But God promised to protect them by becoming a Wall of Fire around the city.

Fire is often associated in the Bible with God's presence and protection. For example, He used a pillar of fire at night to guide His people on their journey through the wilderness (see Exodus 13:21). The prophet Zechariah was assuring the citizens of Jerusalem that they could depend on the Lord's protective presence at this dangerous point in their lives.

> For I, saith the LORD, will be unto her a **wall of fire** round about, and will be the glory in the midst of her.
> ZECHARIAH 2:5

The Wall of Fire Still Burns

"The Lily of the Valley," an old hymn by Charles W. Fry, assures us that God continues to guide and protect His people.

> He will never, never leave me, nor yet forsake me here,
> While I live by faith and do His blessed will;
> A wall of fire about me, I've nothing now to fear,
> With His manna He my hungry soul shall fill.

YAHWEH. See *I Am That I Am*.

PART 2
Names of God the Son

The following 151 names by which Jesus is known show the revolutionary nature of His life and ministry.

He was the Messiah, the One whom God had promised to send to restore the fortunes of His people. But He was more than the earthly ruler that the people expected. He was the divine Son of God, who came into the world as a man to die as an atonement for human sin.

Jesus' work did not end with His crucifixion, resurrection, and ascension into heaven. He continues to intercede for Christians at the right hand of God the Father. And He has promised that we will reign with Him eternally upon His triumphant return.

ADAM. See *Last Adam.*

ADVOCATE

This is the only place in the Bible where Jesus is called by this name. It expresses the idea that He stands before God on our behalf. He serves as our "defense attorney," to represent us before the Father in heaven when Satan, the accuser, charges us with sin. Jesus' argument on our behalf is solid because it is based on His own atoning work—His death on the cross for our sins.

Any attorney will tell you that his client must be totally honest with him about the charges that have brought him into court. Unless the attorney, as the accused's legal repre-sentative, knows everything about the circumstances of the case, he cannot represent his client adequately before the judge and the jury.

In the same way, we as Christians must be honest with our Lord, Jesus, when sin creeps into our lives, if we expect Him to serve as our Advocate before God. Full disclosure, or confession, is essential. As the apostle John expresses it in another place in his first epistle, "If we confess our sins, he [Jesus] is faithful and just to forgive us our sins, and to cleanse us from all unrighteousness" (1 John 1:9).

My little children, these things write I unto you, that ye sin not. And if any man sin, we have an **advocate** with the Father, Jesus Christ the righteous.
1 JOHN 2:1
[NIV: **one who speaks to the Father in our defense**]

A defense attorney speaks on behalf of his client, in a nineteenth-century illustration, "The Advocate," by Honoré Daumier.

ALIVE FOR EVER AND EVER. See *Alive for Evermore*.

ALIVE FOR EVERMORE

> I am he that liveth, and was dead; and, behold, I am **alive for evermore**, Amen; and have the keys of hell and of death.
> REVELATION 1:18
> [NIV: **Alive for ever and ever**]

These words are among the first that Jesus spoke to the apostle John when He revealed Himself to John on the Isle of Patmos. This revelation occurred about fifty or sixty years after Jesus' death and resurrection. He assured John that He was not only alive but that He was Alive for Evermore.

During His brief ministry of about three years, Jesus predicted His death and resurrection on more than one occasion (see Matthew 16:21–28; Mark 10:32–34; Luke 9:43–45). But even His disciples had a hard time believing this would happen.

Even after Jesus appeared to them in His resurrection body, they had doubts. To show that He had flesh and bones and that they were not seeing a ghost or a vision, He asked them to touch His hands and feet. He even ate a piece of fish and a honeycomb, as they looked on, to prove that He had a physical body just like they did (see Luke 24:37–43).

Because Jesus experienced a physical resurrection and is Alive for Evermore, we as Christians have His assurance that death is not the end of life but a glorious new beginning. "I am the resurrection, and the life," He declared. "Whosoever liveth and believeth in me shall never die" (John 11:25–26).

ALL, AND IN ALL

> Where there is neither Greek nor Jew, circumcision nor uncircumcision, Barbarian, Scythian, bond nor free: but Christ is **all, and in all**.
> COLOSSIANS 3:11

Jesus was born into a divided world. Jews looked down on Gentiles. Greeks considered themselves superior in education and culture to the Jews. But the apostle Paul declares in this famous passage that the coming of Jesus changed all that. He is the All in All—the great unifier—who brings all people together at the foot of the cross.

To those who know Jesus, worldly distinctions and social status are no longer important. The only thing that really matters is Christ. He is the sum and substance of life—the absolute and the center of our existence. Because He gave His all to purchase our salvation, our purpose in life is to bring honor and glory to Him.

"Jesus Paid It All," a hymn written by Elvina M. Hall, expresses the all-sufficiency of Christ in the salvation He provides for all believers.

I hear the Savior say,
"Thy strength indeed is small,
Child of weakness, watch and pray,
Find in me thine all in all."
Jesus paid it all,
All to Him I owe;
Sin had left a crimson stain,
He washed it white as snow.

ALMIGHTY

Jesus is referred to as the Almighty only in the book of Revelation (see Revelation 4:8; 16:7; 19:15). This name is also applied to God in both the Old and New Testaments (see Ruth 1:20; 2 Corinthians 6:18; see also *Almighty God* in part 1, Names of God the Father).

Revelation portrays the final victory of Jesus Christ over the forces of evil. As the Almighty, He is to "rule all nations with a rod of iron" (Revelation 12:5). He is also the source of the believer's new life with God the Father in the heavenly Jerusalem (see Revelation 21:22; 22:1).

God as the Almighty has delegated all authority and power to His Son, who is also known as the Almighty. Using His unlimited power, Jesus will bring the world to its conclusion in accordance with God's purpose.

In his famous prophecy about the coming Messiah, Isaiah declares that Jesus will be called the Mighty God (Isaiah 9:6). He also referred to Him as the Mighty One of Israel (Isaiah 30:29) and the Mighty One of Jacob (Isaiah 60:16).

I am Alpha and Omega, the beginning and the ending, saith the Lord, which is, and which was, and which is to come, the **Almighty**.
REVELATION 1:8

Praise for the Almighty

The hymn "Praise to the Lord, the Almighty," by Joachim Neander, invites all people to worship the all-powerful Lord. Both God the Father and God the Son deserve our highest praise.

Praise to the Lord, the Almighty, the King of creation!
O my soul, praise Him, for He is thy health and salvation!
All ye who hear,
Now to His temple draw near;
Praise Him in glad adoration!

> I am **Alpha and Omega**, the beginning and the end, the first and the last.
> REVELATION 22:13

ALPHA AND OMEGA

This is one of four places in the book of Revelation where Jesus is called by this name (see Revelation 1:8, 11; 21:6). In all four places, Jesus uses this name of Himself.

Alpha and omega are the first and last letters of the Greek alphabet—the language in which most of the New Testament was written. Thus, this name is a poetic way of declaring that Jesus is the beginning and the end of all things. We might put it this way in modern terms: "Jesus is the A and Z of life, and everything in between."

No letter stands before alpha, and no letter follows omega. This shows that Jesus defines truth and reality. All other gods that people worship are counterfeit deities. Jesus encompasses everything and rejects all limitations.

Other names for Jesus that mean essentially the same thing as Alpha and Omega are Beginning and the Ending (Revelation 1:8) and First and the Last (Revelation 1:17; 2:8; 22:13).

> And unto the angel of the church of the Laodiceans write; These things saith the **Amen**, the faithful and true witness, the beginning of the creation of God.
> REVELATION 3:14

AMEN

This verse was spoken by Jesus as He prepared to deliver a special message to the church at Laodicea. By designating Himself as the Amen, He claimed to be speaking a truthful, authoritative word for this church.

The word *amen* has a rich biblical history. In the Old Testament, it was used to confirm an oath or consent to an agreement. For example, Nehemiah called on the people of his time not to cheat and defraud one another. The people responded with "amen" to pledge their agreement with Nehemiah's proposal (Nehemiah 5:13).

Jesus often used the word *verily* in His teachings to show that He was about to speak God's words of truth (see Matthew 16:28). This Greek word is rendered as "I tell you the truth" (NIV) or "I assure you" (HCSB) by modern translations. The early church used *amen* to declare "let it be so" or "let it be true" at the close of prayers (see 2 Timothy 4:18), just as we do today.

Because Jesus is the great Amen, we can trust His words and His leadership. He is the sum and substance of Truth (see John 14:6). He will never say or do anything that will cause us to stumble or go astray. He has promised that if we follow Him, we will know the truth, "and the truth shall make you free" (John 8:32).

ANGEL OF HIS PRESENCE

This verse from the prophet Isaiah describes God's patience with His people. Although they sinned and rebelled against Him again and again, He never left them, and He provided the Angel of His Presence as their Savior and Redeemer.

Although angels are mentioned often throughout the Bible, this is the only place where the phrase Angel of His Presence occurs. This is probably a reference to Jesus Christ in His pre-earthly existence. There is no doubt that Jesus existed with God in His pre-incarnate state, long before He was born into the world (see John 1:1–3). So He certainly could have served as God's agent of redemption with His people in the days before His earthly ministry.

This name of Jesus may explain the references to the mysterious Angel of the Lord in the Old Testament. This special agent was sent by God to communicate His message and to assure selected individuals of His presence. This messenger was clearly not the typical angel, but neither was He God the Father. The best explanation is that this special messenger—the Angel of His Presence—was Jesus Christ.

> In all their affliction he was afflicted, and the **angel of his presence** saved them: in his love and in his pity [NIV: mercy] he redeemed them; and he bare them [NIV: lifted them up], and carried them all the days of old.
> ISAIAH 63:9

People to Whom the Angel of the Lord Appeared
- Hagar (Genesis 16:7–11)
- Abraham (Genesis 22:11–12)
- Jacob (Genesis 31:11)
- Moses (Exodus 3:1–2)
- Joshua (Joshua 5:14)
- Gideon (Judges 6:11–12)
- Samson's parents (Judges 13:1–18)
- The prophet Zechariah (Zechariah 1:7–12)

ANOINTED

Psalm 2 is a messianic psalm that predicts the coming of the Messiah. Rebellion against the Lord by the nations of the world is futile, the psalmist declares, because the Lord has appointed Christ, His Anointed, as the King of the earth.

The kings of the earth set themselves [NIV: take their stand], and the rulers take counsel together, against the LORD, and against his **anointed**, saying, Let us break their bands asunder, and cast away their cords [NIV: fetters] from us.
PSALM 2:2–3
[NIV: **Anointed One**]

This name of Jesus ties into the anointing custom of the Old Testament. Priests and kings were anointed by having oil poured on their heads (see Leviticus 8:10–12; 1 Samuel 16:13). This ritual showed that a person had been especially chosen or set apart to perform the responsibilities of his office.

As God's Anointed, Jesus Christ was set apart for His role as the divine Mediator and Redeemer. Through Him we find forgiveness for our sins and the abundant life that God intends for His people. He in turn has anointed us as Christians for the task of declaring His message of hope in a desperate world. The apostle Paul puts it like this: "We are therefore Christ's ambassadors, as though God were making his appeal through us. We implore you in Christ's behalf: Be reconciled to God" (2 Corinthians 5:20 NIV).

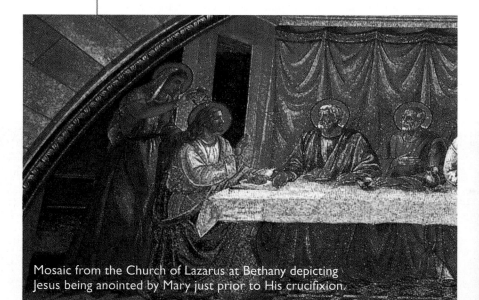

Mosaic from the Church of Lazarus at Bethany depicting Jesus being anointed by Mary just prior to His crucifixion.

ANOINTED ONE. See *Anointed*.

APOSTLE

Jesus selected twelve disciples, or apostles (see Mark 3:14; 6:30), to learn from Him and to carry on His work after He was gone. But here in Hebrews 3, He Himself is called the

Apostle. This is the only place in the Bible where this name of Jesus occurs.

The basic meaning of the word *apostle* is a person sent on a special mission with delegated authority and power. Jesus sent out the twelve disciples to teach and heal, and He gave them the ability to succeed in this mission (see Mark 6:7–13). They continued this teaching and healing ministry even after Jesus' resurrection and ascension to the Father (Acts 2:38–43).

But Jesus was the ultimate Apostle. Under the authority of His Father, He came into the world on a mission of love and grace. This mission wasn't a cushy assignment. He was opposed by the religious establishment of His time. Some people who saw His miracles tried to turn Him into a military deliverer. Even His own "sent ones," the apostles, were slow to understand who He was and what He was about.

But as the author of Hebrews expresses it in these verses, Jesus was "faithful to him that appointed him." He did not falter in the mission on which He was sent. From the cross, He triumphantly declared, "It is finished" (John 19:30). His provision for our salvation was a done deal, but the Good News about His death and resurrection—the gospel—rolls on across the ages.

> Wherefore, holy brethren, partakers of the heavenly calling, consider [NIV: fix your thoughts on] the **Apostle** and High Priest of our profession, Christ Jesus; who was faithful to him that appointed him.
> HEBREWS 3:1–2

The Beat Goes On

In her hymn "I Love to Tell the Story," Katherine Hankey reminds us that Jesus' work as the Apostle goes on through His followers as we tell others about His love and grace.

I love to tell the story of unseen things above,
Of Jesus and His glory, of Jesus and His love:
I love to tell the story because I know 'tis true;
It satisfies my longing as nothing else can do.
I love to tell the story, 'twill be my theme in glory
To tell the old, old story of Jesus and His love.

ATONING SACRIFICE FOR OUR SINS.

See *Propitiation for Our Sins.*

AUTHOR AND FINISHER OF OUR FAITH

Jesus is called *author* in two verses in the King James Version (Hebrews 12:2 [see next page] and Hebrews 5:9: "And being made perfect, he became the *author of eternal salvation* unto all them that obey him" [emphasis added]). In two modern translations, He is also called the Author of Salvation (see Hebrews 2:10, NASB, NIV). An author is someone who creates. Jesus is the author of our faith, or our salvation, in that He has provided us with the only flawless example of what the life of faith is like. The NRSV expresses this idea by calling Him the *pioneer* of our faith. He blazed the trail for all others who seek to follow His example.

But Jesus not only started the journey of faith, He also brought it to completion as the "finisher" (NRSV: perfecter) of faith. He did not stop until He had guaranteed our final redemption, making it possible for us to enjoy eternal life with Him in heaven.

AUTHOR OF SALVATION. See *Captain of Salvation.*

BABE

This verse from Luke brings to mind the Christmas plays that are presented every year at Christmastime. We see shepherds in bathrobes with towels around their heads. Mary and Joseph kneel beside a rough feeding trough that some member of the church has hammered together. Inside the trough is a doll—or a baby if a newborn is available and the parents can be persuaded to lend him for the occasion—representing the baby Jesus. Even though we have seen it all before, we still get a little misty-eyed when we stand at the conclusion of the play and sing "Joy to the World."

The wonder of Christmas is that Jesus came into the world like any newborn of the ancient world. He was a helpless baby, who cried when He was hungry and uncomfortable. He had to be fed, burped, and changed. He probably got His days and nights mixed up like any baby, causing Mary and Joseph to wonder if they would ever again get a good night's sleep.

It's natural for us to wonder why God would choose this way to send His

---

Looking unto Jesus the **author and finisher of our faith**; who for the joy that was set before him endured the cross, despising the shame, and is set down at the right hand of the throne of God.
HEBREWS 12:2
[NASB, NIV: **author and perfecter of our faith**; NRSV: **pioneer and perfecter of our faith**]

And they [shepherds] came with haste, and found Mary, and Joseph, and the **babe** lying in a manger.
LUKE 2:16
[NIV: **baby**; NRSV: **child**]

A familiar image recreated thousands of times each Christmas season—Mary, Joseph, and the baby Jesus.

Son into the world. He could have arrived as a king to the blast of trumpets. He could have dazzled the crowds by riding into town as a triumphant general at the head of a massive army. But perhaps God wanted His Son to experience the helplessness of a little baby so He could sympathize with us in our sin and weakness. Going through the stages of life like all people do, He could participate fully in the humanity of those He came to serve.

The writer of the book of Hebrews expresses it like this: "For we do not have a high priest who is unable to sympathize with our weaknesses, but we have one who has been tempted in every way, just as we are—yet was without sin" (Hebrews 4:15 NIV).

BABY. See *Babe.*

BANNER FOR THE NATIONS. See *Ensign for the Nations.*

BEGINNING AND THE ENDING.
See *Alpha and Omega.*

BEGINNING OF THE CREATION OF GOD

The affirmation of this verse is that Jesus has always been. Before He was born into the world in human form, He existed with God the Father. The Nicene Creed, a famous statement of faith formulated by the church in AD 325, puts it like this: "I believe in one Lord, Jesus Christ. . .born of the Father before all ages." Thus, He is called the Beginning of the Creation of God.

Not only has Jesus existed eternally; but the Bible also affirms that He participated with God in the creation of the universe. On the sixth day of creation, the Lord declared, "Let us make man in *our* image, after *our* likeness" (Genesis 1:26, emphasis added). The plural *our* probably refers to God in His three trinitarian modes of existence: God the Father, God the Son, and God the Holy Spirit.

Two key passages from the New Testament also teach that Jesus Christ was involved in the creation of the universe (see sidebar, next page).

And unto the angel of the church of the Laodiceans write; These things saith the Amen, the faithful and true witness, the **beginning of the creation of God**. REVELATION 3:14 [NIV: **ruler of God's creation**; NRSV: **origin of God's creation**]

Jesus as Creator Before the Beginning

"In the beginning was the Word, and the Word was with God, and the Word was God. The same was in the beginning with God. All things were made by him; and without him was not any thing made that was made" (John 1:1–3).

"For by him were all things created, that are in heaven, and that are in earth. . . . And he is before all things, and by him all things consist" (Colossians 1:16–17).

BEGOTTEN. See *Only Begotten Son.*

BELOVED SON

This verse describes in graphic terms what happened when Jesus was baptized by John the Baptist at the beginning of His public ministry. The heavens opened, the Holy Spirit settled on Jesus, and God identified Him clearly as His Beloved Son, who brought Him joy. God was pleased with Jesus because He had waited patiently on God's timing. Now He was ready to begin the work for which He had been sent into the world.

God repeated these words near the end of Jesus' public ministry following His transfiguration (see Matthew 17:1–5). God's words on this occasion showed He was pleased with what His Beloved Son had done. Only Jesus'

A section of the Jordan River, believed by some to be where Jesus was baptized.

death and resurrection to follow could top the divine work He had already accomplished.

Because Jesus was God's Beloved Son, we as Christians are also known as God's beloved (see Romans 1:7; Ephesians 1:6). We hold a special place in Jesus' heart, because we have been cleansed by His blood and are committed to the work of His everlasting kingdom.

BISHOP OF YOUR SOULS

Only here in the Bible is Jesus called by this name. The word *bishop*, in its New Testament usage, refers to a person who oversees, supervises, or watches over the welfare of others. Thus the translation of this name as "Guardian" or "Overseer" by modern translations.

Notice the mention of "sheep" and "Shepherd" in connection with this name in 1 Peter 2:25. Sheep were helpless animals who often wandered away from the flock. They needed a shepherd—a guardian or overseer—to watch over them and keep them out of danger. The shepherd, or bishop, is a good image for leaders, particularly church leaders. The terms *bishop* and *elder* are often used interchangeably in the Bible to designate those who are responsible for leading God's flock, the church (see Acts 14:23; 1 Timothy 3:1).

It's good to know that we, as wandering sheep, have someone to watch over us. The Bishop of Our Souls is on the job, and He will keep us safe.

BLESSED AND ONLY POTENTATE

In this verse from Paul's first epistle to Timothy, he heaps up three names of God the Son in a row, each showing His unlimited power. The titles King of kings and Lord of lords appear elsewhere in the Bible (see Revelation 17:14; 19:16), but this is the only place where Jesus is called the Blessed and Only Potentate.

The word *potentate* comes from the Latin word *potent*, which means "power." A potentate was a king, monarch, or ruler with total power over his subjects. He shared his power with no one, and no earthly council could question his judgment or veto his decisions.

But Jesus is a Potentate of a different type—a spiritual ruler who will triumph over all the forces of evil when He judges the world at His second coming. He is the *Blessed*

And Jesus, when he was baptized, went up straightway out of the water: and, lo, the heavens were opened unto him, and he saw the Spirit of God descending like a dove, and lighting upon him: and lo a voice from heaven, saying, This is my **beloved Son**, in whom I am well pleased.
MATTHEW 3:16–17
[NIV: **my Son, whom I love**; NRSV: **my Son, the Beloved**]

For ye were as sheep going astray; but are now returned unto the Shepherd and **Bishop of your souls**.
1 PETER 2:25
[NASB, NRSV: **Guardian of your souls**; NIV: **Overseer of your souls**]

Which in his times he shall shew, who is the **blessed and only Potentate**, the King of kings, and Lord of lords.
1 TIMOTHY 6:15
[NASB, NRSV: **blessed and only Sovereign**; NIV: **blessed and only Ruler**]

Potentate: Chosen and blessed by God, He has been given ultimate power and authority. He is the *Only* Potentate: the sole ruler who has the right to reign over the new creation that God will bring into being in the end time.

BLESSED AND ONLY SOVEREIGN. See *Blessed and Only Potentate.*

BLESSED AND ONLY RULER. See *Blessed and Only Potentate.*

BOY JESUS. See *Child Jesus.*

BRANCH OF RIGHTEOUSNESS

The prophet Jeremiah predicted that God's judgment would fall on the nation of Judah because of their sin and rebellion against the Lord. But in this verse, he looked beyond that time of destruction to the day when God would send the Messiah, who would be known as the Branch of Righteousness, and who would rule over God's people with love and mercy.

The Messiah would be like a new shoot or limb that sprang from a dead tree trunk. God had promised King David centuries before Jeremiah's time that a descendant of David's would always rule over His people (see 2 Samuel 7:12–16). This promise was fulfilled in Jesus Christ. He was the new Davidic king, in a spiritual sense, who came to redeem the world from its bondage to sin and the powers of darkness.

In a prophecy about the coming Messiah, the prophet Jeremiah also refers to Jesus as the Righteous Branch (Jeremiah 23:5).

> In those days, and at that time, will I cause the **Branch of righteousness** to grow up unto David [NIV: sprout from David's line]; and he shall execute judgment and righteousness in the land.
> JEREMIAH 33:15
> [NIV, NRSV: **righteous Branch**; NASB: **righteous Branch of David**]

Other Prophecies About the Branch

"In that day shall the branch of the LORD be beautiful and glorious, and the fruit of the earth shall be excellent and comely for them that are escaped of Israel" (Isaiah 4:2).

"I will raise unto David a righteous Branch, and a King shall reign and prosper, and shall execute judgment and justice in the earth" (Jeremiah 23:5).

"I will bring forth my servant the BRANCH" (Zechariah 3:8).

BREAD

John 6 might be called the "bread chapter" of the New Testament. It begins with Jesus' miracle of multiplying five small loaves of bread and two fish to feed a large crowd of hungry people (see John 6:2–13). It continues across seventy-one verses as Jesus talks with the crowds and the religious leaders about the spiritual bread that He came to provide for the world.

In this long chapter, Jesus uses four different names for Himself that involve the imagery of bread: Bread from Heaven (verse 32), Bread of God (verse 33), Bread of Life (verse 35), and Living Bread (verse 51).

Jesus probably used these names for Himself because bread made from wheat or barley was the staple food of His day. The common people could identify with this comparison. Bread was also closely identified with some of the major events from Israel's history. When the Israelites left Egypt in the Exodus, they baked their bread without leaven, because they didn't have time to wait for the bread to rise (see Exodus 12:30–34). They commemorated this event in future years with a religious festival known as the Feast of Unleavened Bread (see Exodus 13:3–10). The Lord also kept His people alive in the wilderness after the Exodus by providing manna, a bread substitute, for them to eat (see Numbers 11:6–9).

Just as God provided food in the wilderness, He also provides spiritual sustenance for His people. Jesus is the Bread from Heaven that was sent by God Himself. As the Living Bread and the Bread of Life, Jesus provides eternal life for

> My Father giveth you the **true bread from heaven**.
> JOHN 6:32

> For the **bread of God** is he which cometh down from heaven, and giveth life unto the world.
> JOHN 6:33

> I am the **bread of life**: he that cometh to me shall never hunger.
> JOHN 6:35

> I am the **living bread** which came down from heaven. . . and the bread that I will give is my flesh, which I will give for the life of the world.
> JOHN 6:51

Bread from Thebes in Egypt, dating as far back as 1550 BC.

those who claim Him as their Lord and Savior. "This is that bread which came down from heaven," Jesus declared. "Not as your fathers did eat manna, and are dead: he that eateth of this bread shall live for ever" (John 6:58).

In her hymn "Break Thou the Bread of Life," Mary A. Lathbury expresses the deep desire of all Christians for fellowship with Christ, the Living Bread.

Break thou the bread of life, dear Lord, to me,
As thou didst break the loaves beside the sea;
Beyond the sacred page I seek thee, Lord;
My spirit pants for Thee, O living Word.

BREAD FROM HEAVEN. See *Bread.*

BREAD OF GOD. See *Bread.*

BREAD OF LIFE. See *Bread.*

BRIDEGROOM

And Jesus said unto them, Can the children of the bridechamber [NIV: guests of the bridegroom] mourn, as long as the **bridegroom** is with them? but the days will come, when the **bridegroom** shall be taken from them, and then shall they fast.
MATTHEW 9:15

Jesus responded with these words when the followers of John the Baptist asked why He and His disciples did not participate in the ritual of fasting. His answer picked up imagery from a Jewish wedding, with Jesus referring to Himself as the Bridegroom and His disciples as the wedding guests ("children of the bridechamber").

It was not appropriate, Jesus said, for His disciples to fast or mourn while He as the Bridegroom was physically present with them. They should save their fasting for the time when He would be taken up to heaven by God the Father after His death and resurrection.

We are accustomed to thinking of Jesus as the King, Redeemer, or Savior. But Bridegroom? This name strikes us as a little strange. What did He mean when He applied this name to Himself?

One possibility is that He used this name to identify closely with God the Father, who referred to Himself as the Husband of His people (see *Husband* in part 1, Names of God the Father). Jesus as the Bridegroom will provide for His followers, just as any bridegroom assumes responsibility for taking care of his wife and children.

Another possibility is that Jesus was looking ahead to the birth of the church, which is spoken of symbolically as His bride (see Revelation 21:9). The apostle Paul points out that, just as "the husband is head of the wife," so "Christ is the head of the church" (Ephesians 5:23). Jesus loved the church so much that He laid down His life for it (see Ephesians 5:25). Every single member of His kingdom has experienced this sacrificial love.

Maybe Bridegroom is not such a strange name for Jesus, after all.

BRIGHT AND MORNING STAR

This is one of the last names of God the Son mentioned in the Bible, since it appears in the final chapter of the last book of the Bible. How appropriate that Jesus should call Himself the Bright and Morning Star, a name associated with a heavenly body and its light.

The people of ancient times did not know as much about stars, planets, and heavenly bodies as we know today. To them, the last star to disappear in the eastern sky as the sun began to rise was known as the morning star. Scholars and astronomers of modern times have identified this "star" as the planet Venus, Earth's closest neighbor. Because of its closeness, Venus is the third brightest object in the sky, outshone only by the sun and the moon.

When the light from all the other stars disappears in the early morning, Venus twinkles on, signaling the beginning of

I Jesus have sent mine angel to testify unto you these things in the churches. I am the root and the offspring of David, and the **bright and morning star**.
REVELATION 22:16

Venus, the "morning star," shines along with the crescent moon.

a new day. The birth of Jesus also marked the beginning of a new day. This truth should bring joy to our hearts. What better way to greet the dawning of each new day than to breathe a prayer of thanks to God for sending His Bright and Morning Star into the world.

Another name of God the Son that means basically the same thing as Bright and Morning Star is Day Star (2 Peter 1:19).

BRIGHTNESS OF GOD'S GLORY

The Old Testament contains many references to God's glory, referring to His excellence and majesty (see *Father of Glory* in part 1, Names of God the Father). But the writer of Hebrews in this verse says, in effect, "You don't know divine glory until you experience the glory that appears in Jesus Christ." He is the Brightness of God's Glory. In Him, the glory of God appeared as it had never appeared before.

As God's Son, Jesus shared in the Father's glory, or His divine nature. He was born into the world by supernatural conception in Mary's womb (see Luke 1:34–35). His teachings and His miracles were performed under God's authority, causing people to exclaim, "We have never seen anything like this!" (Mark 2:12 NIV). His glorious resurrection demonstrated His power over the forces of evil and death.

But the greatest demonstration of Jesus' glory is reserved for the future. In the end time, at His return, the apostle Paul declares, "every knee should bow. . .and every tongue confess that Jesus Christ is Lord, to the glory of God the Father" (Philippians 2:10–11 NIV).

Another name of God the Son that expresses basically the same idea as Brightness of God's Glory is Lord of Glory (James 2:1).

> Who being the **brightness of his glory**, and the express image of his person, and upholding all things by the word of his power [NIV: sustaining all things by his powerful word], when he had by himself purged our sins, sat down on the right hand of the Majesty on high.
> HEBREWS 1:3
> [NASB: **Radiance of His glory**; NIV: **Radiance of God's glory**; NRSV: **reflection of God's glory**]

Jesus and His Glory

"And the Word was made flesh, and dwelt among us, (and we beheld his glory)" (John 1:14).

"Father, I will that they also, whom thou has given me [Jesus' disciples], be with me where I am; that they may behold my glory" (John 17:24).

"God. . .hath shined in our hearts, to give the light of the knowledge of the glory of God in the face of Jesus Christ" (2 Corinthians 4:6).

CAPSTONE. See *Head of the Corner.*

CAPTAIN OF SALVATION

This is the only place in the Bible where Jesus is called the Captain of Salvation. The Greek word behind *captain* in this verse is rendered as "author" in Hebrews 12:2 (see *Author and Finisher of Our Faith* above). Other meanings of this word are "prince" and "leader" (see NRSV).

    In what sense is Jesus the Captain or Leader of Salvation? For one thing, this verse from Hebrews goes on to say that He was made "perfect in sufferings." A genuine leader does not ask his followers to do something that he is not willing to do himself. He sets the example for those whom he leads. This is what Jesus did when He died on the cross for us. We as Christians will never suffer more by following Him than He did to make it possible for us to be cleansed of our sins.

    A leader also guides, encourages, inspires, and motivates the people in his charge. We can rest assured that we are in good hands when we follow our Captain of Salvation.

> For it became him, for whom are all things, and by whom are all things, in bringing many sons unto glory, to make the **captain of their salvation** perfect through sufferings.
> HEBREWS 2:10
> [NASB, NIV: **author of their salvation**; NRSV: **pioneer of their salvation**]

Following the Lord's Leadership

God the Father and His Son, Jesus Christ, are trustworthy leaders who will lead us in the right paths. This sentiment was expressed beautifully by Joseph H. Gilmore in his hymn "He Leadeth Me! O Blessed Tho't!"

He leadeth me! O blessed tho't!
O words with heav'nly comfort fraught!
Whate'er I do, where'er I be,
Still 'tis God's hand that leadeth me!
He leadeth me, He leadeth me,
By His own hand He leadeth me:
His faithful foll'wer I would be,
For by His hand He leadeth me.

CAPTAIN OF THE HOST OF THE LORD

This is the name by which the mysterious messenger of the Lord identified Himself to Joshua as the Israelites prepared to enter Canaan. The best explanation of this verse is that the messenger was the Angel of the Lord, also called the Angel of His Presence in Isaiah 63:9 (see *Angel of His Presence* above).

    In the third century of the modern era, the scholar

Origen identified this messenger as Jesus Christ in a pre-incarnate appearance. This approach to the passage has been followed by many modern Bible students. One strong argument for this interpretation is that Joshua bowed down and worshipped this Captain of the Host of the Lord. This indicates that He was a divine being of high stature, not just a messenger of a lower angelic order.

> And he said, Nay; but as **captain of the host of the LORD** am I now come. And Joshua fell on his face to the earth, and did worship, and said unto him, What saith my Lord unto his servant?
> JOSHUA 5:14
> [NIV, NRSV: **commander of the army of the LORD**]

This name of God the Son uses military imagery. The NIV and NRSV render it as "Commander of the Army of the Lord." After Moses died, Joshua became the new leader of Israel. He faced the daunting task of leading Israel against the Canaanites and claiming the land of promise for God's people. The appearance of the Captain of the Host of the Lord assured Joshua that he would be successful in this campaign. This would happen not because of their military might, but because God would go before them into battle.

CARPENTER

During His ministry, Jesus paid a visit to His hometown of Nazareth. This verse describes the skeptical response to His teachings by the people who had known Him for many years. To them, He was nothing but "the carpenter," a skilled tradesman who had grown up in their midst and who was nothing special.

> Is not this the **carpenter**, the son of Mary, the brother of James, and Joses, and of Juda, and Simon? and are not his sisters here with us? And they were offended at him.
> MARK 6:3

This is the only place in the Bible where this name is applied to Jesus. The people of His hometown used it in a derogatory way, but it is actually a name of honor and dignity. Jesus probably learned this skill from His earthly father, Joseph. He must have worked at this trade for at least fifteen or twenty years before He began His public ministry at about thirty years of age (see Luke 3:23).

The word *carpenter* in our society applies generally to a skilled workman who constructs buildings. But in New Testament times, this occupation was more likely what we know today as woodworking. Jesus probably worked with Joseph in a woodworking shop, making and repairing furniture and tools for the citizens of Nazareth.

As the Carpenter of Nazareth, who worked with His hands, Jesus dignified labor and identified with the common people of His day. He spoke in language they could understand, driving home His teachings with parables drawn from everyday life. No wonder "the common people heard him gladly" (Mark 12:37).

In Matthew's Gospel, the skeptical people of Nazareth refer to Jesus not as "the carpenter" but as "the carpenter's son" (Matthew 13:55).

CARPENTER'S SON. See *Carpenter.*

CHIEF CORNERSTONE

With these words, the apostle Paul assured the believers in the church at Ephesus that they were recipients of God's grace. Their faith in Christ had brought them into God's kingdom, because He was the Chief Cornerstone on which this kingdom was built.

Jesus as the Cornerstone of our faith is one of the most important images of God the Son in the Bible. It is rooted in a famous messianic passage that was written several centuries before Jesus was born. In Psalm 118:22, the psalmist declares, "The stone which the builders refused is become the head stone of the corner."

Jesus identified with this messianic passage during the final days of His ministry. He knew that He would be rejected as the Messiah and executed by the religious leaders

> Now therefore ye are no more strangers and foreigners, but fellowcitizens with the saints [NIV: God's people], and of the household of God. And are built upon the foundation of the apostles and prophets, Jesus Christ himself being the **chief corner stone**.
> EPHESIANS 2:19–20 [NIV, NRSV: **cornerstone**)

George Washington lays the cornerstone of the U.S. Capitol in a painting by DeLand.

of His nation. So he told them: "Did ye never read in the scriptures, The stone which the builders rejected, the same is become the head of the corner: this is the Lord's doing, and it is marvellous in our eyes? Therefore. . .the kingdom of God shall be taken from you, and given to a nation bringing forth the fruits thereof" (Matthew 21:42–43).

Jesus was referring to the non-Jewish or Gentile nations that would accept Him as Lord and Savior. This is exactly what happened as the gospel was proclaimed throughout the Roman world after Jesus' death and resurrection. The leader of this movement was a Jewish zealot and persecutor of the church—the apostle Paul—who was gloriously converted to Christianity and transformed into the "apostle to the Gentiles" (see Acts 9:15).

In the stone buildings of Bible times, a cornerstone was used to hold two opposing rows of stones together at the point where they came together. Jesus as the Chief Cornerstone is the force on which our faith is based. Though He may be rejected by the non-believing world, He is our hope in this life and the life to come.

In a famous prophecy about the coming Messiah, Isaiah also refers to Jesus as the Precious Corner Stone and the Tried Stone (Isaiah 28:16).

CHIEF SHEPHERD. See *Good Shepherd.*

CHILD. See *Babe.*

CHILD JESUS

This verse is part of the only account we have in the Gospels about the childhood of Jesus. According to Luke 2:41–52, when Jesus was twelve, He made a trip to Jerusalem with His parents to observe the Passover Feast. Joseph and Mary were traveling with a group back to Nazareth when they discovered that the boy Jesus was missing. He had "tarried behind" in Jerusalem.

Joseph and Mary returned quickly to the Holy City, where they discovered Jesus in the temple among the Jewish teachers and scholars, listening to them expound on the scriptures and asking them questions. Everyone was amazed at His religious insights at such a young age.

And when they had fulfilled the days [NIV: After the Feast was over], as they returned, the **child Jesus** tarried [NIV: stayed] behind in Jerusalem; and Joseph and his mother knew not of it.
LUKE 2:43
[NASB, NIV, NRSV: **boy Jesus**]

This account tells us that, even as a child, Jesus was aware of His special mission as the Son of God. When His mother scolded Him for staying behind in Jerusalem and causing her and Joseph such anxiety, He replied, "Why were you searching for me? . . . Didn't you know I had to be in my Father's house?" (Luke 2:49 NIV).

This account in Luke goes on to report that Jesus returned to Nazareth with His earthly parents, and He "increased in wisdom and stature, and in favour with God and man" (Luke 2:52). In other words, He grew up like any typical Jewish boy of the first century. As the Child Jesus, He went through all the normal stages of life—from birth, to infancy, to childhood, to adulthood. He is a Savior who can identify with us in all our human experiences.

In Peter's remarks to the Jewish Sanhedrin after healing a lame man near the temple, he referred to Jesus as the Holy Child Jesus (Acts 4:27, 30).

CHOSEN BEFORE THE CREATION OF THE WORLD. See *Foreordained before the Foundation of the World.*

CHOSEN OF GOD

Chosen of God is the name that the religious leaders and the scoffing crowd assigned to Jesus as He was dying on the cross. The irony is that the name that they used in ridicule was a perfect description of Jesus and the mission from His Father that had brought Him into the world.

For generations, the Jewish people had looked for a Messiah sent from God, who would serve as a Deliverer for His people. Jesus was that Chosen One, but He was not the type of champion they expected. He came not as a military conqueror, but as a spiritual Savior who died to deliver people from their sin. His work as the Chosen One of God continues to this day, as He calls people to take up their crosses and follow Him (see Matthew 16:24).

And the people stood beholding [NIV: watching]. And the rulers also with them derided [NIV: sneered at] him, saying, He saved others; let him save himself, if he be Christ, the **chosen of God**.
LUKE 23:35
[NASB, NIV, NRSV: **Chosen One**]

Others Chosen of God

Jesus was deemed the Chosen of God in a special sense. But He followed in the tradition of many people in the Bible who were said to be chosen of God. These include

- Descendants of Jacob, or the Israelites (1 Chronicles 16:13)
- King Solomon (1 Chronicles 29:1)
- Moses (Psalm 106:23)
- Zerubbabel (Haggai 2:23)
- The apostle Paul (Acts 9:15)
- All Christians (Ephesians 1:4; 1 Peter 2:9)

CHOSEN ONE. See *Chosen of God; Elect.*

CHRIST

And Simon Peter answered and said, Thou art the **Christ**, the Son of the living God. MATTHEW 16:16 [NRSV: **Messiah**]

Then charged he his disciples that they should tell no man that he was Jesus the **Christ**. MATTHEW 16:20 [NRSV: **Messiah**]

These two verses are part of the account of Peter's recognition and confession of Jesus as the Messiah in the Gospel of Matthew (see Matthew 16:13–20).

Notice the use of the article *the* ("the Christ") in both verses. The English word *Christ* comes from the Greek word *christos*, which means "anointed." Thus, Peter was declaring that Jesus was the Anointed One, a special agent who had been sent into the world under divine appointment by God Himself. He was the Son of God, the Messiah, the great Deliverer for whom the Jewish people had been looking for many years.

Jesus commended Peter for his recognition of Him as God's Anointed One. But why did He want His identity as the Messiah to be kept a secret?

He probably charged His disciples to keep quiet about His messiahship because the Jewish people expected their Messiah to be a military and political champion. They thought He would rally the people, raise an army, deliver their nation from Roman tyranny, and restore Israel to its glory days.

Jesus could not live up to these expectations, because He was a Messiah in a spiritual sense. He had been sent to teach about the kingdom of God, to heal the sick, and to deliver the people from their sin. He would eventually reveal Himself as the Son of God (see Luke 22:70–71), but only after He had completed the spiritual mission on which He had been sent.

Jesus is called *Christ* (the Messiah or the Anointed One) hundreds of times throughout the New Testament. Often this name or title is grouped with other names. For example, *Jesus Christ* actually means "Jesus the Anointed One" or "Jesus the Messiah." *Christ of God* (see Luke 9:20) means "the Anointed One of God." *Christ Jesus* appears often in the epistles, especially in those written by the apostle Paul (see Romans 3:24; 1 Corinthians 1:2). This reversal of the two names places emphasis on the messiahship of God's Son.

Because Jesus was the Anointed One of God, we as His followers are also commissioned to continue His work in the world. The apostle Paul declares, "Now he which stablisheth us with you in Christ, and hath anointed us, is God" (2 Corinthians 1:21).

A Name to Carry Proudly

The name or title *Christ* is carried by all Christians—those who belong to Jesus Christ. This name—Christians—appears only three times in the New Testament. According to the book of Acts, it was first applied to the believers in the church at Antioch (see Acts 11:26). An unbeliever, King Agrippa, used it when he told the apostle Paul, "Almost thou persuadest me to be a Christian" (Acts 26:28). And the apostle Peter encouraged the persecuted Christians to whom he wrote with these words: "Yet if any man suffer as a Christian, let him not be ashamed; but let him glorify God on this behalf" (1 Peter 4:16).

CHRIST CRUCIFIED

This is the only place in the Bible where this name of God the Son appears. Since the name or title *Christ* means "the Anointed One" or "the Messiah" (see *Christ* above), the literal meaning of this name is "the Messiah Crucified."

In Jewish tradition, the coming Messiah was to be a powerful leader who would defeat all their enemies and rule over a restored Israel in splendor and glory. That this Messiah would die on a Roman cross like a common criminal was something they found totally unacceptable—a "stumblingblock" that prevented them from accepting Jesus as the Messiah.

A crucified Savior who died in our place to set us free from bondage to sin is still a foreign concept to many people.

But we preach **Christ crucified**, unto the Jews a stumblingblock, and unto the Greeks foolishness.
1 CORINTHIANS 1:23

Like the rich young ruler, they want to know "what good thing" (Matthew 19:16) they must do in order to be assured of eternal life. But there is nothing we can do that will buy us God's favor. We must accept by faith the provision for our salvation that God has already made through the death of His Son.

The apostle Paul puts it like this: "For by grace are ye saved through faith; and that not of yourselves: it is the gift of God: not of works, lest any man should boast" (Ephesians 2:8–9).

Jesus' death on the cross may be one of the most painted and sculpted events of human history.

CHRIST JESUS. See *Christ*.

CHRIST JESUS OUR LORD

This is one of the more inspiring passages in all the writings of the apostle Paul. Generations of Christians have claimed its promise that no force on earth or heaven is strong enough to break the grip of God's love on their lives.

This passage is also unusual because Paul strings together three separate names or titles of God the Son—*Christ*, *Jesus*, and *Lord*—to express this truth in such a powerful way. *Christ* means "the Anointed One" or "the Messiah" (see *Christ* above). *Jesus* was His personal name, which means "God Is Salvation" (Luke 1:31; 2:21). *Lord* expresses His unlimited dominion and power, a characteristic that Jesus shares with God His Father.

With Paul, we can declare that Christ Jesus Our Lord walks with us through every experience of life, and His love will never let us go.

Other variations on this name are Lord and Saviour Jesus Christ (2 Peter 3:18), Lord Christ (Colossians 3:24), and Lord Jesus Christ our Saviour (Titus 1:4).

CHRIST OF GOD. See *Christ*.

COMMANDER OF THE ARMY OF THE LORD. See *Captain of the Host of the Lord*.

CONSOLATION OF ISRAEL

A few weeks after Jesus was born, Joseph and Mary took Him to the temple in Jerusalem to dedicate Him to the Lord. A man named Simeon was moved by the Holy Spirit to come to the temple while they were there. He immediately recognized the young Jesus as the Messiah who had been sent as the Consolation of Israel.

The word *consolation* means "comfort" or "relief." God had promised in the Old Testament that He would send His Messiah to His people someday. Simeon was convinced that he would not die before he had seen this promise fulfilled (see Luke 2:26). God apparently showed him by divine revelation that the baby Jesus was the Promised One for whom the nation of Israel had been waiting.

> For I am persuaded, that neither death, nor life, nor angels, nor principalities, nor powers, nor things present, nor things to come, nor height, nor depth, nor any other creature, shall be able to separate us from the love of God, which is in **Christ Jesus our Lord**.
> ROMANS 8:38–39

> And, behold, there was a man in Jerusalem, whose name was Simeon; and the same man was just [NIV: righteous] and devout, waiting for the **consolation of Israel**: and the Holy Ghost was upon him.
> LUKE 2:25

But this good news had a dark side. Simeon told Mary and Joseph that many people would accept their Son as the Messiah, but many would not (see Luke 2:34). He also revealed to Mary that "a sword shall pierce through thy own soul also" (Luke 2:35)—a prediction of Jesus' future crucifixion.

Today, as then, Jesus' birth was a good news/bad news scenario—good news for those who accepted His messiahship, and bad news for those who refused to believe He had been sent by God the Father. Our task as Christians is to help others find the consolation that Jesus can bring into their lives.

Simeon's Prayer When He Saw the Infant Jesus

"Lord, now lettest thou thy servant depart in peace, according to thy word: For mine eyes have seen thy salvation, which thou hast prepared before the face of all people; a light to lighten the Gentiles, and the glory of thy people Israel" (Luke 2:29–32).

CORNERSTONE. See *Chief Cornerstone; Head of the Corner.*

COUNSELLOR

This verse is probably the most familiar messianic prophecy in the book of Isaiah. It is especially quoted at Christmastime when we gather with other believers to celebrate the birth of Jesus.

Most modern translations drop the comma between *Wonderful* and *Counselor* and render this name as Wonderful Counselor. But no matter how many words are included in the name, Counselor is one of the most significant titles of God the Son in the Bible.

The word *counsel* refers to guidance, advice, or instruction. The Bible is filled with models of good counsel and bad counsel and counselors who fall into both categories.

For example, on the good side, Daniel provided wise counsel to Arioch, an aide to King Nebuchadnezzar of Babylon, when the king issued an order to have all his wise men put to death (see Daniel 2:10–16). But on the foolish side, King Rehoboam of Judah rejected the wise counsel of the older leaders of the nation and listened to the foolish counsel of his young associates (see 1 Kings 12:8). This led to the rebellion of the northern tribes and the division of the united

For unto us a child is born, unto us a son is given: and the government shall be upon his shoulder: and his name shall be called Wonderful, **Counsellor**, The mighty God, The everlasting Father, The Prince of Peace.
ISAIAH 9:6
[NASB, NIV, NRSV: **Wonderful Counselor**]

kingdom of Solomon into two separate nations (see 1 Kings 12:16–19).

We can depend on Jesus, our wise Counselor, to always provide us with good instruction. He guides us with grace and righteousness. He will never give us bad advice that would cause us to go astray.

A counselor provides guidance to a troubled patient.

COVENANT OF THE PEOPLE

The forty-second chapter of Isaiah is one of the famous "servant songs" of his book. This Servant is Jesus, the Messiah, who will bring salvation to all people.

In 42:6, the prophet refers to the Messiah as a Covenant of the People. He will do more than establish a new covenant of God with the people. He *is* the new covenant. Through the Messiah, and His death and resurrection, God provides the means by which people can have unbroken fellowship with the Lord of the universe. Jesus is the only mediator between man and God that people need.

I the LORD have called thee in righteousness, and will hold thine hand, and will keep thee, and give thee for a **covenant of the people**, for a light of the Gentiles.
ISAIAH 42:6

Standing on the Solid Rock

"The Solid Rock," a hymn by Edward Mote, declares that the blood of Jesus seals the new covenant between God and His people.

His oath, His covenant, His blood
Support me in the whelming flood;
When all around my soul gives way,
He then is all my hope and stay.
On Christ, the solid Rock, I stand;
All other ground is sinking sand,
All other ground is sinking sand.

DAWN FROM ON HIGH. See *Dayspring from on High.*

DAYSMAN

Neither is there any **daysman** betwixt us, that might lay his hand upon us both.
JOB 9:33
[NASB, NRSV: **Umpire**; NIV: **someone to arbitrate**]

This verse is part of Job's complaint that God was punishing him without cause. Job was convinced that he had done nothing to deserve his suffering. To make matters worse, God was all-powerful and Job was but a weak human being, who had no right to question God. So he longed for a Daysman—a referee, mediator, or impartial judge—who could speak to God on his behalf.

Job's desire for someone to represent him before God the Father was eventually fulfilled with the coming of Jesus Christ into the world. As the God-man, Jesus is fully human and fully divine. He communicates directly with the Father, because He is God's Son. But He identifies with us humans in our frailties, because He came to earth in human form. As Job expressed it, Jesus is able to "lay his hand upon us both"—God and man.

It's difficult for us to comprehend how Jesus could be both human and divine at the same time. But just because we don't understand it doesn't mean it isn't true. Here's how the apostle Paul expressed this great truth: "Let this mind be in you, which was also in Christ Jesus: who, being in the form of God, thought it not robbery to be equal with God:

Today, we would call a "daysman" an "umpire"—a term even the most casual baseball fan understands.

but made himself of no reputation, and took upon him the form of a servant, and was made in the likeness of men: and being found in fashion as a man, he humbled himself, and became obedient unto death, even the death of the cross" (Philippians 2:5–8).

DAYSPRING FROM ON HIGH

This verse is part of the passage in the Gospel of Luke known as the "Benedictus" (see Luke 1:68–79). This passage consists of a prayer uttered by Zacharias, father of John the Baptist, after John was born. An angel had revealed to Zacharias, even before John's birth, that his son would be the forerunner of the Messiah. In this prayer, Zacharias praises God for sending the Messiah, Jesus, whom he calls the Dayspring from on High.

The English word *dayspring* comes from a Greek word that means "a rising up." It is generally used to describe the rising of the sun in the morning and the appearance of stars in the night sky. Thus, Zacharias thought of Jesus the Messiah as a bright light that God was preparing to send into a dark world.

The phrase *on high* reveals the origin of this Daystar. Jesus did not come into the world on His own as a "Lone Ranger." He was on a mission of redemption from God the Father.

The prophet Malachi uses a similar name for Jesus in his prophecy about the coming Messiah. He calls Him the Sun of Righteousness who would "arise with healing in his wings" (Malachi 4:2).

DAY STAR. See *Bright and Morning Star.*

DELIVERER

In this verse, Paul refers to Psalm 14:7, a portion of a messianic psalm written many years before. This psalm is attributed to David, who declares that the salvation of God's people would come from Zion, or Jerusalem.

This is an unusual reference to the Messiah, because Jesus was born in Bethlehem, not Jerusalem. But Jesus was crucified and resurrected in Jerusalem. This is also the place where the church was born on the day of Pentecost (see Acts 2:1–41) following Jesus' ascension to God the Father. These facts are probably what Paul had in mind when he declared that Jesus as our Deliverer came out of Jerusalem.

Through the tender mercy of our God; whereby the **dayspring from on high** hath visited us.
LUKE 1:78
[NASB: **Sunrise from on high**; NIV: **rising sun**; NRSV: **dawn from on high**]

And so all Israel shall be saved: as it is written, There shall come out of Sion [NIV: Zion] the **Deliverer**, and shall turn away ungodliness from Jacob.
ROMANS 11:26

The great work that Jesus performs as our Deliverer is to rescue us from sin. He sets us free from the guilt that accompanies our sin and separates us from God (see Isaiah 59:2). He delivers us from the power of Satan, who tempts us constantly to fall back into sin (see Ephesians 6:11–13). And He will deliver us from a world filled with sin when He returns to claim us as His own (see Galatians 1:4).

God is also referred to in the Old Testament as our Deliverer (see *Deliverer* in part 1, Names of God the Father). His deliverance in that section of the Bible is expressed mainly in physical terms. But His work as our Deliverer in a spiritual sense continues through His Son.

DESCENDANT OF DAVID. See *Root and Offspring of David.*

DESIRE OF ALL NATIONS

> And I will shake all nations, and the **desire of all nations** shall come: and I will fill this house with glory, saith the LORD of hosts.
> HAGGAI 2:7
> [NASB: **wealth of all nations**; NIV: **desired of all nations**; NRSV: **treasure of all nations**]

The prophet Haggai spoke these words to the Jewish exiles who had returned to Jerusalem after their period of captivity in Babylonia and Persia. He challenged them to get busy at the task of rebuilding the Jewish temple that had been destroyed about eighty years before by the invading Babylonian army. The temple is apparently the "house" referred to in this verse.

But Haggai's words also look beyond his time to the distant future when Israel's Messiah would become the Desire of All Nations. At the Messiah's return in glory in the end time, all nations will pay Him homage and recognize his universal rule throughout the earth.

Jesus is not only the desire of Christians; He is the hope of the entire world. As the apostle Paul declares, "At the name of Jesus every knee should bow. . .and every tongue confess that Jesus Christ is Lord, to the glory of God the Father" (Philippians 2:10–11 NIV).

In his hymn "Jesus Shall Reign Where'er the Sun," Isaac Watts expresses his sentiments about the universal rule of Christ in the end time.

Jesus shall reign where'er the sun
Does his successive journeys run;
His kingdom stretch from shore to shore,
Till moons shall wax and wane no more.

DESTINED BEFORE THE FOUNDATION OF THE WORLD. See *Foreordained before the Foundation of the World.*

DOCTOR. See *Physician.*

DOOR

This is one of several "I Am" statements made by Jesus in the Gospel of John (see sidebar). A door is an opening or entryway into a building or a shelter. By affirming that He was the Door, Jesus made it clear that he was the only way to salvation and eternal life.

In His Sermon on the Mount, Jesus also addresses this topic by talking about two gates (Matthew 7:13–14). The broad gate, representing the way of the world, is so wide that people can drift through it without any conscious thought about what they are doing. But the narrow gate, representing Jesus and His teachings, requires commitment and sacrifice from those who want to enter this way and follow Him.

Maybe you have heard people say, "It doesn't matter what you believe as long as you're sincere," or "All religions are basically the same; they just take us to heaven by different paths."

Don't you believe it. Jesus declares, "I am the way, the truth, and the life: no man cometh unto the Father but by me" (John 14:6).

> I am the **door**: by me if any man enter in, he shall be saved, and shall go in and out, and find pasture.
> JOHN 10:9
> [NIV, NRSV: **gate**]

Other "I Am" Statements of Jesus
- "I am the bread of life" (John 6:35).
- "I am the light of the world" (John 8:12).
- "I am the door of the sheep" (John 10:7).
- "I am the good shepherd" (John 10:11, 14).
- "I am the resurrection, and the life" (John 11:25).
- "I am the true vine" (John 15:1).

DOOR OF THE SHEEP. See *Good Shepherd.*

ELECT

This is another verse from one of the "servant song" chapters in the book of Isaiah (see *Covenant of the People* above). In this verse, the prophet uses the name *Elect* to describe the relationship of Jesus to God the Father. God elected or chose to send His Son Jesus into the world on a mission of redemption.

The concept of *election* is one of the richer theological themes in the Bible. It refers simply to God's gracious calling of people to become part of His kingdom and participate in His work.

God elected the nation of Israel to become a special recipient of His grace, and to serve as a channel of His blessing to the rest of the world (see Genesis 12:1–3). When Israel failed at this task, God elected to send His own Son to serve as His agent of grace and salvation.

God is still in the election business. The church of Jesus Christ is the channel through which He continues His work. We as Christians are His elect, and we work under the authority of Jesus as the supreme Elect One. We are called to bear witness for Him in a dark and unbelieving world.

> Behold my servant, whom I uphold; mine **elect**, in whom my soul delighteth; I have put my spirit upon him: he shall bring forth judgment to the Gentiles.
> ISAIAH 42:1
> [NASB, NIV: **chosen one**; NRSV: **chosen**]

EMMANUEL. See *Immanuel/Emmanuel*.

END OF THE LAW

This is the only place in the Bible where Jesus is referred to by this name. The NIV clarifies the meaning of this verse by stating that He is the End of the Law, "so that there may be righteousness for everyone who believes." This name of Jesus has a double meaning.

First, Jesus is the End of the Law because He did everything required by the Old Testament law to become a righteous person. He lived a sinless life and obeyed all of God's commandments, although He was tempted to do wrong, like any human being (see Luke 4:1–13; Matthew 26:36–42; Hebrews 4:15).

Second, Jesus is the End of the Law because He brought an end to law-keeping as the way for people to find justification in God's sight. Belief in Jesus as Lord and Savior is the only way to deal with sin and eliminate the separation between God and mankind.

Some things outlive their usefulness and ought to be brought to an end or transformed into something better. Aren't you glad that Jesus as the End of the Law offers all believers a glorious new beginning?

> For Christ is the **end of the law** for righteousness to every one that believeth.
> ROMANS 10:4

Jesus, the Believer, and the Law

- "For sin shall not have dominion over you: for ye are not under the law, but under grace" (Romans 6:14).
- "We have believed in Jesus Christ, that we might be justified by the faith of Christ, and not by the works of the law" (Galatians 2:16).
- "For the law made nothing perfect, but the bringing in of a better hope did; by the which we draw nigh unto God" (Hebrews 7:19).

ENSIGN FOR THE NATIONS

The eleventh chapter of Isaiah is one of the more pronounced messianic passages in the prophet's book. In this verse from that chapter, Isaiah portrays the coming Messiah as an Ensign, or Banner, not only for the Jewish people (Israel and Judah) but for all nations of the world.

The prophet probably had in mind a battle flag under which warriors of Bible times fought (see *Jehovah-nissi* in part 1, Names of God the Father). An army was distinguished from its enemies, and from the fighting units of its allies, by the banner under which it marched. Their flag was visible to all members of the unit, and it served as a rallying point for the soldiers during the heat of battle.

As the Ensign for the Nations, Jesus calls on all Christians to fall in step behind Him and spread the Good News of the Gospel throughout the world. The Great Commission (see Matthew 28:19–20) is our call to action.

And he shall set up an **ensign for the nations**, and shall assemble the outcasts of Israel, and gather together the dispersed of Judah from the four corners of the earth. ISAIAH 11:12 [NASB: **standard for the nations**; NIV: **banner for the nations**; NRSV: **signal for the nations**]

Marching Under the Royal Banner

The hymn "Onward, Christian Soldiers," by Sabine Baring-Gould, is a stirring call to arms for all who belong to the army of the Lord.

Onward, Christian soldiers, marching as to war,
With the cross of Jesus going on before!
Christ, the royal Master, leads against the foe;
Forward into battle, see His banners go!
Onward, Christian soldiers, marching as to war,
With the cross of Jesus going on before!

This "ensign" identifies a British ship.

ETERNAL FATHER. See *Everlasting Father.*

ETERNAL LIFE

Jesus is described as the provider of eternal life in several places in the New Testament. For example:

- "The gift of God is eternal life through Jesus Christ our Lord" (Romans 6:23).
- "This is the promise that he hath promised us, even eternal life" (1 John 2:25).
- "Looking for the mercy of our Lord Jesus Christ unto eternal life" (Jude 1:21).

But 1 John 5:20 is the only verse in the Bible where Jesus Himself is given the name Eternal Life. The apostle John was probably thinking about the resurrection of Jesus, His ascension to the Father, and His declaration, "I am alive for evermore" (Revelation 1:18).

Jesus tasted death like all mortal human beings. But He was gloriously raised and restored to His place of honor with God the Father in heaven. As the perfect model of Eternal Life, Jesus promises that all who place their trust in Him will live forever. The apostle Paul puts it like this: "For as in Adam all die, even so in Christ shall all be made alive" (1 Corinthians 15:22).

EVERLASTING FATHER

We are accustomed to making the distinction between God and Jesus by referring to God as the Father and to Jesus as the Son. But in this famous messianic passage from Isaiah, the prophet seems to blur these neat lines by referring to Jesus as the Father—the Everlasting Father.

This name of Jesus focuses attention on the dilemma we face as Christians in trying to explain the Trinity, or God's existence in three different modes or essences—Father, Son, and Holy Spirit. Just where does the God mode stop and where do the Son and Spirit essences begin?

Some people explain the Trinity by using the analogy of water. We know that water is one substance, but it can exist in three different forms—liquid, ice, and vapor. In the same way, so this analogy goes, God exists in the three different modes known as the Trinity—one substance in three different forms.

> And we know that the Son of God is come, and hath given us an understanding, that we may know him that is true, and we are in him that is true, even in his Son Jesus Christ. This is the true God, and **eternal life**.
> 1 John 5:20

> For unto us a child is born, unto us a son is given: and the government shall be upon his shoulder: and his name shall be called Wonderful, Counsellor, The mighty God, The **everlasting Father**, The Prince of Peace.
> Isaiah 9:6
> [NASB: **Eternal Father**]

Rather than resorting to analogies like this, we are better off if we admit that there is no neat and easy way to explain the Trinity. This concept is filled with mystery that defies logical explanation. But this doesn't mean it isn't true.

So, was Jesus God's Son? Yes. Was Jesus also God, the Everlasting Father, as Isaiah declared? Yes. This doesn't make sense to our scientific, analytical minds, but faith in God's Word comes to our rescue. We believe that Jesus was separate from God but one with Him at the same time, because He Himself declared, "I and my Father are one" (John 10:30).

EVERLASTING LIGHT

In this verse, the prophet Isaiah looks ahead to the end time, when Christ will dwell with His people in heaven, or the New Jerusalem. There will be no need for the sun or moon in that time, because Jesus will serve as the Everlasting Light for His people.

The apostle John, in the book of Revelation, picks up on this prophecy, repeating Isaiah's declaration that no light would be needed in heaven except the light that Jesus will provide (see Revelation 21:23; 22:5).

It's difficult for earthbound human beings to realize that any light source could replace the sun. This hot, life-giving, luminous body has provided most of the light we have enjoyed throughout our lives. But scientists tell us that the sun is not immortal. They predict it will burn out in about five billion years.

Jesus, however, is the Everlasting Light. When the sun grows dark and disappears from the sky, Jesus' reign will continue, and we as Christians will be with him in this New Jerusalem.

> The sun shall be no more thy light by day; neither for brightness shall the moon give light unto thee: but the LORD shall be unto thee an **everlasting light**, and thy God thy glory.
> ISAIAH 60:19

EXACT IMPRINT OF GOD'S VERY BEING. See *Express Image of God.*

EXACT REPRESENTATION OF GOD'S BEING. See *Express Image of God.*

EXACT REPRESENTATION OF GOD'S NATURE. See *Express Image of God.*

EXPRESS IMAGE OF GOD

Who being the brightness of his glory, and the **express image** of his person, and upholding all things by the word of his power [NIV: sustaining all things by his powerful word], when he had by himself purged our sins, sat down on the right hand of the Majesty on high.

HEBREWS 1:3

[NASB: **exact representation of His nature**; NIV: **exact representation of his being**; NRSV: **exact imprint of God's very being**]

This name occurs at the beginning of the book of Hebrews, where the writer declares that Jesus is the climax of God's revelation of Himself to mankind (see Hebrews 1:1–3). In the past, God had communicated to His people through the prophets; but now He has "spoken unto us by His Son" (Hebrews 1:2).

The Greek word behind the phrase *express image* referred in New Testament times to engravings in wood, impressions in clay, or stamped images on coins. The imagery of this verse from Hebrews implies that Jesus was an exact duplicate of His Father in His attitudes, character, and actions. Physical features are not included in this resemblance, because God is a spiritual being (see John 4:24).

This name, the Express Image of God, tells us that Jesus perfectly represents God, His Father. If we want to know what God looks like, we should examine the life and ministry of His Son.

Have you ever heard someone say, "That boy is just like his father"? Sometimes this pronouncement can cause embarrassment for a father because of his son's bad behavior. But God was always pleased with the actions of His Son (see Luke 3:22).

Other names of God the Son that express the same meaning as this name are Image of God (2 Corinthians 4:4) and Image of the Invisible God (Colossians 1:15).

FAITHFUL

Faithful is he that calleth you, who also will do it [NIV: The one who calls you is **faithful** and he will do it].

1 THESSALONIANS 5:24

According to the dictionary, a person who is faithful displays "firm determination to stick to a cause or purpose." This definition is a perfect description of Jesus' earthly life and ministry. No wonder the apostle Paul applies the name Faithful to Him in this verse from his first epistle to the Thessalonians.

Throughout His brief earthly ministry, Jesus refused to be turned aside from His mission as the Messiah sent by the Father to bring people into His kingdom of grace. He resisted Satan's temptation at the beginning of His ministry to become a "bread Messiah" and dazzle the crowds with death-defying stunts (see Matthew 4:1–11). He also did not become the military conqueror or political hero that the Jewish people thought the Messiah should be. While on the cross, He did not try to save Himself, although He could have done so. He chose instead to die for our sins (see Luke 23:35). He was faithful to His mission as the Suffering Servant to the very end.

Dogs are well-loved as faithful companions.

He who was faithful in His earthly existence continues to be the Faithful One to those who follow Him. We as Christians have His promise that we will enjoy eternal life with Him in heaven. As the apostle Paul declares, "He which hath begun a good work in you will perform it until the day of Jesus Christ" (Philippians 1:6).

Jesus Christ, the Faithful One

- "If we confess our sins, he is faithful and just to forgive us our sins, and to cleanse us from all unrighteousness" (1 John 1:9).
- "The Lord is faithful, and he will strengthen and protect you from the evil one" (2 Thessalonians 3:3 NIV).
- "God is faithful, by whom ye were called unto the fellowship of his Son Jesus Christ our Lord" (1 Corinthians 1:9).

FAITHFUL AND TRUE

In this verse near the end of the book of Revelation, the apostle John sees Jesus appear as the heavens are opened. The white horse on which He is seated symbolizes His triumph over all His enemies. As the Faithful and True, He is coming to earth in judgment against all forms of unrighteousness and injustice.

This verse contains images that are similar to the portrayal of God as the divine Judge in the Old Testament (see *Judge* in part 1, Names of God the Father). For example, in Psalm 96:13, the psalmist looks forward to the time when God will judge the earth. He will "judge the world with righteousness, and the people with his truth." Because God is the standard of truth, He has the right to set the standards by which the world will be judged.

In this verse from Revelation, God has delegated to His Son the authority to judge the world. Jesus is faithful to God's promise of judgment, and He is the True One who will judge by God's standard of ultimate truth.

As Christians, we recognize that truth does not always win out in an unjust and unrighteous world. But the final work of judgment belongs to God and His Son—the Faithful and True.

And I saw heaven opened, and behold a white horse; and he that sat upon him was called **Faithful and True**, and in righteousness he doth judge and make war.
REVELATION 19:11

> And unto the angel of the church of the Laodiceans write; These things saith the Amen, the **faithful and true witness**, the beginning of the creation of God.
> REVELATION 3:14

FAITHFUL AND TRUE WITNESS

Witness is one of the words used again and again by the apostle John in his writings—the Gospel of John, his three epistles, and the book of Revelation. It occurs about seventy times in these five books. In this verse from Revelation, John applies this word to Jesus, calling Him the Faithful and True Witness.

A witness is a person who gives testimony to others about something he has seen, felt, or experienced. The best modern example of a witness is a person who is summoned by the justice system to present testimony in a legal proceeding, such as a trial. The task of a witness is to tell the court what he knows from personal experience that is relevant to the case under investigation.

The witness that Jesus bore about God grew out of His personal experience. He is the only person who has ever seen God the Father. Thus He knows God like no one has ever known Him. He came into the world

Witnesses in court swear to speak the truth—and face penalties if found guilty of perjury, or lying under oath.

to show that His Father is a merciful God who relates to His people in love and grace. By dying on the cross, Jesus showed just how much God the Father and God the Son love us.

Those of us who have been transformed by God's love are also charged to give testimony about His love to others (see Luke 24:45–48). Jesus told His disciples, "This gospel of the kingdom shall be preached in all the world for a witness unto all nations" (Matthew 24:14). This witnessing work continues in our time through the church and individual Christians. If you know Jesus as Lord and Savior, you have no choice in the matter—you are automatically in the witnessing business.

FAITHFUL CREATOR

The apostle Peter wrote his first epistle to Christians who were undergoing persecution because of their commitment to Christ. Peter encouraged them to place their hope in their Faithful Creator, Jesus, and to "continue to do good" (NIV). This is the only place in the Bible where Jesus is called by this name.

Jesus as a participant in the physical creation with God the Father is described in other New Testament passages (see John 1:1–3; Colossians 1:16; see also *Beginning of the Creation of God* above). But the emphasis of this verse from 1 Peter is on Jesus' role as spiritual Creator. According to the apostle Paul, we become "new creatures" (2 Corinthians 5:17) when we accept Christ as Savior. As our Faithful Creator, Jesus not only gives us a new nature, but He also keeps us from falling back into sin and He leads us toward the goal of eternal life with Him in heaven.

All Christians can affirm with the apostle Paul, "The Lord will rescue me from every evil attack and will bring me safely to his heavenly kingdom" (2 Timothy 4:18 NIV).

FAITHFUL HIGH PRIEST. See *Great High Priest*.

FINISHER OF OUR FAITH. See *Author and Finisher of Our Faith*.

FIRST AND THE LAST. See *Alpha and Omega*.

FIRSTBEGOTTEN

The word *he* in this verse refers to God the Father, and *firstbegotten* refers to His Son, Jesus Christ. But because Jesus has existed from eternity with the Father (see *Beginning of the Creation of God* above), how could Jesus be the firstborn or "firstbegotten into the world"?

Firstbegotten refers to Jesus' incarnation, or His appearance in human flesh. True, He has existed with the Father from the beginning; but there was a specific point in time when He was conceived by the Holy Spirit in Mary's womb and then born nine months later like any human infant (see Luke 1:35; 2:7). This is one sense in which the name Firstbegotten is applied to Jesus.

> Wherefore let them that suffer according to the will of God commit the keeping of their souls to him in well doing, as unto a **faithful Creator**.
> 1 PETER 4:19

> And again, when he bringeth in the **firstbegotten** into the world, he saith, And let all the angels of God worship him.
> HEBREWS 1:6
> [NASB, NIV, NRSV: **firstborn**]

The word also refers to rank or order. To say that Jesus is God's Firstbegotten is to declare that He ranks above all other earthly or divine beings, except God Himself. This verse from Hebrews makes the point that Jesus is higher than all of God's angels, because they are told to bow down and worship Him. Similar names of God the Son that express the idea of His preeminence and superiority are Firstborn (Psalm 89:27), Firstborn Among Many Brethren (Romans 8:29), and Firstborn of Every Creature (Colossians 1:15).

As God's Firstbegotten or Firstborn, Jesus is worthy of our honor and praise. The apostle Peter declares that all Christians should glorify Jesus Christ, "to whom be praise and dominion for ever and ever" (1 Peter 4:11).

Rights and Responsibilities of the Firstborn

Jesus as the Firstbegotten or Firstborn picks up on a key term that appears often throughout the Old Testament. The firstborn offspring of both humans and animals were considered special blessings of God, and they were to be devoted to Him (see Exodus 13:2). The firstborn son in a Jewish family inherited a larger share of the family property than the other sons, but he also assumed responsibility for taking care of the family after his father's death.

As the Firstborn, Jesus is exalted as head of the church, but He is also responsible for its welfare. Aren't you glad our well-being rests in such capable hands?

FIRST BEGOTTEN OF THE DEAD.
See *Firstborn from the Dead.*

FIRSTBORN. See *Firstbegotten.*

FIRSTBORN AMONG MANY BRETHREN. See *Firstbegotten.*

FIRSTBORN OF EVERY CREATURE.
See *Firstbegotten.*

FIRSTBORN FROM THE DEAD
The apostle Paul applies this name to Jesus in his description of Jesus as head of the church in his epistle to the Colossian Christians. *Firstborn from the Dead* expresses the same

essential meaning as the name *First Begotten of the Dead* in the book of Revelation (see Revelation 1:5).

This name obviously refers to Jesus' resurrection. But in what sense was He the Firstborn from the Dead? Jesus was not the first person in the Bible to be brought back to life following physical death. The prophet Elisha raised back to life the son of a family in Shunem (see 2 Kings 4:18–37). Jesus Himself raised three people from the dead: the daughter of Jairus (see Matthew 9:18–26), the son of a widow in the village of Nain (see Luke 7:11–15), and His friend Lazarus (see John 11:1–44).

But all of these resurrections were temporary stays of death. These resurrected people eventually died again. Jesus rose from the grave never to die again. He was the first person to overcome death and to appear in a glorified body (see Luke 24:36–39). He also rose as the head of a new creation, the church. As the Firstborn from the Dead, Jesus has the authority and power to provide bodily resurrection and eternal life for all who commit their lives to Him (see 1 Corinthians 15:12–26).

> And he is the head of the body, the church: who is the beginning, the **firstborn from the dead**; that in all things he might have the preeminence.
> COLOSSIANS 1:18

Jesus raises a young man—son of a widow from Nain—from the dead. But the young man would die again. Jesus was the first to come back to life permanently, as "firstborn from the dead."

But now is Christ risen from the dead, and become the **firstfruits of them that slept**. 1 CORINTHIANS 15:20 [NIV: **firstfruits of those who have fallen asleep**; NRSV: **first fruits of those who have died**]

But every man in his own order: Christ the **firstfruits**; afterward they that are Christ's at his coming. 1 CORINTHIANS 15:23

FIRSTFRUITS

These references to Jesus as the Firstfruits occur in the apostle Paul's famous passage about the resurrection of Jesus and His promise of a similar resurrection for all believers (see 1 Corinthians 15:12–57).

Some people in the church at Corinth apparently were teaching that the resurrection was spiritual, not physical, in nature, or that the resurrection of the dead had already happened. They may have even been denying the resurrection altogether, because Paul scolds them: "How say some among you that there is no resurrection of the dead?" (1 Corinthians 15:12).

Paul based his argument for Jesus' physical resurrection on the fact that He had been seen by His disciples as well as many other believers during the days after He rose from the dead (see 1 Corinthians 15:3–7). He was the Firstfruits of the resurrection, or the model that had blazed the trail for them.

The Jewish people thought of the firstfruits, or the first of their crops to be gathered, as God's harvest. These were presented as offerings to God on the day of the firstfruits—part of the festival known as Pentecost, which celebrated the harvest (see Numbers 28:26; 2 Chronicles 31:5).

Harvest time was cause for great celebration when the "firstfruits" appeared.

To Paul, Jesus in His resurrection was the Firstfruits of a spiritual harvest known as eternal life. Believers in Jesus would be the rest of the harvest, which would be gathered in at the appointed time. Just as Jesus had been raised from the dead to reign with His Father in glory, so too the believers' bodies would be "raised incorruptible" (1 Corinthians 15:52) at Christ's second coming, and they would live with Him forever in heaven.

FIRSTFRUITS OF THOSE WHO HAVE DIED. See *Firstfruits*.

FLESH

This bold affirmation of the apostle John in his Gospel is the strongest declaration in the New Testament about the humanity of Jesus. And it carries the authority of an eyewitness.

John knew that Jesus existed in the flesh, because he had lived and worked with Him. As one of Jesus' disciples, John had walked with Him along the dusty roads of Palestine, watched His interaction with people, and learned from His teachings across a period of about three years. Certainly, John must have been impressed by Jesus' miracles and His claim to be the divine Son of God. But he was also convinced that Jesus was fully human.

In John's later years, his personal association with Jesus in the flesh was a valuable asset to the church. False teachers had begun to teach that Jesus did not exist in human form, and that He only seemed to be a man. John rejected this heresy with these strong words: "Every spirit that confesseth that Jesus Christ is come in the flesh is of God: and every spirit that confesseth not that Jesus Christ is come in the flesh is not of God: and this is that spirit of antichrist" (1 John 4:2–3).

We find it hard to understand how Jesus could be both divine and human in the same body. But this is the clear affirmation of the New Testament, and the church has upheld this doctrine for almost two thousand years, despite ridicule by the world. Even the apostle Paul admitted that it was a deep mystery, but he accepted it by faith. "And most certainly, the mystery of godliness is great," he said. "He was manifested in the flesh, justified in the Spirit, seen by angels, preached among the Gentiles, believed on in the world, taken up in glory" (1 Timothy 3:16 HCSB).

Other names of God the Son that emphasize the human side of Jesus' nature are God Manifest in the Flesh (1 Timothy 3:16), Man Approved of God (Acts 2:22), and Man Christ Jesus (1 Timothy 2:5).

> And the Word was made **flesh**, and dwelt among us, (and we beheld his glory, the glory as of the only begotten of the Father,) full of grace and truth.
> JOHN 1:14

Evidences from Mark's Gospel of Jesus' Existence in the Flesh

- His fatigue (Mark 4:38)
- His amazement (Mark 6:6)
- His disappointment (Mark 8:12)
- His displeasure (Mark 10:14)
- His anger (Mark 11:15–17)
- His sorrow (Mark 14:34)

FOREKNOWN BEFORE THE FOUNDATION OF THE WORLD. See

Foreordained before the Foundation of the World.

FOREORDAINED BEFORE THE FOUNDATION OF THE WORLD

This verse from the apostle Peter's first epistle is the only place in the Bible where Jesus is called by this name. It echoes the words of Peter on the day of Pentecost, when three thousand people became believers in Christ (see Acts 2:41). In his sermon on that occasion, Peter told the crowd that Jesus had been sent into the world by "the determinate counsel and foreknowledge of God" (Acts 2:23).

The words *foreordained* and *foreknowledge* show that Jesus was especially chosen by God the Father for the redemptive mission on which He was sent. His coming to earth was no accident; it was part of God's plan. The phrase "before the foundation of the world" tells us that Jesus had existed with God the Father from the beginning (see John 1:1–3). Even before He created the world, God had designated His Son as the agent of salvation for all humankind.

This is difficult for us earthbound humans to understand. But aren't you glad that God didn't wait until we had perfect understanding before He sent Jesus to deliver us from the bondage of sin?

A name of Jesus similar in meaning to Foreordained before the Foundation of the World is Man Whom God Hath Ordained (Acts 17:31).

> Who verily was **foreordained before the foundation of the world**, but was manifest [NIV: revealed] in these last times for you.
> 1 PETER 1:20
> [NASB: **foreknown before the foundation of the world**; NIV: **chosen before the creation of the world**; NRSV: **destined before the foundation of the world**]

FORERUNNER

A forerunner is an advance agent, the lead person on a team. He goes ahead on a scouting mission to spot possible dangers and to prepare the way for others who will follow. Two good examples of forerunners in the Bible are the twelve spies sent by Moses to investigate the land of Canaan (see Numbers 13:1–3) and the forerunner of Jesus, John the Baptist (see Mark 1:1–8).

But the ultimate Forerunner, according to the author of Hebrews, was Jesus Christ. He came to prepare the way so we could become citizens of God's kingdom. Following His death and resurrection, He returned to His Father in heaven (see Acts 1:9). There, He has prepared a place for us. We as

> Whither the **forerunner** is for us entered, even Jesus, made an high priest for ever after the order of Melchisedec.
> HEBREWS 6:20

Christians have His word that we will live in heaven with Him forever. "If I go and prepare a place for you," He promised, "I will come again, and receive you unto myself, that where I am, there ye may be also" (John 14:3).

An advance scout serves as "forerunner" to his fellow soldiers.

FOUNDATION

In his first letter to the believers at Corinth, the apostle Paul dealt with divisions in the church (see 1 Corinthians 1:10–15). The people were following four different authority figures—Paul, Apollos, Cephas, and Christ. Paul made it clear in this verse (3:11) that the one Foundation on which they should be basing their faith was Jesus Christ.

For other **foundation** can no man lay than that is laid, which is Jesus Christ.
1 CORINTHIANS 3:11

The Ultimate Foundation

The old hymn "How Firm a Foundation" declares that Christians can rely on Jesus Christ and the promise of His abiding presence.

How firm a foundation, ye saints of the Lord,
Is laid for your faith in His excellent Word!
What more can He say than to you He hath said,
To you who for refuge to Jesus have fled?

Jesus Himself addressed this issue during His earthly ministry. In the parable of the two foundations, He described two men who built houses on two different sites (see Matthew 7:24–27). The house built on sand collapsed in the first storm that came up. The second house held firm in violent weather, because "it was founded upon a rock" (Matthew 7:25).

The message of this parable is that almost any foundation will do when the weather is good. But only a faith based on the solid Foundation known as Jesus Christ can withstand the gales and floods of life.

Several centuries before Jesus was born, the prophet Isaiah looked ahead to the coming of the Messiah and referred to Him as the Sure Foundation (Isaiah 28:16).

FOUNTAIN

This verse from the prophet Zechariah looks forward to the day when the nations of Israel and Judah would be restored to moral purity. They had rebelled against God and were worshipping false gods. The Lord would provide a fountain in which they could wash and be cleansed of their sin.

> In that day there shall be a **fountain** opened to the house of David and to the inhabitants of Jerusalem for sin and for uncleanness [NIV: to cleanse them from sin and impurity].
> ZECHARIAH 13:1

The word *fountain* in the Bible generally refers to a spring or some source of fresh water, such as a well or a free-flowing stream. This type of water was preferable to standing water that was stored in cisterns. The prophet Isaiah used this image of a fountain in referring to God (see *Fountain of Living Waters* in part 1, Names of God the Father).

This passage from Zechariah has been interpreted as a reference to Jesus Christ. He is the Fountain whose blood provides cleansing from sin. This Fountain is available to everyone—nobles ("the house of David") as well as commoners ("the inhabitants of Jerusalem").

As the Fountain of salvation, Jesus invites us to drink freely of the living water that He provides. "Whosoever drinketh of the water that I shall give him shall never thirst," He told the woman at the well. "The water that I shall give him shall be in him a well of water springing up into everlasting life" (John 4:14).

Jesus as the Fountain of Life is memorialized in the hymn "There Is a Fountain," written by William Cowper.

> There is a fountain filled with blood
> Drawn from Immanuel's veins;
> And sinners plunged beneath that flood
> Lose all their guilty stains.
> Lose all their guilty stains,
> Lose all their guilty stains;
> And sinners plunged beneath that flood
> Lose all their guilty stains.

FRIEND OF PUBLICANS AND SINNERS

With these words, Jesus condemned the Pharisees, who were criticizing Him for associating with people whom they considered the outcasts of society.

But Jesus took their criticism as a compliment. He had been sent into the world to become the Savior of sinners. On one occasion, He told the scribes and Pharisees, "They that are whole have no need of the physician, but they that are sick: I came not to call the righteous, but sinners to repentance" (Mark 2:17).

In addition to befriending all sinners, Jesus was also a special friend to His disciples—the twelve ordinary men whom He trained to carry on His work after He was gone. In His long farewell address to them in the Gospel of John, He tells them, "Henceforth I call you not servants. . .but I have called you friends; for all things that I have heard of my father I have made known unto you" (John 15:15).

Most of us get to know a lot of people during our lifetime—teachers, neighbors, fellow church members, work associates. But few of these become true friends. In this select group whom we consider friends, one stands out above all others—our Lord Jesus Christ. He is the Friend who made the ultimate sacrifice on our behalf. "Greater love hath no man than this," He declared, "that a man lay down his life for his friends" (John 15:13).

> The Son of man came eating and drinking, and they say, Behold a man gluttonous, and a winebibber [NIV: Here is a glutton and a drunkard], a **friend of publicans and sinners**.
> MATTHEW 11:19
> [NASB, NIV, NRSV: **friend of tax collectors and sinners**]

"Jesus Is All the World to Me," a hymn by Will L. Thompson, focuses on the never-failing friendship of Jesus for all believers.

Jesus is all the world to me,
My life, my joy, my all;
He is my strength from day to day,
Without Him I would fall:
When I am sad, to Him I go,
No other one can cheer me so;
When I am sad
He makes me glad,
He's my friend.

FULLERS' SOAP

This verse from the next to last chapter in the Old Testament refers to the coming Messiah. The Jewish people expected Him to be a conquering hero. But the prophet Malachi declared that He would come in judgment against the sinful nation of Israel.

A fuller, or launderer, made his living by washing and dyeing clothes or cloth. Soap as we know it did not exist in Bible times, so the fuller used a strong alkaline substance to get clothes clean. It was made from a plant that was reduced to ashes to form potash or lye.

The name Fullers' Soap emphasizes the judgment side of Jesus' ministry. He will return to earth in judgment against those who refuse to accept Him as Lord and Savior (see 2 Corinthians 5:10).

GATE. See *Door*.

GIFT OF GOD

Jesus answered and
said unto her, If thou
knewest the **gift of
God**, and who it
is that saith to thee,
Give me to drink; thou
wouldest have asked
of him, and he would
have given thee
living water.
JOHN 4:10

Jesus spoke these words to the woman at the well outside the village of Sychar (see John 4:5–26). In His long conversation with this sinful woman, Jesus made it clear that He was the Gift of God who had been sent into the world by God the Father as His agent of salvation.

The dictionary defines a gift as "something voluntarily transferred by one person to another without compensation." This is a fancy way of saying that a gift is something a person gives without expecting anything in return. Speaking in spiritual terms, we might add the element of grace to this definition: God through His Son gave us a gift that we could never earn and certainly did not deserve.

Some earthly gifts are better than others. Most of us have received gifts that we couldn't use or that had to be returned to the store because they were the wrong size or the wrong color. But not so with God's gift of His Son. We needed this gift more than anything in the world; it was selected with great care; and it was given in love. This familiar verse from the Gospel of John says it all: "For God so loved the world, that he gave his only begotten Son, that whosoever believeth in him should not perish, but have everlasting life" (John 3:16).

Another name of God the Son that means essentially the

same thing as Gift of God is Unspeakable Gift (2 Corinthians 9:15).

God's Greatest Gift
- "For the wages of sin is death; but the gift of God is eternal life through Jesus Christ our Lord" (Romans 6:23).
- "For by grace are ye saved through faith; and that not of yourselves: it is the gift of God: not of works, lest any man should boast" (Ephesians 2:8-9).

GLORY OF ISRAEL

This verse is part of the prayer of Simeon in the temple when he recognized the infant Jesus as the Messiah whom God had sent into the world (see *Consolation of Israel* above). God revealed to Simeon that Jesus would grow up to become not only a light to the Gentiles but the Glory of Israel as well.

> For my eyes have seen thy salvation. . . a light to lighten the Gentiles [NIV: a light for revelation to the Gentiles], and the **glory of thy people Israel**.
> LUKE 2:30, 32

As God's chosen people, the nation of Israel was charged with the responsibility of leading other nations to come to know and worship the one true God. Jesus was born into the world as a Jew and a native of Israel. In this sense, He was the Glory of Israel, showing that God had not given up on His promise to bless the entire world through Abraham and his descendants (see Genesis 12:1–3).

The tragedy is that Jesus was rejected by His own people. They were tripped up by their expectations of a Messiah who would restore Israel to its golden days as a political power. But God's purpose was not turned aside by their refusal to ac-

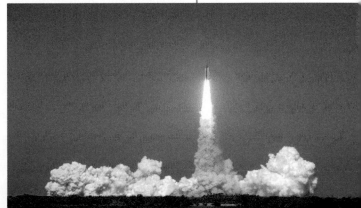

The impressive and brilliant flame of a rocket launch is nothing compared to the "glory of Israel," the spiritual light that Jesus brings!

cept Him and His spiritual mission. The glory of one nation, Israel, went on to become a light to the Gentiles, as Simeon predicted. At His return He will become the Glorified One among all the peoples of the world (see Philippians 2:11).

> Then saith he to Thomas, Reach hither thy finger [NIV: Put your finger here], and behold [NIV: see] my hands, and reach hither thy hand [NIV: reach out your hand], and thrust it into my side: and be not faithless, but believing [NIV: stop doubting and believe]. And Thomas answered and said unto him, my Lord and my **God**.
>
> JOHN 20:27–28

GOD

These verses from the Gospel of John describe an appearance of Jesus to His disciples after His resurrection. He had revealed Himself to them before at a time when Thomas the disciple was not present. Thomas had declared that he would not believe that Jesus was alive unless he could see Him with his own eyes.

When Thomas finally saw the resurrected Lord, he not only believed, but he also acknowledged Jesus as God in the flesh. This is one of the clearest statements in all the New Testament of the divinity of Jesus and His oneness with the Father.

Thomas, like all the other disciples of Jesus, had lived and worked with Him for about three years. They had walked with Him among the people, observing His miracles and listening to His teachings on the kingdom of God. But they were slow to understand that Jesus was actually God come to earth in human form. Theologians call this the doctrine of incarnation, a word that derives from a Latin term, *in carne*, meaning "in flesh."

As the God-man, Jesus is both the all-powerful Father, for whom nothing is impossible, and the man of sorrows, who can sympathize with us in our human weakness. He is the all-sufficient Savior.

Other names of God the Son that express His divinity and oneness with the Father are God Blessed For Ever (Romans 9:5), God Manifest in the Flesh (1 Timothy 3:16), God Our Saviour (1 Timothy 2:3), and True God (1 John 5:20).

Jesus' Oneness with God in John's Gospel

- "In the beginning was the Word, and the Word was with God, and the Word was God" (John 1:1).
- "I and my Father are one" (John 10:30).
- "He that hath seen me hath seen the Father" (John 14:9).

GOD BLESSED FOREVER. See *God*.

GOD MANIFEST IN THE FLESH.
See *Flesh*; *God*.

GOD OUR SAVIOUR. See *God*.

GOD WITH US. See *Immanuel/Emmanuel*.

GOOD MASTER

This account of Jesus' encounter with a man seeking eternal life appears in all three Synoptic Gospels—Matthew, Mark, and Luke. Matthew tells us that the man was young (see Matthew 19:22); Mark reveals that he was rich (see Mark 10:22); and Luke informs us that he was a ruler (see Luke 18:18). Thus, the man is known as the rich young ruler.

This young man called Jesus "Good Master" and bowed before Him. This shows that he was respectful toward Jesus and recognized Him as a teacher of some authority. But Jesus gently corrected him for calling Him "good." "There is none good but one," He replied, "that is, God" (Mark 10:18).

Why did Jesus resist this name? Perhaps He saw it as meaningless flattery. Or, it may have been His way of testing the young ruler's commitment to God the Father, who held the keys to eternal life—the very thing the man was seeking. He wanted to know what he could *do* to have eternal life. Jesus made it clear that it is a gift that God bestows on those who follow His commands.

The message of this account is that flattery gets us no-where with God. He grants His grace to those who commit to follow Him in absolute obedience. The rich young ruler was more committed to his riches than he was to following the Lord. This kept him from finding the eternal life that he sought.

> And when he was gone forth into the way, there came one [NIV: a man] running, and kneeled to him, and asked him, **Good Master**, what shall I do that I may inherit eternal life?
> MARK 10:17
> [NASB, NIV, NRSV: **Good Teacher**]

GOOD SHEPHERD

This verse is part of a long monologue by Jesus, in which He compares His followers to sheep and identifies Himself as the Shepherd who leads His flock (see John 10:1–16).

In the Old Testament, God is also known by this name (see *Shepherd* in part 1, Names of God the Father). Sheep are helpless animals that have no natural defenses against preda-tors such as wolves and lions. They wander away from the flock and find themselves in danger unless they are watched constantly. They have to be led from one grassy area to an-other to find new sources of food and water. Sheep need a vigilant leader—a shepherd—to provide all these resources.

But Jesus is more than just another shepherd. He is the *Good* Shepherd. The "good" in this name shows that Jesus

> I am the **good shepherd**: the **good shepherd** giveth his life for the sheep.
> JOHN 10:11

was deliberately contrasting Himself with the religious leaders of Israel—the scribes and Pharisees—who were leading the people astray. They were like "hirelings" (John 10:12), or hired hands who were paid to do a job but had no personal interest in the sheep they were leading. But Jesus is different.

- He knows His sheep personally and calls them by name (John 10:3).
- He doesn't drive His sheep; He guides them by showing the way (John 10:4).
- He is the door of the sheepfold that offers shelter and safety for His sheep (John 10:9).
- Unlike hired shepherds, He is willing to put His own life on the line for His sheep (John 10:11–12).
- He loves His sheep (John 10:13–15).

Some people might consider it an insult if we referred to them as sheep. But Christians don't mind, because we, as God's sheep, are in the care of the Good Shepherd.

Other names of God the Son that use the imagery of a shepherd are Chief Shepherd (1 Peter 5:4), Door of the Sheep (John 10:7), Great Shepherd of the Sheep (Hebrews 13:20), and Shepherd of Your Souls (1 Peter 2:25).

Led by the Good Shepherd

In her hymn "Saviour, Like a Shepherd Lead Us," Dorothy A. Thrupp prays for the tender leadership of the Good Shepherd.

Saviour, like a shepherd lead us,
Much we need thy tender care;
In thy pleasant pastures feed us,
For our use thy folds prepare.
Blessed Jesus, blessed Jesus,
Thou hast bought us, Thine we are.
Blessed Jesus, blessed Jesus,
Thou hast bought us, Thine we are.

The image of Christ as the "Good Shepherd" was captured in art by the early Christian church as represented in statuettes like this one from the 4th century.

GOOD TEACHER. See *Good Master.*

GOVERNOR

When Jesus was born in Bethlehem, wise men came from a far country to find Him after a strange star appeared in the eastern sky. They stopped in Jerusalem to find out where this new ruler had been born. The Jewish scholars of Jerusalem quoted this verse from the prophet Micah to tell these wise men that this ruler was supposed to be born in Bethlehem (see Micah 5:2). The name that they used for Jesus was Governor, a generic term for a ruler, administrator, leader, or civil official.

> And thou Bethlehem, in the land of Juda, art not the least [NIV: are by no means least] among the princes [NIV: rulers] of Juda: for out of thee shall come a **Governor**, that shall rule my people Israel.
> MATTHEW 2:6

The world into which Jesus was born knew all about governors. These officials were sent by Rome to rule over the provinces—territories similar to states—into which the Roman government had divided its empire. A provincial governor was responsible for collecting taxes for the Roman treasury, keeping the peace, and administering the rule of Rome in the territory to which he was assigned. Three Roman governors are mentioned in the New Testament: Cyrenius (Luke 2:2), Pontius Pilate (Matthew 27:2), and Felix (Acts 23:24).

But Jesus is a Governor of a different type. He was sent as a spiritual ruler to guide and direct His people in the ways of the Lord. He rules by love and not by force. As Christians, our lives should reflect more of His rule every day as we grow in our commitment to Him and His teachings.

Governors of states and nations come and go, but Jesus' rule over His followers is eternal. As the prophet Isaiah declares, "Of the increase of his government and peace there will be no end" (Isaiah 9:7 NIV).

In other passages about the Messiah's rulership, Jesus is called a Leader and Commander (Isaiah 55:4) and a Ruler in Israel (Micah 5:2).

GREATER THAN JONAS/GREATER THAN SOLOMON

In these verses, Jesus condemns the scribes and Pharisees for their unbelief. Although they had seen Him perform many miracles, they were biased against Him and His teachings. They kept asking Him to perform more spectacular signs. Jesus uses two case studies from the Old Testament to make a point about their hopeless skepticism.

First, Jesus asks them to think about the citizens of the pagan city of Nineveh, who had repented at the preaching of the reluctant prophet Jonah. These pagan Ninevites were a judgment against Jesus' generation. He was Greater Than Jonah would ever be, but still the scribes and Pharisees refused to accept Him or His message.

Then Jesus reminds them of the queen of Sheba and draws a contrast between her attitude and theirs. She had traveled many miles to learn from King Solomon (and did so gladly), but the Jewish religious leaders were unwilling to listen to Jesus, who stood among them as a ready and accessible teacher. The queen of Sheba was eager to learn from Solomon, but the scribes and Pharisees were hardened in their attitude toward Jesus. The queen also stood in judgment against Jesus' generation because they had rejected the teachings of the One who was Greater Than Solomon.

The problem with the scribes and Pharisees was that their minds were like concrete—permanently set. For generations, they had been expecting God to send the Messiah into the world; yet, when He stood among them, they didn't recognize Him. They were trapped by their expectations of what the Messiah would be like.

Jesus always has been and always will be a "greater than" personality. His grace exceeds our understanding. He always has more truth to teach us than we are willing to accept. He has prepared a place for us in heaven that is more glorious than we can imagine. This means that we as Christians need open and teachable minds. Hold on for the ride; God is not finished with us yet.

GREAT HIGH PRIEST

The worship rituals of Old Testament times were presided over by the priesthood. Priests offered various types of sacrifices on behalf of the people to atone for their sins. This name of Jesus from the book of Hebrews picks up on this priestly imagery.

At the top of the priestly hierarchy stood the high priest. His responsibility as supreme priest was to see that all the functions of the priesthood were carried out appropriately (see 2 Chronicles 19:11). Below him were the priests, who performed sacrificial rituals at the altar. On the lower end of

---

The men of Nineveh shall rise in judgment with this generation. . . because they repented at the preaching of Jonas [NIV: Jonah]; and, behold, a **greater than Jonas** is here. The queen of the south shall rise up in the judgment with this generation. . .for she came from the uttermost parts [NIV: ends] of the earth to hear the wisdom of Solomon; and, behold, a **greater than Solomon** is here.
MATTHEW 12:41–42

Seeing then that we have a **great high priest**, that is passed into the heavens, Jesus the Son of God, let us hold fast our profession [NIV: hold firmly to the faith we profess].
HEBREWS 4:14

the priesthood were the Levites, who performed menial jobs as assistants to the priests, doing such chores as preparing animals for sacrifice, cleaning sacrificial vessels, and taking care of the tabernacle and the temple.

In this verse from Hebrews, the writer adds another level to this priesthood hierarchy by referring to Jesus as the Great High Priest. He stands above even the high priest of Israel, because He laid down His own life as the perfect sacrifice for sin.

The book of Hebrews might be called the priestly book of the New Testament. It is filled with references to Jesus as our Priest or our High Priest (see sidebar). In modern terms, a priest is usually understood as a religious leader who intercedes between God and man on behalf of sinful people. As Christians, we need no human intermediary to represent us before God. We can come directly into His presence through "one mediator between God and men, the man Christ Jesus" (1 Timothy 2:5).

Other priestly names of God the Son that express basically the same idea as Great High Priest are High Priest For Ever (Hebrews 6:20), High Priest of Our Profession (Hebrews 3:1), Merciful and Faithful High Priest (Hebrews 2:17), and Priest For Ever (Hebrews 7:17).

> The High Priest in Bibles times was overseer of all the priestly functions, including the sacrifices. Jesus stands above all other priests as the True High Priest who also came to lay down his life as the one true sacrifice for sin.

EARTHLY PRIESTS COMPARED TO JESUS' PRIESTHOOD

Human Priests	Jesus Our Priest
Became priests through human succession (Hebrews 5:1)	Appointed a priest by God (Hebrews 5:5, 10)
Required to offer sacrifice for their own sin (Hebrews 7:27–28)	Had no sin (Hebrews 4:15)
Animal blood could not take away sin (Hebrews 10:1–4)	Offered His own blood as atonement for human sin (Hebrews 9:12)
Subject to death (Hebrews 7:23)	Has an eternal priesthood; lives forever (Hebrews 7:24–25)

And there came a fear on all [NIV: they were all filled with awe]: and they glorified God, saying, That a **great prophet** is risen up among us; and, That God hath visited his people.
LUKE 7:16

GREAT PROPHET

This verse describes the reaction of the people of Nain when Jesus brought back to life the son of a widow of that town. Perhaps they were comparing Jesus to Elijah, the famous prophet of Old Testament times, who also brought back from the dead the son of a poor widow (see 1 Kings 17:17–24).

Their reaction was similar to that of those whom Jesus fed when He multiplied five loaves and two fish to feed more than five thousand people. They declared, "This is of a truth that prophet that should come into the world" (John 6:14). They were referring to a promise God had made to Moses many centuries before that a prophet similar to Moses would one day appear among His people (see Deuteronomy 18:18). Jesus was the promised Prophet.

Jesus was the ultimate Prophet in a long line of prophets whom God had sent to His people, the Israelites, across many centuries. The classic definition of a prophet in the Jewish tradition is that he should declare God's message to His people and he should foretell the future. Jesus fit this definition perfectly.

As the Master Teacher, He expounded God's timeless truth to people as they had never been taught before. He taught about the kingdom of God and how people could become citizens of this heavenly realm. He also drew back the curtain to reveal the end time, encouraging people to get ready for the time when God would bring the world to its appointed conclusion.

A true prophet must be committed to declaring God's truth, no matter how his message is received. He accepts the fact that he will never be the most popular person in town. It was no different with Jesus. Some of the saddest words He ever uttered were spoken after He was rejected by the people of His own hometown: "Only in his hometown and in his own house is a prophet without honor" (Matthew 13:57 NIV).

Other names of God the Son that emphasize his role as Prophet are Prophet Mighty in Deed and Word (Luke 24:19) and Prophet of Nazareth of Galilee (Matthew 21:11).

GREAT SHEPHERD OF THE SHEEP.

See *Good Shepherd.*

GUARDIAN OF YOUR SOULS. See *Bishop of Your Souls*.

HEAD OF ALL PRINCIPALITY AND POWER

In this verse, the apostle Paul deals with a false teaching in the church at Colossae. Some were claiming that Jesus was a member of an order of angels, thus a created being like all other things created by God. Paul declared that Jesus was actually the Head of All Principality and Power—a non-created being who was above all heavenly beings, with the exception of God Himself. And even in His relationship to God, Jesus reflected "all the fulness of the Godhead."

Just as Jesus is supreme in the heavens, He also exercises dominion over all the earth. This truth should drive us to our knees in worship and praise. In her hymn "Praise Him! Praise Him!" this is how Fanny J. Crosby expresses it:

Praise Him! Praise Him! Jesus our blessed Redeemer!
Sing, O Earth, His wonderful love proclaim!
Hail Him! Hail Him! highest archangels in glory;
Strength and honor give to His holy name!

Other names of God the Son that express His supreme headship are Head of Every Man (1 Corinthians 11:3) and Head Over All Things (Ephesians 1:22).

HEAD OF EVERY MAN. See *Head of All Principality and Power*.

HEAD OF EVERY RULER AND AUTHORITY. See *Head of All Principality and Power*.

HEAD OF THE CHURCH

Only here and in one other place in the New Testament (see Colossians 1:18) is Jesus called the Head of the Church. This is not surprising, because very little is said about the church in any of the New Testament writings. But there is little doubt that Jesus had the church in mind from the very beginning of His ministry.

The first evidence of His commitment to the church was His selection of twelve disciples to join Him in ministry. The word *disciple* means "learner"—and that's exactly what they

For in him dwelleth all the fulness of the Godhead bodily [NIV: in Christ all the fullness of the Deity lives in bodily form]. And ye are complete in him, which is the **head of all principality and power**. COLOSSIANS 2:9–10 [NASB: **head over all rule and authority**; NIV: **head over every power and authority**; NRSV: **head of every ruler and authority**]

For the husband is the head of the wife, even as Christ is the **head of the church**: and he is the saviour of the body. EPHESIANS 5:23

were. They learned from Jesus—who He was, the mission on which He had been sent, the characteristics of citizens of the kingdom of God, and God's love for all people, Gentiles included. Jesus trained these common, ordinary men to carry on His work after He was gone.

Jesus also spoke openly several times about the church. On one occasion, he told Peter, "Upon this rock I will build my church" (Matthew 16:18). Peter had just declared his belief that Jesus was the long-awaited Messiah and "the Son of the living God" (Matthew 16:16). Jesus was saying that His church would be built on confessions of faith just like the one Peter had made. The church would consist of people who accepted Jesus as Savior and Lord and committed themselves to His work of redemption in the world.

Other clues about Jesus' commitment to the church appear in the Gospel of John. He promised His disciples that He would send the Holy Spirit to comfort and guide them after He returned to God the Father (see John 14:16–18). He sealed this promise some time later with

Church buildings come in every color, shape, and size. But if they truly worship Jesus, they all have the same "head."

a fervent prayer on their behalf. He asked God to protect His disciples and keep them committed to the mission for which He had trained them. "As you sent me into the world," He prayed, "I have sent them into the world" (John 17:18 NIV).

The church is still the key element in Jesus' strategy to bring the world into the kingdom of God. He is the Head of the Church, and we as believers make up the body. A body without a head is useless, but a body joined to a head becomes a living, breathing, working organism. There's no limit to what it can accomplish for the cause of Christ our Head.

Love for the Church

If Jesus loved the church enough to die for it, Christians should love it, too. This is the message of "I Love Thy Kingdom, Lord," a hymn by Timothy Dwight.

I love Thy kingdom, Lord,
The house of Thine abode,
The church our blessed Redeemer saved
With His own precious blood.
For her my tears shall fall;
For her my prayers ascend;
To her my cares and toils be given
Till toils and cares shall end.

HEAD OF THE CORNER

Jesus directed these words to the religious leaders of His day who were questioning His authority. He quoted Psalm 118:22–23, an Old Testament passage that they probably knew well. His point was that He was destined to be rejected by them as the Messiah.

But He, the rejected Stone, would become the centerpiece of a new building that would include all people who accepted Him as Savior and Lord. This building would be the church, a fresh, new organism that would be born out of the ashes of the old religious order based on the Jewish law.

The apostle Peter also quoted this same verse from the Psalms (see 1 Peter 2:7). Peter went on to say that Jesus, the rejected Stone, was also a Stone of Stumbling and a Rock of Offence (see 1 Peter 2:8) to those people who thought the Messiah would be a powerful political and military leader. It was unthinkable to them that He would come as a spiritual deliverer who would suffer and die on a cross.

Jesus as the Head of the Corner expresses the same idea as His name, Cornerstone (see *Chief Cornerstone* above).

HEAD OVER ALL RULE AND AUTHORITY. See *Head of All Principality and Power.*

HEAD OVER ALL THINGS. See *Head of All Principality and Power.*

Jesus saith unto them, Did ye never read in the scriptures, The stone which the builders rejected, the same is become the **head of the corner**: this is the Lord's doing, and it is marvellous in our eyes?
MATTHEW 21:42
[NASB: **CHIEF CORNER STONE**; NIV: **capstone**; NRSV: **cornerstone**]

HEAD OVER EVERY POWER AND AUTHORITY. See *Head of All Principality and Power.*

HEIR OF ALL THINGS

> God, who. . .spake in time past unto the fathers by the prophets, hath in these last days spoken unto us by his Son, whom he hath appointed **heir of all things**, by whom also he made the worlds.
> HEBREWS 1:1–2

The dictionary defines an heir as "one who receives or is entitled to receive some endowment or quality from a parent or predecessor." Most heirs receive only a small amount of property or cash that their parents have managed to accumulate during a lifetime of working and saving. But the writer of Hebrews declares that Jesus is the Heir of All Things, and this endowment was granted to Him by none other than God the Father.

The heirship of Jesus is both material and spiritual. He participated with God in the creation of the world (see John 1:3), so God has granted Him ownership and dominion over the universe. In the spiritual sense, He sets the terms by which all people will be judged for their sins. Then He Himself became the means by which people could be made righteous in God's sight. This was accomplished through His death on the cross.

La lecture du Testament.

The great thing about Jesus' spiritual heirship is that He shares His inheritance with us. As the apostle Paul expresses it, we are "joint-heirs with Christ" (Romans 8:17) because He lives eternally with the Father and He has made it possible for us to enjoy eternal life with Him.

Heirs nervously hear "The Reading of the Will," the name of this nineteenth-century illustration by Boilly. While human beings often fight over wills, Jesus gladly shares His heavenly inheritance with all who believe in Him.

HIGH PRIEST. See *Great High Priest.*

HIGH PRIEST ACCORDING TO THE ORDER OF MELCHIZEDEK. See *High Priest after the Order of Melchisedec.*

HIGH PRIEST AFTER THE ORDER OF MELCHISEDEC

This name of Jesus refers to one of the most mysterious personalities of the Bible. Melchisedec was the king of Salem—

an ancient name for Jerusalem—and a priest of the Most High God. He appeared to Abraham and his servants after they defeated several kings who had carried Abraham's nephew, Lot, away as a captive.

When Abraham returned from battle with the spoils of war he had taken from these kings, Melchisedec met him, blessed him, and gave him and his hungry men bread and wine to eat. In return, Abraham presented Melchisedec with a tithe—one-tenth of the spoils of war he had taken from the conquered kings (see Genesis 14:12–20).

The author of Hebrews calls Jesus a High Priest after the Order of Melchisedec because Melchisedec did not become a priest by virtue of his birth. He was not a descendant of Aaron, the first high priest of Israel through whose family line all succeeding priests of Israel emerged.

Like Melchisedec, Jesus did not inherit His priestly responsibilities. He was appointed to this role by God the Father. His priesthood is eternal, without beginning or end, and thus superior to the priests and the sacrificial system of the Old Testament (see Hebrews 7:16, 24).

> And being made perfect, he became the author of eternal salvation unto all them that obey him; called of God an **high priest after the order of Melchisedec**.
> HEBREWS 5:9–10
> [NASB, NRSV: **high priest according to the order of Melchizedek**; NIV: **high priest in the order of Melchizedek**]

HIGH PRIEST FOR EVER. See *Great High Priest*.

HIGH PRIEST IN THE ORDER OF MELCHIZEDEK. See *High Priest after the Order of Melchisedec*.

HIGH PRIEST OF OUR PROFESSION. See *Great High Priest*.

HOLY CHILD JESUS. See *Child Jesus*.

HOLY AND RIGHTEOUS ONE. See *Holy One/Holy One of God*.

HOLY ONE/HOLY ONE OF GOD

This name of Jesus is also applied to God and the Holy Spirit (see *Holy One* in part 1, Names of God the Father, and part 3, Names of God the Holy Spirit). In Paul's sermon in the book of Acts, he calls Jesus by this name to contrast the righteousness of Jesus with the unrighteousness of Barabbas, a

> But ye denied the **Holy One** and the Just, and desired a murderer to be granted unto you.
> ACTS 3:14
> [NASB, NIV, NRSV: **Holy and Righteous One**]

> Saying, Let us alone; what have we to do with thee, thou Jesus of Nazareth? art thou come to destroy us? I know thee who thou art, the **Holy One of God**.
> MARK 1:24

criminal whom the crowd released instead of Jesus on the day of Christ's crucifixion (see Matthew 27:15–26). In the verse from Mark's Gospel, even the evil spirit that Jesus casts out of a demented man recognizes Jesus as the Holy One of God.

Jesus can be called the Holy One because He is the only sinless person who ever lived. Perfect in holiness before He was born, He managed to resist sin throughout His entire life because of His close relationship with God the Father.

We as Christians will never achieve complete holiness in this life. We will always struggle with temptation and our sinful human nature. But we ought to be growing more and more like Jesus in this important dimension of the Christian life. The apostle Peter admonishes us, "Just as he who called you is holy, so be holy in all you do" (1 Peter 1:15 NIV).

In a messianic passage in the book of Daniel, Jesus is also called the Most Holy (Daniel 9:24).

Actor Max von Sydow performs an exorcism in the 1973 film *The Exorcist*. It was a demon-possessed man who identified Jesus as "the Holy One of God."

HOPE OF GLORY

> To whom God would make known what is the riches of the glory of this mystery among the Gentiles; which is Christ in you, the **hope of glory**.
> COLOSSIANS 1:27

The apostle Paul is known as the apostle to the Gentiles, but he could also be called the apostle of hope. His writings abound with the theme of the hope that believers have in the promises of Jesus Christ (see sidebar).

In this verse from his letter to the Colossian church, he called Jesus the Hope of Glory. If we know Christ as our Savior and Lord, we are assured that we will live with Him in His full glory when we reach our heavenly home.

To hope in something is to look forward to its fulfillment with confident expectation. Notice that Paul says in this verse that "Christ in you" is your Hope of Glory. With Jesus as a constant presence in your life, you can be as certain of heaven as if you were already there.

Jesus as Our Hope in Paul's Writings
- "Now the God of hope fill you with all joy and peace in believing, that ye may abound in hope" (Romans 15:13).
- "Be not moved away from the hope of the gospel, which ye have heard" (Colossians 1:23).
- "Being justified by his grace, we should be made heirs according to the hope of eternal life" (Titus 3:7).

HORN OF SALVATION

These verses are part of the song of praise, known as the "Benedictus," that Zacharias sang at the birth of his son John, the forerunner of Jesus (see Luke 1:67–79). This name was also applied to God by the psalmist David in Psalm 18 (see *Horn of My Salvation* in part 1, Names of God the Father).

An animal horn was used as a container for the oil that was poured on the head of a king in an anointing ceremony (see 1 Samuel 16:13). Thus, Zacharias implied that Jesus was the King of salvation from the kingly line of David. A horn was also considered a symbol of strength (see Psalm 112:9). This imagery, as applied to Jesus, declares that He would be a powerful Savior.

As the Horn of Salvation, Jesus is the all-sufficient Savior, who sprang from the line of David. In Bible times, a trumpet (*shofar*, or ram's horn) was made from an animal horn, so

> Blessed be the Lord God of Israel: for he hath visited and redeemed his people, and hath raised up an **horn of salvation** for us in the house of his servant David.
> LUKE 1:68–69
> [NRSV: **mighty savior**]

Since early Bible times the "shofar" has been used on many Jewish holidays to remind the hearers that God is King and Rescuer.

we can carry this horn analogy one step further: Our role as Christians is to "sound the trumpet" about God's love and grace to an unbelieving world.

Another name of Jesus on the theme of salvation is Salvation of God (Luke 3:6).

I AM

This name that Jesus called Himself is the equivalent of the name with which God identified Himself to Moses at the burning bush (see *I Am That I Am* in part 1, Names of God the Father).

> Jesus said unto them, Verily, verily [NIV: I tell you the truth], I say unto you, Before Abraham was, **I am**. Then took they up stones to cast at him: but Jesus hid himself, and went out of the temple, going through the midst of them, and so passed by.
> JOHN 8:58–59

Just like the great I Am of the Old Testament, Jesus was claiming to be eternal, timeless, and unchanging. He had always been and He would always be. In other words, He was of the same divine essence as God the Father.

This claim of divinity was seen as blasphemy by the Jewish religious leaders, so they picked up stones to execute Jesus—the penalty for such a crime as spelled out in the Old Testament law (see Leviticus 24:16). But Jesus' escape proved the claim He was making. He easily avoided their death threat as He slipped miraculously "through the midst of them." Only when the time was right, in accordance with God's plan, would He allow Himself to be captured and crucified.

IMAGE OF GOD. See *Express Image of God.*

IMAGE OF THE INVISIBLE GOD.

See *Express Image of God.*

IMMANUEL/EMMANUEL

This prophecy from the prophet Isaiah was gloriously fulfilled with the birth of Jesus, as described in these two verses from Matthew's Gospel. Matthew adds the phrase that gives the meaning of the name Immanuel: "God with us."

Even before Jesus was born, this name was given to Him by an angel who appeared to Joseph. Joseph needed divine assurance that Mary's pregnancy was an act of the Holy Spirit, and that he should proceed to take her as his wife.

The promise of God's presence among His people goes back to Old Testament times. For example, when God called Moses to return to Egypt to free His people from slavery, He told him, "I will be with you" (Exodus 3:12 NIV). Likewise, when God called the prophet Jeremiah to the difficult task of delivering a message of judgment to His wayward people, He promised the prophet, "I am with you and will rescue you" (Jeremiah 1:8 NIV).

King David declared that God's presence would follow him wherever he went: "If I take the wings of the morning, and dwell in the uttermost parts of the sea; even there shall thy hand lead me, and thy right hand shall hold me" (Psalm 139:9–10).

These promises of God's presence with His people reached their peak in His Son, Jesus Christ, who came to earth in the form of a man to show mankind that God is for us in our weak, sinful, and helpless condition. As a man, Jesus understands our temptations and shortcomings. As God, He can meet all these needs through His love and grace.

Just as Matthew's Gospel begins with the affirmation that God is with us, so it ends with Jesus' promise of His abiding presence: "Lo, I am with you always, even unto the end of the world" (Matthew 28:20).

> Therefore the Lord himself shall give you a sign; Behold, a virgin shall conceive, and bear a son, and shall call his name **Immanuel**.
> ISAIAH 7:14
>
> Now all this was done, that it might be fulfilled which was spoken of the Lord by the prophet. . . . And they shall call his name **Emmanuel**, which being interpreted is, God with us.
> MATTHEW 1:22–23
> [NASB, NIV: **Immanuel**]

Saint Patrick, a missionary to Ireland in the fourth century, expressed the reality of Jesus as God with Us in this beautiful prayer:

> Christ be beside me, Christ be before me,
> Christ be behind me, King of my heart;
> Christ be within me, Christ be below me,
> Christ be above me, never to part.
> Christ on my right hand, Christ on my left hand,
> Christ all around me, shield in the strife;
> Christ in my sleeping, Christ in my sitting,
> Christ in my rising, light of my life.

INNOCENT MAN. See *Just Man.*

INSTRUCTOR. See *Master.*

JESUS

Jewish custom dictated that a male child be circumcised and named on the eighth day after he was born. Mary and Joseph followed this custom with Jesus. They had been told by an angel, even before Jesus was born, that His name would be Jesus (Matthew 1:21; Luke 1:31). They followed the angel's

> And when eight days were accomplished for the circumcising of the child, his name was called **JESUS**, which was so named of the angel before he was conceived in the womb.
> LUKE 2:21

instruction by giving Him this name.

The name *Jesus* is the equivalent of the Old Testament name rendered variously as Jehoshua (Numbers 13:16), Jeshua (Ezra 2:2), and Joshua (Exodus 17:9). It means "Jehovah (or Yahweh) Is Salvation." Thus, Jesus' personal name indicated from the very beginning that He was to be God's agent of salvation in a dark and sinful world.

Jesus was actually a common name among the Jewish people when He was born, similar to the popularity or John or Robert in our society. For example, a believer named Jesus Justus was mentioned by the apostle Paul in his letter to the Christians at Colossae (see Colossians 4:11). But the name has become so closely associated with Jesus of Nazareth, the Son of God, that few people are given this name in our time. In the words of Paul, it is the "name. . .above every name" (Philippians 2:9).

The name Jesus appears often by itself in the Gospels (see Matthew 17:18; Mark 14:62; Luke 10:37; John 20:14). But outside the Gospels, it often appears in combination with other names such as Jesus Christ (Acts 8:37), Jesus Christ Our Lord (Romans 6:11), Lord Jesus (Colossians 3:17), and Lord Jesus Christ (James 2:1).

His Wonderful Name

Christians never seem to tire of hearing the name of Jesus, according to the hymn "There Is a Name I Love to Hear," written by Frederick Whitfield.

> There is a Name I love to hear,
> I love to sing its worth;
> It sounds like music in mine ear,
> The sweetest Name on earth.
> Oh, how I love Jesus,
> Oh, how I love Jesus,
> Oh, how I love Jesus,
> Because He first loved me.

JESUS CHRIST. See *Christ*; *Jesus*.

JESUS CHRIST OUR LORD. See *Christ*; *Jesus*.

JESUS OF GALILEE/JESUS OF NAZARETH

Galilee was one of three provinces, or regions, into which Palestine was divided during New Testament times. Nazareth, the hometown of Jesus (see Luke 2:51), was a small, insignificant village in the province of Galilee.

The verse from Matthew in which Jesus was called Jesus of Galilee, describes the final days of His ministry in Jerusalem. This city was located in the southernmost province of Judea, about ninety miles from the province of Galilee. This young

> Now Peter sat without in the palace [NIV: out in the courtyard]: and a damsel [NIV: servant girl] came unto him, saying, Thou also wast with **Jesus of Galilee**.
> MATTHEW 26:69
> [NASB, NRSV: **Jesus the Galilean**]

People at the time of Christ would not recognize Nazareth today. It has changed from a small village not much larger than a football field to one of Israel's larger cities.

woman questioned Peter about his association with Jesus because Galilee to the north was Jesus' home province and the place where He had spent most of His time of ministry.

In the verse from John's Gospel, Phillip's reference to Jesus as a person from Nazareth shows his prejudice against this tiny village. He was convinced that no one of any importance could come from this little "hick town."

But Nathanael changed his mind when he met Jesus in person. When Jesus told him that He knew all about him, Nathanael acknowledged Him as "the Son of God" and "the King

> Philip findeth Nathanael, and saith unto him, We have found him, of whom Moses in the law, and the prophets, did write, **Jesus of Nazareth**, the son of Joseph.
> JOHN 1:45

of Israel" (John 1:49). Nathanael eventually became one of Jesus' disciples—the one referred to as Bartholomew (see Mark 3:18).

The significance of these names—Jesus of Galilee and Jesus of Nazareth—is that they attest to the historicity of Jesus Christ. He was not a make-believe figure who emerged from a fiction writer's imagination. He was a real person, who grew up in humble circumstances and spent most of His ministry among the common people. Some skeptics may say otherwise, but Christians declare that the Gospels are eyewitness accounts of the life of a miracle-working Savior, who hailed from a little village in a backwater province.

If Jesus had been created by a fiction writer, He probably would have been born into society's upper class in the influential city of Jerusalem. He certainly would not have been executed on a Roman cross like a common criminal.

JESUS THE GALILEAN. See *Jesus of Galilee/Jesus of Nazareth.*

JUDGE OF QUICK AND DEAD

This name of Jesus appears in the sermon that the apostle Peter preached to the Roman centurion Cornelius, a Gentile (see Acts 10:25–43). Peter made it clear to Cornelius that Jesus had been appointed by God the Father as the supreme Judge of all things—the living and the dead.

God's activity as Judge is one of the key themes of the Old Testament (see *Judge* and *Judge of All the Earth* in part 1, Names of God the Father). But after God sent His Son, Jesus, into the world, He established a new way of rendering His judgment. According to the Gospel of John, with the coming of Jesus, God the Father "committed all judgment unto the Son" (John 5:22). Jesus is now the agent through whom divine judgment is handed down.

As the Judge of Quick and Dead, Jesus is the great dividing line in history. At the great white throne judgment in the end time, He will send into eternal punishment those who have refused to accept Him as Savior and Lord (see Revelation 20:11–15). Christians will not be involved in this judgment, because they have accepted by faith the sacrifice that Jesus has made on their behalf.

But Christians will not totally escape divine judgment; they will be subjected to an evaluation known as the judgment seat of Christ. At this judgment, the service they have rendered for Jesus Christ will be judged and rewarded accordingly (see sidebar). The exact nature of this judgment and the rewards are unclear. But the fact that we will face this time of accountability before the Lord should motive us to loyal service in the cause of God's kingdom.

Another name of Jesus that emphasizes His role as Judge is Righteous Judge (2 Timothy 4:8).

> And he commanded us to preach unto the people, and to testify that it is he which was ordained of God to be the **Judge of quick and dead**. ACTS 10:42 [NASB, NIV, NRSV: **Judge of the living and the dead**]

Paul's Teachings on Christians Facing the Judgment Seat of Christ

- "For we must all appear before the judgment seat of Christ, that each one may receive what is due him for the things done while in the body, whether good or bad" (2 Corinthians 5:10 NIV).
- "So then, each of us will give an account of himself to God" (Romans 14:12 NIV).
- "His work will be shown for what it is, because the Day will bring it to light. . . . If what he has built survives, he will receive his reward. If it is burned up, he will suffer loss; he himself will be saved, but only as one escaping through the flames" (1 Corinthians 3:13–15 NIV).

JUDGE OF THE LIVING AND THE DEAD. See *Judge of Quick and Dead.*

JUST MAN

Pontius Pilate, the Roman governor who condemned Jesus to death, received this message from his wife while Jesus was on trial. She tried to get Pilate to release Jesus, because it had been revealed to her in a dream that He was innocent of the charges against Him.

Pilate also knew that Jesus was not guilty, but he caved in to political pressure from the Jewish religious leaders and pronounced the death penalty against Jesus. Pilate washed his hands before the crowd and declared, "I am innocent of the blood of this just person" (Matthew 27:24).

The word *just*, as applied to Jesus by Pilate and his wife, means "innocent." But in other contexts in the New Testament, the names Just (Acts 3:14) Just One (Acts 7:52; 22:14), and Righteous Man (Luke 23:47) refer to Jesus' righteousness and holiness.

Jesus, the Sinless and Righteous One, was not guilty of any crime or wrongdoing. This makes His death on our behalf all the more meaningful. He willingly laid down His life on the cross as the sacrifice for our sin.

KING

When Jesus made His triumphal entry into Jerusalem, He was hailed as King by the crowds that had seen His miracles during His public ministry. They acknowledged Him as the wonder-working Messiah, whom God had been promising to send to His people for many centuries.

In the Old Testament, God the Father is also referred to by this name (see *King* in part 1, Names of God the Father). But the Jewish people rejected God's kingship in favor of rule by an earthly king in the time of the prophet Samuel (see 1 Samuel 8:4–9).

Saul, Israel's first king, was followed by many other kings throughout history. But by Jesus' time, no king had ruled over the Jews for a period of about five hundred years. They thought their long-promised Messiah would be a powerful king who would restore their nation to its glory days as a political power. When the crowds greeted Jesus as King when

He entered Jerusalem, they were thinking of Him in these terms.

Jesus faced this problem throughout His ministry. After the miracle of the feeding of the five thousand, He realized that the crowds "would come and take him by force, to make him a king" (John 6:15). He avoided them by slipping away to a secluded spot on a nearby mountain.

There was nothing Jesus could do to avoid the crowds on the day when He entered Jerusalem. But He rode a donkey, a symbol of humility and peace, rather than a prancing white horse, the steed of choice for military heroes of the day (see Matthew 21:1–5). This showed that He was not a political king but a spiritual King—one who had come into the world to conquer sin and death.

This artwork is from the Church of Bethpage, located on the Mount of Olives, and represents how the people saw Jesus as King on His triumphal entry into Jerusalem.

KING OF ISRAEL. See *King of the Jews.*

KING OF KINGS

The nineteenth chapter of Revelation describes the return of Jesus Christ to earth in the end time, when He will triumph

And he hath on his vesture [NIV: robe] and on his thigh a name written, **KING OF KINGS**, AND LORD OF LORDS.
REVELATION 19:16

over all His enemies. According to verse 16, He will wear a banner across His royal robe. It will be emblazoned with the phrase "King of Kings." This name, emphasizing His supreme rule over all the earth, will be prominently displayed for everyone to see.

In Old Testament times, the title "king of kings" was assigned to a ruler with an empire that covered a wide territory. Often, a king of an empire would allow the rulers of conquered nations or tribes to keep their royal titles for political and economic reasons. But it was clear that the "king of kings" was the undisputed ruler of his vast domain. Thus, the Persian ruler Artaxerxes referred to himself as "king of kings" in a letter that he sent to Jerusalem with Ezra the priest (Ezra 7:12).

When Jesus returns in glory, He will be the sole ruler of the universe. Meanwhile, He rules over His kingdom, known as the church. If we belong to Him, we are subjects of His kingdom. He should already be King of Kings in our lives.

In a passage that looked forward to the birth of the Messiah, the prophet Zechariah called Jesus the King over All the Earth (Zechariah 14:9).

Our Matchless King

The hymn "Crown Him with Many Crowns," by Matthew Bridges and Godfrey Thring, praises the Lord Jesus for His role as King of Kings in the lives of Christians.

Crown Him with many crowns,
The Lamb upon His throne;
Hark! How the heavenly anthem drowns
All music but its own:
Awake, my soul, and sing
Of Him who died for thee,
And hail Him as thy matchless King
Through all eternity.

KING OF SAINTS

Most people think of saints as people who have been beatified and honored by a church body because of their dedicated service to God. But *saints* when it appears in the New Testament is a term for Christians. Any person who has accepted Jesus as Savior and who follows Him as Lord of his life is a saint. Christians as saints make up the church, the body of Christ.

Thus, Jesus' name as King of Saints is similar to his title as Head of the Church. He watches over His saints and energizes them through His Holy Spirit for the task of carrying out His work in the world.

In this verse from Revelation, the saints of God sing two songs—the song of Moses and the song of the Lamb. These songs celebrate redemption and deliverance. Just as Moses' song celebrates Israel's deliverance from Egyptian slavery (see Exodus 15:1–19), so the song of the Lamb rejoices in our deliverance from Satan and the bondage of sin and death.

> And they sing the song of Moses the servant of God, and the song of the Lamb, saying, Great and marvellous are thy works, Lord God Almighty; just and true are thy ways, thou **King of saints**. REVELATION 15:3 [NASB, NRSV: **King of the nations**; NIV: **King of the ages**]

KING OF THE JEWS

This question asked by Pontius Pilate, the Roman official who condemned Jesus to death, appears in all four Gospels (see Mark 15:2; Luke 23:3; John 18:33). The Gospel writers considered this name important, because it was the basis of the charge that led to Jesus' execution.

The Jewish religious leaders who turned Jesus over to Pilate were enraged by what they considered His blasphemy, or His claim to be the divine Son of God (see Matthew 26:63–66). But they knew that the Romans would never condemn Jesus to death on the basis of their religious laws alone (see John 18:29–32). So they claimed that Jesus was guilty of sedition against the Roman government by claiming to be a king (see Luke 23:2). The implication of this charge is that Jesus was plotting to overthrow Roman rule.

This charge against Jesus was guaranteed to get action from Pilate. One thing his superiors in Rome would not tolerate was unrest or rebellion in the territory over which he ruled.

Jesus never claimed to be a political king (see *King* above). So why didn't He deny that He was the King of the Jews when Pilate asked Him if the charge against Him was true? He refused to answer this question to Pilate's satisfaction because He knew the time for His sacrificial death had

> And Jesus stood before the governor: and the governor asked him, saying, Art thou the **King of the Jews**? And Jesus said unto him, Thou sayest [NIV: Yes, it is as you say]. MATTHEW 27:11

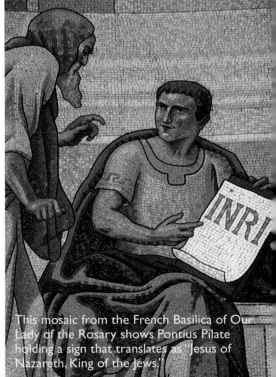

This mosaic from the French Basilica of Our Lady of the Rosary shows Pontius Pilate holding a sign that translates as "Jesus of Nazareth, King of the Jews."

arrived. He would allow events to run their course without any intervention on His part, because it was His destiny to die on the cross. He would be sacrificed willingly as the King of the Jews in order to provide salvation for the entire world.

Another name of Jesus that is similar to King of the Jews is King of Israel (John 1:49; 12:13).

The Right Time for Redemption

During His earthly ministry, Jesus was aware that the timing of His death would be in accordance with God's plan. For example, He told His skeptical brothers, who wanted Him to declare His purpose openly to others: "The right time for me has not yet come" (John 7:6 NIV). But just a few days before His crucifixion, He told His disciples, "My appointed time is near" (Matthew 26:18 NIV).

Looking back on the cross and Jesus' sacrificial death, the apostle Paul declares, "When the fulness of time was come, God sent forth his Son, made of a woman, made under the law, to redeem them that were under the law, that we might receive the adoption of sons" (Galatians 4:4–5).

KING OF THE AGES. See *King of Saints.*

KING OF THE NATIONS. See *King of Saints.*

KING OVER ALL THE EARTH. See *King of Kings.*

LAMB

In this verse from the book of Revelation, the apostle John describes Jesus as the sacrificial Lamb who laid down His life as redemption for the sins of the world. Notice the things that John declares Jesus the Lamb is worthy to receive.

- Power. The Lamb exercises ultimate power over the universe as well as the lives of Christians.
- Riches. All the material possessions we have accumulated belong to Him.
- Wisdom. Jesus is the all-wise One who grants wisdom to those who follow Him.
- Strength. Our physical powers should be dedicated to the service of the Lamb.

And I beheld, and I heard the voice of many angels round about the throne and the beasts and the elders. . .saying with a loud voice, Worthy is the **Lamb** that was slain to receive power, and riches, and wisdom, and strength, and honour, and glory, and blessing.
REVELATION 5:11–12

- Honor. Our behavior as Christians should bring honor to the One whom we profess to follow.
- Glory. Jesus' glory, His excellence and moral superiority, is magnified when Christians are fully devoted to Him and His cause.
- Blessing. In this context, *blessing* means "praise." We should praise the Lamb with our lives as well as our words.

Jesus as the Lamb is one of the major themes of the book of Revelation. As the Lamb, He is worthy to open the scroll that describes God's judgment against the world (see Revelation 5:4; 6:1). The Lamb provides the light for the heavenly city, or New Jerusalem (see Revelation 21:22–23). Those who belong to Jesus have their names written in the Lamb's book of life (see Revelation 21:27).

LAMB OF GOD

On two successive days John the Baptist, forerunner of Jesus, referred to Jesus by this name (see John 1:35–36). Of all the names John could have used—King, Messiah, Prophet— he chose to identify Jesus as the Lamb of God. Lambs were choice young sheep that were used as sacrificial animals in Jewish worship rituals (see Leviticus 14:11–13; 1 Samuel 7:9). Thus, at the very beginning of Jesus' ministry, John

The next day John seeth Jesus coming unto him, and saith, Behold the **Lamb of God**, which taketh away the sin of the world.
JOHN 1:29

The image of Jesus as the Lamb of God carried more meaning at the time of Christ as lambs like this were part of the Jewish religious life, central to the Temple sacrifices.

realized the sacrificial role that Jesus was destined to fill.

The prominence of lambs in the Jewish sacrificial system began with the deliverance of the Israelites from Egyptian slavery, many centuries before Jesus' time. The Lord commanded the people to smear the blood of lambs on the doorposts of their houses. This indicated that they would be passed over when God struck the land with the death of the firstborn (see Exodus 12:21–23). The Jewish festival known as Passover was commemorated from that day on with the eating of unleavened bread and the sacrifice of lambs.

One of the great messianic passages of the Old Testament predicted that Jesus would die like a sacrificial lamb. About seven hundred years before Jesus was born, the prophet Isaiah declared of Him, "He was oppressed, and he was afflicted, yet he opened not his mouth: he is brought as a lamb to the slaughter, and as a sheep before her shearers is dumb, so he opened not his mouth" (Isaiah 53:7).

On the night before His crucifixion, Jesus picked up on the sacrificial lamb imagery that John the Baptist had used of Him when He began His public ministry. He gathered with His disciples to eat a meal that was part of the observance of the Jewish Passover. But He turned it into a meal that we know as the Memorial Supper or the Lord's Supper.

Just as the blood of the first Passover lamb had been an agent of deliverance for the Israelites in Egypt, so the shed blood of Jesus would provide divine redemption for the entire world. As Jesus passed the cup among His disciples, He told them, "This is my blood of the new testament, which is shed for many for the remission of sins" (Matthew 26:28).

Saved by the Blood of the Lamb of God

- "In Christ Jesus ye who sometimes were far off are made nigh by the blood of Christ" (Ephesians 2:13).
- "Neither by the blood of goats and calves, but by his own blood he entered in once into the holy place, having obtained eternal redemption for us" (Hebrews 9:12).
- "Ye were not redeemed with corruptible things. . .but with the precious blood of Christ, as of a lamb without blemish and without spot" (1 Peter 1:18–19).
- "The blood of Jesus Christ. . .cleanseth us from all sin" (1 John 1:7).

LAMB SLAIN FROM THE FOUNDATION OF THE WORLD

The affirmation of this verse is that Jesus was not only the Lamb who was sacrificed for our sins, but He also was selected for this task before the world was created (see *Foreordained before the Foundation of the World* above).

God the Father looked down through the centuries and determined that His Son, Jesus, would die at some time in the future as an atonement for sin. Jesus' death was no accident of history, and no afterthought in the mind of God. It was the fulfillment of God's eternal plan.

How long did it take for this plan to work itself out? As long as it took. This answer may seem nonsensical and ridiculous, but it's as close as we can get to understanding God and His mysterious ways. The apostle Peter expresses it like this: "One day is with the Lord as a thousand years, and a thousand years as one day" (2 Peter 3:8).

LAST. See *Alpha and Omega.*

LAST ADAM

This is the only place in the Bible where Jesus is called by this name. The apostle Paul in this verse draws a contrast between Jesus as the Last Adam and the Adam of the book of Genesis, who was the first man created. This contrast appears at several points throughout the fifteenth chapter of 1 Corinthians.

After God created Adam and placed him in the Garden of Eden, He told him he could eat the fruit from every tree in the garden except one—"the tree of the knowledge of good and evil" (Genesis 2:17). But Adam deliberately disobeyed God and ate the forbidden fruit (see Genesis 3:6). This act of rebellion placed Adam and all his descendants—including everyone born since Adam's time—under the curse of sin and death.

But according to Paul, God had good news for those who were tainted by Adam's sin. He sent another Adam—the Last Adam, Jesus Christ—to undo what the first Adam had caused. Paul expresses it like this: "As in Adam all die, even so in Christ shall all be made alive" (1 Corinthians 15:22). The first Adam's legacy of death has been nullified by the Last Adam's perfect obedience to God the Father, and His sacrificial death on our behalf.

And all that dwell upon the earth shall worship him, whose names are not written in the book of life of the **Lamb slain from the foundation of the world**.
REVELATION 13:8
[NIV: **Lamb. . .Slain from the creation of the world**]

And so it is written, The first man Adam was made a living soul; the **last Adam** was made a quickening spirit.
1 CORINTHIANS 15:45

As Paul continues in this passage from 1 Corinthians, he refers to Jesus as the Second Man. Adam (the first man) was a created being, formed from the dust of the earth (see Genesis 2:7), and thus, "of the earth, earthy" (1 Corinthians 15:47); but Jesus, as the Second Man, came from heaven.

LAUNDERER'S SOAP. See *Fullers' Soap.*

LEADER. See *Master; Prince.*

LEADER AND COMMANDER TO THE PEOPLE

The fifty-fifth chapter of Isaiah is one of many messianic passages in his book. In this verse, the coming Messiah is portrayed as One who will serve as a Leader and Commander for the people to whom He is sent by the Lord.

> Behold, I have given him for [NIV: made him] a witness to the people, a **leader and commander to the people**.
> ISAIAH 55:4

A leader is a person who guides others in the pursuit of a goal. He enlists others to work toward the goal, motivates and inspires them, encourages them through personal example, and keeps them focused on their objective. The name *commander* conjures up a military image. He is more directive in his approach to leadership. He knows what has to be done to win a battle, and he marshals his troops to engage the enemy in such a way that victory is assured.

As Christians, we have both a Leader and a Commander in Jesus Christ. His objective is to bring others into His kingdom. Our task is to follow His leadership as we bear witness for Him in the world. As our Commander, He has the right to demand our unquestioning obedience.

LIFE

We are accustomed to thinking of Jesus in terms of the eternal life that He promises to believers. But in this verse from the apostle Paul's letter to the Colossians, he describes Jesus as the Life of believers in the here-and-now. We don't have to wait until we die to enjoy life with Jesus. He is our Life today—in this present world.

> When Christ, who is our **life**, shall appear, then shall ye also appear with him in glory.
> COLOSSIANS 3:4

With Jesus as our Life, we can live each day with joy, in spite of the problems and frustrations that come our way. He is the very essence of the truly good life, and He promises the same to those who follow Him: "I am come that they might have life, and that they might have it more abundantly" (John 10:10).

Other names of God the Son that emphasize the meaningful life He offers Christians are Prince of Life (Acts 3:15) and Word of Life (1 John 1:1).

Walking with Jesus Every Day

The old gospel hymn "Ev'ry Day with Jesus," by Robert C. Loveless, expresses the joy of life with Jesus, our Life, during every day of our earthly journey.

Ev'ry day with Jesus
Is sweeter than the day before,
Ev'ry day with Jesus
I love Him more and more;
Jesus saves and keeps me,
And He's the One I'm waiting for;
Ev'ry day with Jesus
Is sweeter than the day before.

LIFE-GIVING SPIRIT. See *Quickening Spirit.*

LIGHT

These verses from the prologue of John's Gospel contain one of the more meaningful names of God the Son in the entire New Testament. Jesus was the Light whom God sent into a world that was stumbling around in the darkness of sin.

This name of Jesus is also used for God the Father (see *Light* in part 1, Names of God the Father) because God is the Creator of light. The earth was shrouded in darkness until He declared, "Let there be light" (Genesis 1:3), and light appeared to illuminate the earth.

Light is something we take for granted until it disappears. Most of us know what it's like to grope around in a dark house after the electricity goes out unexpectedly. We are virtually helpless until we locate that flashlight we had placed in a closet for just such an emergency.

As the Light, Jesus pushes back the darkness and helps us find our way in a chaotic world. He reveals God in all His righteousness, and He bridges the gap that separates sinful humankind from a holy God. He gives us insights from God's written Word, the Bible, that enable us to make wise

There was a man sent from God, whose name was John. The same came for a witness, to bear witness of the **Light**, that all men through him might believe.
JOHN 1:6–7

decisions and live in accordance with His will.

Just as Jesus is the Light of our lives, He expects us as Christians to reflect His light to others. In His Sermon on the Mount, He called us "the light of the world" (Matthew 5:14). Then He challenged us to "let your light so shine before men, that they may see your good works, and glorify your Father which is in heaven" (Matthew 5:16).

The apostle John also refers to Jesus as the True Light (John 1:9).

LIGHT OF THE GENTILES. See *Light of the World.*

LIGHT OF THE WORLD

Jesus referred to Himself by this name in a conversation with the Pharisees, His constant critics. They thought He was nothing but a religious quack and a troublemaker. But Jesus claimed to be the Son of God, who had been sent on a redemptive mission as the Light of the World. He also used this name for Himself after restoring the sight of a blind man (see John 9:5).

The Jewish people of Jesus' time—especially religious leaders such as the Pharisees—were filled with religious and national pride. They realized that God had blessed them as His special people. They thought of His favor as something they deserved because of their moral superiority to the people of other nations. But they forgot that God had blessed them because He wanted them to serve as His witnesses to the rest of the world. Centuries before, God had told their ancestor Abraham, "I will make of thee a great nation. . .in thee shall all families of the earth be blessed" (Genesis 12:2–3).

Jesus was born into the world as a Jew, but His commitment as Savior was to the entire world. This is one reason why He was rejected by the Jewish religious leaders of His time. How could God the Father possibly love the pagan peoples of the world as much as He loved them? They wanted to put limits on God's love and concern.

This problem is still with us today. Some people want to make Jesus into the Light of the middle class, or the Light of Western society, or the Light of the beautiful. But He refuses to be bound by such restrictions. He is also the Light of the poor, the Light of the Third World, and the Light of the

> Then spake Jesus again unto them, saying, I am the **light of the world**: he that followeth me shall not walk in darkness, but shall have the light of life.
> JOHN 8:12

homely. No matter what your earthly circumstances, Jesus is *your* Light.

Another name of Jesus that expresses the same truth as Light of the World is Light of the Gentiles. To the Jews, "Gentiles" was a catch-all term for all non-Jewish peoples. In a famous messianic passage, the prophet Isaiah declared that Jesus would come into the world as a Light of the Gentiles (see Isaiah 42:6).

Light for a Dark World

Jesus is the Light for a dark world, according to the hymn "The Light of the World Is Jesus" by Philip P. Bliss.

The whole world was lost in the darkness of sin,
The Light of the world is Jesus;
Like sunshine at noonday His glory shone in,
The Light of the world is Jesus.
Come to the Light, 'tis shining for thee;
Sweetly the Light has dawned upon me,
Once I was blind, but now I can see:
The Light of the world is Jesus.

LION OF THE TRIBE OF JUDAH

This name of Jesus appears in one of the visions of the apostle John in the book of Revelation. Only Jesus as the Lion of the Tribe of Judah is worthy to open the scroll that contains God's judgment against the world in the end time. God the Father has delegated to His Son the authority and power to serve as supreme Judge over all things.

The lion, known as the "king of beasts," is legendary for its strength and ferocious nature. Lions do not roam the land of Israel today, but they were common in Bible times. For example, David killed a lion that was threatening his father's sheep (see 1 Samuel 17:37). The judge Samson, one of the superheroes of the Bible, killed a young lion with his bare hands (see Judges 14:5–6). God the Father also compared His forthcoming judgment against His rebellious people—the nation of Israel (spoken of symbolically as Ephraim) and the nation of Judah—to the fierceness of a lion (see Hosea 5:14).

Jesus as the Lion of the Tribe of Judah probably has its origin in the prophecy of Jacob in the book of Genesis. He declared that his son Judah was destined to become the

And one of the elders saith unto me, Weep not: behold, the **Lion of the tribe of Judah**, the Root of David, hath prevailed [NIV: triumphed] to open the book, and to loose the seven seals thereof.
REVELATION 5:5

This statue of the "Lion of Judah" stands in the Ethiopian capital of Addis Ababa.

greatest among all his twelve sons, whose descendants would become the Israelites, God's chosen people. Jacob described Judah, symbolically, as a lion, or a fearless ruler, who would lead God's people (see Genesis 49:8–12).

This prophecy was fulfilled dramatically throughout the Bible. The tribe of Judah, composed of Judah's descendants, took the lead on the Israelites' trek through the wilderness after they left Egypt (see Numbers 10:14). Moses' census of the people in the wilderness revealed that the tribe of Judah was the largest of the twelve tribes (see Numbers 1:27; 26:22). King David, the popular ruler of Israel, against whom all future kings were measured, was a Judahite, a native of Bethlehem in the territory of Judah (see 1 Samuel 16:1).

Most significantly of all, Jesus the Messiah sprang from the line of Judah. The genealogy of Jesus in the Gospel of Matthew traces His lineage back to Judah (spelled "Judas" in the KJV; see Matthew 1:2–3). Thus, Jesus is the Lion of the Tribe of Judah, who rules among His people as supreme Savior and Lord.

LIVING BREAD. See *Bread*.

LIVING STONE

In this verse, the apostle Peter compares Jesus to a stone used in the construction of a building. The imagery of a stone is also applied to Jesus in other New Testament passages (see *Chief Cornerstone* and *Head of the Corner* above). But Peter refers to Jesus here as a Living Stone, emphasizing His resurrection from the dead and His close relationship with believers as the living Christ.

In the next verse, Peter describes Christians as "lively stones" (1 Peter 2:5). Just as Jesus is the living and breathing Head of the Church, so believers make up the body of the church. Thus, the church is a living organism devoted to the service of Jesus and His kingdom in the time between His ascension to God the Father and His second coming.

Peter summarizes the mission of the church by stating

To whom coming, as unto a **living stone**, disallowed [NIV: rejected] indeed of men, but chosen of God, and precious [NIV: precious to him].
1 PETER 2:4

that Christians are "a chosen generation, a royal priesthood, an holy nation, a peculiar people; that ye should shew forth the praises of him who hath called you out of darkness into his marvellous light" (1 Peter 2:9).

Maybe you never thought about it before, but if you belong to Jesus, you have the spirit of the Living Stone in your life. We bring honor to Him when we serve as "lively stones" in the world.

A large crowd of Christians "shew forth the praises" of their Living Stone, Jesus.

LORD

Lord is one of the most popular names of God the Son in the New Testament, appearing hundreds of times. These two verses show that this name, from the Greek word *kurios*, is used in two distinct ways in the New Testament.

In the first verse, from Luke's Gospel, the "Lord" used of Jesus is a term of respect, similar to our use of *mister* or *sir* in modern society. This "certain man" respected Jesus, but he apparently had no intention of committing his life to Him as his spiritual Lord and Master. He did not reply when Jesus told him about the sacrifice He required of His followers (see Luke 9:58).

Even Jesus' disciples sometimes called Him Lord in this polite, respectful sense. For example, Jesus once told a parable about the need for people to wait and watch expectantly for

And it came to pass, that, as they went in the way, a certain man said unto him, **Lord**, I will follow thee whithersoever thou goest [NIV: wherever you go].
LUKE 9:57

> Therefore, my beloved brethren, be ye stedfast, unmoveable, always abounding in the work of the **Lord**, forasmuch as ye know that your labour is not in vain in the **Lord**.
> 1 CORINTHIANS 15:58

His return. Peter approached Him and asked, "Lord, speakest thou this parable unto us, or even to all?" (Luke 12:41).

As Jesus' earthly ministry unfolded, the polite title of Lord that people used of Him was transformed into a declaration of faith in Him as the divine Son of God the Father. This is the sense in which the apostle Paul calls Jesus "Lord" in 1 Corinthians 15:58.

After His resurrection and ascension, Jesus became the Lord of history, the Lord of the church, and the Lord of individual Christians. When we declare that "Jesus is Lord," we submit to His lordship and crown Him as the supreme ruler over our lives.

LORD AND SAVIOUR JESUS CHRIST.
See *Christ Jesus Our Lord.*

LORD CHRIST. See *Christ Jesus Our Lord.*

LORD FROM HEAVEN

> The first man is of the earth, earthy: the second man is the **Lord from heaven**.
> 1 CORINTHIANS 15:47

This verse appears in the apostle Paul's famous passage about Jesus' sinlessness in contrast to Adam's sin as the first man (see *Last Adam* above). Here, Adam's origin as a being created from the dust of the earth (see Genesis 3:19) is contrasted with Jesus' divine origin as the Lord from heaven.

When Jesus completed His mission on earth as our Redeemer, He returned to His Father in heaven (see Acts 1:9–11). He is now seated in heaven at God's right hand (see Colossians 3:1), where He intercedes on our behalf with God the Father (see Romans 8:34).

The One from Heaven

Jesus' coming to earth from heaven the first time, as well as His future return, is celebrated in the hymn "One Day," by J. Wilbur Chapman.

> One day when heaven was filled with His praises,
> One day when sin was as black as could be,
> Jesus came forth to be born of a virgin,
> Dwelt among men, my example is He!
> Living, He loved me; dying, He saved me;
> Buried, He carried my sins far away;
> Rising, He justified freely forever:
> One day He's coming—O glorious day!

Just as Jesus came into the world from heaven when the time was right (see Galatians 4:4), so, too, will He return one day to bring the earth as we know it to its conclusion, in accordance with God's plan. As Christians, we should be looking forward with watchful readiness to that glorious day (see Matthew 25:13).

LORD JESUS. See *Jesus.*

LORD JESUS CHRIST. See *Jesus.*

LORD JESUS CHRIST OUR SAVIOUR.
See *Christ Jesus Our Lord.*

LORD OF GLORY. See *Brightness of God's Glory.*

LORD OF LORDS

This name emphasizes Jesus' supreme authority in the end time, when He returns to earth in victory over all His enemies. He is also called Lord of Lords in two other places in the New Testament (see 1 Timothy 6:15; Revelation 17:14; see also *King of Kings* above).

> And he hath on his vesture [NIV: robe] and on his thigh a name written, **KING OF KINGS, AND LORD OF LORDS.** Revelation 19:16

As Lord of Lords, Jesus is superior in power and authority to all the rulers of the earth. Some monarchs of the ancient world were worshipped as divine by their subjects. But only Jesus, as Lord of Lords, is worthy of our worship and total commitment.

Here is how the apostle Paul expresses the meaning of this name in his letter to the believers at Philippi: "God also hath highly exalted him, and given him a name which is above every name: that at the name of Jesus every knee should bow, of things in heaven, and things in earth, and things under the earth; and that every tongue should confess that Jesus Christ is Lord, to the glory of God the Father" (Philippians 2:9–11).

LORD OF PEACE

As the apostle Paul brought to a close his second letter to the Thessalonian Christians, he blessed them with this beautiful benediction. He wanted these Christians, who were going through disagreement and turmoil, to experience the peace that Jesus promises to those who abide in Him.

> Now the **Lord of peace** himself give you peace always by all means [NIV: at all times and in every way]. The Lord be with you all.
> 2 Thessalonians 3:16

The dictionary defines peace as "freedom from disquieting or oppressive thoughts or emotions." This definition assumes that peace is the *absence* of elements such as conflict or negative feelings. But we as Christians know that peace is actually the *presence* of something. This presence is Jesus Christ, who brings peace and inner tranquillity to those who have placed their trust in Him. With Jesus as the Lord of Peace in our lives, we can have peace even in the midst of troubling circumstances.

When Jesus was born in Bethlehem, the angels celebrated His arrival by declaring "peace, good will toward men" (Luke 2:14). Jesus also told His disciples on one occasion, "Let not your heart be troubled: ye believe in God, believe also in me" (John 14:1). We don't have to go around with troubled looks on our faces if the Lord of Peace reigns in our hearts.

The apostle Paul referred to Jesus as Our Peace (Ephesians 2:14). The prophet Isaiah called the coming Messiah the Prince of Peace (Isaiah 9:6).

Promises from the Lord of Peace

- "Peace I leave with you, my peace I give unto you" (John 14:27).
- "Being justified by faith, we have peace with God through our Lord Jesus Christ" (Romans 5:1).
- "He is our peace, who hath. . .broken down the middle wall of partition between us" (Ephesians 2:14).
- "The peace of God, which passeth all understanding, shall keep your hearts and minds through Christ Jesus" (Philippians 4:7).

LORD OF THE DEAD AND LIVING

> Whether we live therefore, or die, we are the Lord's. For to this end [NIV: For this very reason] Christ both died, and rose, and revived [NIV: returned to life], that he might be **Lord** both **of the dead and living**.
> Romans 14:8–9

In this verse from Paul's letter to the believers at Rome, he refers to those who know, and have known, Christ as Lord and Savior. Jesus is the Lord of the millions of Christians who have lived in the past and who have now passed on to their reward. He is also the Lord of all believers still living who look forward to eternal life with Him in heaven after their days on earth are over.

Whether we are alive or dead, there is no better place to be than in the hands of our loving Lord.

LORD OF THE HARVEST

These verses describe the reaction of Jesus to the crowds in the region of Galilee who came to Him for help. His reputation as a healer and teacher had spread throughout the area. He was moved with compassion when He saw their needs. He longed for more workers to help Him as the Lord of the Harvest with the spiritual harvest that pressed in from every side.

Jesus had unlimited power, so why didn't He just take care of all these needs Himself, rather than ask His disciples to pray for more workers? Perhaps it was because He knew His time on earth was limited. Even if He healed all the sick and taught all those who flocked after Him, others in the same condition would take their place after He was gone. He needed other committed workers, such as His disciples, who would carry on His work after His death, resurrection, and ascension.

Jesus is still in the harvesting business. His work on earth continues through His church, under the power of the Holy Spirit. He still needs workers to gather the harvest. When we get so concerned about the spiritual needs of others that we begin to pray to the Lord of the Harvest for more workers, we might just become the answer to our own prayers.

> Pray ye therefore the **Lord of the harvest**, that he will send forth labourers into his harvest.
> MATTHEW 9:38

Agriculture was a way of life in Bible times. The image of laborers harvesting in the ripened fields was an easy metaphor for those who heard Christ speak about a spiritual harvest. Scenes like this can still be seen in modern day Israel.

LORD OF THE SABBATH

This verse from Mark's Gospel describes Jesus' response to the Pharisees when they criticized Him for picking grain on the Sabbath to feed Himself and His hungry disciples. He

> And he said unto them, The sabbath was made for man, and not man for the sabbath: Therefore the Son of man is **Lord** also **of the sabbath**.
> MARK 2:27–28

also claimed to be the Lord of the Sabbath when He was criticized for healing people on this sacred day (see Matthew 12:8–14; Luke 6:5–11).

The original law about Sabbath observance stated simply, "Remember the sabbath day, to keep it holy" (Exodus 20:8). The law went on to restrict people from working on this day—Saturday, the seventh day of the week—in the Jewish religious system.

Over the years, the Pharisees had added all sorts of rules or traditions to this simple law about honoring the Sabbath. For example, one restriction forbade people from traveling more than about one-half mile—or a "Sabbath's day journey" (Acts 1:12)—from their homes on this day. These silly rules had reduced the Sabbath from a spiritual principle to little more than an external observance.

When Jesus claimed to be the Lord of the Sabbath, He declared that He would not be bound by the human rules about Sabbath observance that the Pharisees had established. To Jesus, doing good on the Sabbath by healing people was more important than obeying ritualistic rules (see Matthew 12:12).

Jesus' claim to be the Lord of the Sabbath also placed Him on the same level as God the Father. It was God who had established the Sabbath (see Genesis 2:2–3). Jesus as the agent of Creation (John 1:1–3) was the authority over the Sabbath. The Creator is always greater than anything He has created.

LORD OVER ALL

The name of Jesus in this verse—Lord over All—may seem to express the same idea as Lord of Lords (see above). But there is an important distinction between these two names.

> For there is no difference between the Jew and the Greek: for the same **Lord over all** is rich unto all [NIV: richly blesses all] that call upon him.
> ROMANS 10:12

Lord of Lords refers to Jesus' supreme rule throughout the earth at His second coming. Lord over All declares that every person, whether Jew or Gentile, is on the same level in relationship to Jesus Christ. The apostle Paul declares in this verse that Jesus does not have one plan of salvation for the Jewish people and another for Greeks or non-Jews. Every person comes to salvation by accepting by faith the price Jesus paid on the cross to redeem us from our sin.

In New Testament times, the Jews looked upon Greeks, or Gentiles, as pagans who were excluded from God's favor. The learned Greeks, in turn, thought of all people who were not Greek citizens as uncultured barbarians. But Paul declared that Jesus wiped out all such distinctions between people. The ground was level at the foot of the cross. Everyone stood before God as wayward sinners who had no hope except the forgiveness they could experience at the feet of the crucified Savior.

Paul also makes it clear in this verse that something is required of sinners who want the salvation that Jesus provides. They must "call upon" Jesus the Son. This involves repenting of their sins, confessing Him as Savior, and committing their lives to His lordship. This is the New Testament equivalent of "calling upon" God the Father, which runs like a refrain throughout the Old Testament (see Genesis 12:8; 1 Samuel 12:17; Psalm 4:3; Isaiah 55:6).

"Whosoever" Means Everyone

"Whosoever Will," a hymn written by Philip P. Bliss, declares that everyone is included in Jesus' summons to accept Him as Savior and Lord.

"Whosoever heareth," shout, shout the sound!
Spread the blessed tidings all the world around;
Tell the joyful news wherever man is found,
"Whosoever will may come."
"Whosoever will, whosoever will!"
Send the proclamation over vale and hill;
'Tis a loving Father calls the wanderer home:
"Whosoever will may come."

LORD'S CHRIST

The "him" in this verse refers to Simeon, a man who came to the temple when the infant Jesus was dedicated to the Lord by Mary and Joseph (see *Consolation of Israel* above). Simeon recognized the young child as the Lord's Christ.

The word *Lord's* in this context refers to God the Father. *Christ* derives from a Greek word *christos*, meaning "anointed" (see *Christ* above). Thus, Simeon recognized Jesus as God's Anointed One, or the Messiah, whom the Jewish people had been expecting God the Father to send since Old Testament times.

Even though Jesus was just a little baby in His mother's arms, Simeon realized the moment he saw Him that He was the Messiah. This insight came from the Holy Spirit. So all

And it was revealed unto him by the Holy Ghost, that he should not see death, before he had seen the **Lord's Christ**.
LUKE 2:26

three persons of the Godhead—God the Father, God the Son, and God the Holy Spirit—were present at this event. This makes Jesus' dedication at the temple one of the more dramatic passages on the Trinity in the entire New Testament.

MAN APPROVED OF GOD. See *Flesh.*

MAN CHRIST JESUS. See *Flesh.*

MAN OF GOD'S RIGHT HAND

> Let thy hand be upon the **man of thy right hand**, upon the son of man whom thou madest strong for thyself [NIV: you have raised up for yourself].
> PSALM 80:17

In this verse, the psalmist asks God the Father to strengthen the One whom He has selected for a special task. This Man of God's Right Hand refers to Jesus, the Messiah and the agent of God's redemption in the world.

A person who sat at the right side of a king in Bible times was the most important official in the royal court. He was often the second in command, who acted as the chief administrator of the king's affairs. Even today, a leader's most important and trusted aide is often referred to as his "right-hand man."

As the Man of God's Right Hand, Jesus came into the world as the dispenser of divine justice and forgiveness. God the Father delegated to Him the task of restoring sinful humankind to fellowship with Him through His death on the cross. When this task was accomplished, the Father summoned His Son back to heaven, where He is seated in the place of authority at His Father's right hand (see Ephesians 1:20).

You've probably heard the old saying, "Don't send a boy to do a man's job." Aren't you glad that Jesus was man enough and faithful enough and determined enough and prayerful enough to accomplish the task that His Father sent

Jesus at His Father's Right Hand
- "It is Christ. . .who is even at the right hand of God, who also maketh intercession for us" (Romans 8:34).
- "Seek those things which are above, where Christ sitteth on the right hand of God" (Colossians 3:1).
- "This man, after he had offered sacrifice for sins for ever, sat down on the right hand of God" (Hebrews 10:12).
- "Who is. . .on the right hand of God; angels and authorities and powers being made subject to him" (1 Peter 3:22).

Him to do? No person has ever been sent on a more important mission, and He handled it perfectly as the Man of God's Right Hand.

MAN OF SORROWS

In our society, the words *sorrow* or *sorrows* suggest a state of deep remorse or regret over the loss of something or someone highly loved and esteemed. For example, we might say about a couple who have lost a child: "They are still in sorrow a year after the death."

If we apply this modern definition to this name of Jesus in Isaiah's prophecy—Man of Sorrows—we sense that an alternative translation of this name might be in order. Perhaps, as the NRSV suggests, Jesus was a Man of Suffering more than a Man of Sorrows.

Jesus was not a person who was immersed in a state of remorse or regret over a loss that He had experienced. He was an overcomer—a victorious person—in spite of the problems He faced during His earthly ministry. Even the suffering that led to His death on the cross was swallowed up in victory

> He is despised and rejected of men; a **man of sorrows**, and acquainted with grief: and we hid as it were our faces from him; he was despised, and we esteemed him not. Surely he hath borne our griefs, and carried our sorrows: yet we did esteem him [NIV: considered him] stricken, smitten of God, and afflicted.
> ISAIAH 53:3–4
> [NRSV: **man of suffering**]

An angel comforts Jesus as He prays the night before His crucifixion (Luke 22:43).

when He drew His last breath and declared, "It is finished" (John 19:30). He had accomplished the purpose for which He had been sent into the world.

There is no doubt that Jesus' suffering on the cross was real. So is the pain that we as Christians feel when we are ridiculed for our faith by an unbelieving world. But this should not drive us to sorrow or despair. The Man of Suffering has already "borne our griefs, and carried our sorrows" by dying on the cross in our place. He invites us to cast our cares upon Him during each day of our earthly journey.

Our inspiration for doing so is Jesus Himself, "who for the joy that was set before him endured the cross, despising the shame, and is set down at the right hand of the throne of God" (Hebrews 12:2).

MAN OF SUFFERING. See *Man of Sorrows.*

MAN WHOM GOD ORDAINED. See *Foreordained before the Foundation of the World.*

MASTER

This name that Jesus used of Himself appears in the famous "woe" chapter of Matthew's Gospel, in which Jesus condemns the Pharisees. He was particularly critical of their hypocrisy and religious pride. They enjoyed being greeted in the streets with titles that recognized them for their learning and expertise in the Jewish law; but Jesus declared that He as God's Son was the only person who deserved the title of Master.

Master in this verse is a derivative of a Greek word that means "commander" or "ruler." Modern translations sometimes render this word as "teacher." But Jesus was claiming to be more than a teacher. He made it clear to His disciples and others who were listening that He had the right to serve as the supreme authority in their lives.

In New Testament times, slave owners were sometimes

> And call no man your father upon the earth: for one is your Father, which is in heaven. Neither be ye called masters: for one is your **Master**, even Christ.
> MATTHEW 23:9–10
> [NASB: **Leader**; NIV: **Teacher**; NRSV: **instructor**]

In the Master's Service

"O Master, Let Me Walk with Thee," Washington Gladden's famous hymn, expresses the believer's desire to serve others in the cause of Jesus Christ and His kingdom.

O Master, let me walk with thee
In lowly paths of service free;
Tell me Thy secret, help me bear
The strain of toil, the fret of care.
Help me the slow of heart to move
By some clear, winning word of love;
Teach me the wayward feet to stay,
And guide them in the homeward way.

called "masters" (see Colossians 4:1), implying their supreme control over every aspect of their slaves' lives. As Christians, we are also subject to the will of our Master, the Lord Jesus, who has redeemed us for His service.

MEDIATOR

A mediator is a person who serves as a middleman or go-between to bring two opposing parties together. For example, a mediator is often used in labor disputes. Both labor and management leaders agree to abide by the decision of an independent mediator. This avoids the expense and hassle of a lawsuit and often brings a quick resolution to the problem.

> For there is one God, and one **mediator** between God and men, the man Christ Jesus.
> 1 TIMOTHY 2:5

According to the apostle Paul, in this verse from his first letter to Timothy, Jesus also fills the role of spiritual Mediator in the world. He is the middleman, or go-between who reconciles God to mankind.

Man by nature is a sinner. In his sinful state, he is estranged from a holy God, who will not tolerate anything that is unholy or unclean. But Jesus eliminated this gap between God and man by sacrificing His life on the cross for our sins and purchasing our forgiveness. Cleansed of our sin through the blood of Jesus, we now have fellowship with God the Father. We have been reconciled to God through His Son's work as our Mediator.

Jesus is the perfect Mediator between God and man, because He had both divine and human attributes. As God, He understood what God the Father demanded of people in order to be acceptable in His sight. As a man, He realized the desperate situation of sinful human beings. He was the God-man who was able to bring these two opposites together in a way that brought glory to God and gave man access to God's blessings and His eternal presence.

U.S. President Jimmy Carter served as mediator, bringing Egyptian President Anwar Sadat and Israeli Prime Minister Menachem Begin together in a 1978 peace agreement.

Jesus our Mediator also expects His followers to serve as "middlemen" for others in a sinful world. Our job as Christians is to point others to Jesus Christ, who wants everyone to enjoy fellowship with God the Father. The apostle Paul expresses it like this: "All things are of God, who hath reconciled us to himself by Jesus Christ, and hath given to us the ministry of reconciliation" (2 Corinthians 5:18).

MEDIATOR OF A BETTER COVENANT. See *Mediator of the New Testament.*

MEDIATOR OF A NEW COVENANT.
See *Mediator of the New Testament.*

MEDIATOR OF THE NEW TESTAMENT

Testament is another word for covenant or agreement. Thus the "new testament" that the writer of Hebrews mentions here is the new covenant that God established with His people, based on the sacrificial death of Jesus Christ. Jesus is the Mediator of this new covenant.

> And for this cause [NIV: for this reason] he is the **mediator of the new testament**, that by means of death, for the redemption of the transgressions that were under the first testament, they which are called might receive the promise of eternal inheritance.
> HEBREWS 9:15
> [NASB, NIV, NRSV: **mediator of a new covenant**]

The first covenant of God with His people was formalized in Old Testament times. God agreed to bless the Israelites and serve as their Guide and Protector if they would follow and worship Him. But the Jewish people broke this covenant time and time again as they fell into rebellion and idolatry.

Finally, God promised through the prophet Jeremiah that He would establish a new covenant with His people. This would be a spiritual covenant written on their hearts rather than a covenant of law (see Jeremiah 31:31–34). This covenant would accomplish for God's people what the old covenant had failed to do—bring them forgiveness and give them a new understanding of God the Father.

On the night before His crucifixion, Jesus declared that He was implementing this new covenant that had been promised by His Father. This covenant would be based on His blood, which would be shed to provide redemption and forgiveness of sin for God's people (see Matthew 26:28).

Unlike the old covenant, this new covenant has never been replaced. The Mediator of the New Covenant has promised that those who belong to Him will enjoy eternal life with Him in heaven. What could be better than that? We are willing to bet our lives that Jesus will deliver on His promise.

In Hebrews, Jesus is also called the Mediator of a Better Covenant (Hebrews 8:6) and the Surety of a Better Testament (Hebrews 7:22). These names express the same idea as Mediator of the New Testament.

MELCHISEDEK. See *High Priest after the Order of Melchisedec.*

MERCIFUL AND FAITHFUL HIGH PRIEST. See *Great High Priest.*

MESSENGER OF THE COVENANT

Jesus not only established the new covenant that God had promised for His people (see *Mediator of the New Testament* above). He was also the Messenger whom God sent to announce that this new covenant was now a reality. In this messianic passage, the prophet Malachi declares that Jesus the Messiah would come as the Messenger of the Covenant.

Throughout the history of Israel, God had sent many agents to deliver His message to His people. The greatest of His messengers were the prophets, who often delivered unpopular messages of divine judgment against the nation's sin and rebellion. But Jesus was the divine Messenger who stood out above all the others. He was the Messenger of the covenant of grace that God the Father had established with a sinful world.

About six hundred years before Jesus was born, the prophet Isaiah announced that God the Father would send His servant with a message of joy and comfort for all people. At the beginning of His public ministry, Jesus identified with this prophecy. He stood in the synagogue in his hometown of Nazareth and read these words from Isaiah: "The Spirit of the Lord is upon me, because he hath anointed me to preach the gospel to the poor; he hath sent me to heal the broken-hearted, to preach deliverance to the captives, and recovering of sight to the blind, to set at liberty them that are bruised, to preach the acceptable year of the Lord" (Luke 4:18–19). Then He declared, "This day is this scripture fulfilled in your ears" (Luke 4:21).

For more than three years, Jesus served as the faithful Messenger of God's new covenant of grace that He had been sent to establish. Then His earthly ministry ended with His death on the cross and His glorious resurrection. God's plan from the beginning was that His Messenger would eventually become the Message—the good news (gospel) about God's love for sinners.

Behold, I will send my messenger, and he shall prepare the way before me: and the LORD, whom ye seek, shall suddenly come to his temple, even the **messenger of the covenant**, whom ye delight in: behold, he shall come, saith the LORD of hosts.
MALACHI 3:1

The woman saith unto him, I know that **Messias** cometh, which is called Christ: when he is come, he will tell us all things. Jesus saith unto her, I that speak unto thee am he.
JOHN 4:25–26
[NIV: **Messiah**]

MESSIAH

These two verses are part of the account in John's Gospel of Jesus' conversation with the Samaritan woman at the well. He admitted openly to her that He was the Messiah, the deliverer whom God had been promising to send to His people for hundreds of years.

The only other place in the New Testament where the word *Messiah* appears is also in John's Gospel. After meeting Jesus, Andrew told his brother, Simon Peter, "We have found the Messias" (John 1:41).

It's not surprising that *Messiah* appears rarely in the New Testament, because Jesus discouraged others from referring to Him by this title (see Matthew 16:20). The Jewish people expected their Messiah to be a political and military deliverer who would throw off the yoke of Rome and restore the fortunes of Israel. Jesus had come into the world as a spiritual Messiah, but He avoided this name because it would lead the people to expect Him to be something He was not.

Though the word *Messiah* is rare in the New Testament, the concept appears on almost every page. The Greek term *christos*, rendered as "Christ," means "anointed" or "anointed one"—a word referring to the Messiah or God's Chosen One (see *Chosen of God* and *Christ* above).

Even when the Messiah is mentioned in the Old Testament, the word itself is seldom used. Usually this leader who was to come is described as a Prince (Daniel 8:25), Ruler (Micah 5:2), or Servant (Isaiah 53:11). The rare exception is the book of Daniel, which contains a reference to Messiah the Prince (Daniel 9:25).

MESSIAH THE PRINCE. See *Messiah*.

MIGHTY GOD. See *Almighty*.

MIGHTY ONE OF ISRAEL. See *Almighty*.

MIGHTY ONE OF JACOB. See *Almighty*.

MIGHTY SAVIOUR. See *Horn of Salvation*; *Saviour*.

MINISTER OF THE TRUE TABERNACLE

One of the major themes of the book of Hebrews is the supremacy of Christ's priesthood over the Old Testament sacrificial system. In this verse, the writer of Hebrews claims that the priesthood established during Aaron's time (see Exodus 40:12–15) was only a shadow of the eternal priesthood provided for believers in heaven. Jesus is the priest of the heavenly sanctuary that God has established for His people; He is the Minister of the True Tabernacle.

The most sacred place in the Jewish religious system was the inner sanctuary of the tabernacle or temple, known as "the most holy" (NIV: Most Holy Place; NASB: holy of holies), which represented God's holy and awesome presence. Only the high priest could enter this section of the temple, and even he could do so only once a year, on the Day of Atonement. On this special occasion, he offered a sacrifice—first for his own sins and then for the sins of the people (see Leviticus 16:1–6).

When Jesus died on the cross, the heavy veil or curtain that sealed off this section of the temple was torn from top to bottom (see Matthew 27:50–51). This symbolized that all people now had access to God's presence and forgiveness through the sacrificial death of His Son, Jesus.

Jesus is now the perfect priest or Minister of the True Tabernacle in heaven. There, He conducts His ministry of intercession for all believers. "He is able to save completely those who come to God through him," the writer of Hebrews declares, "because he always lives to intercede for them" (Hebrews 7:25 NIV).

> We have such an high priest, who is set on the right hand of the throne of the Majesty in the heavens; a **minister** of the sanctuary, and **of the true tabernacle**, which the Lord pitched [NIV: set up], and not man.
> HEBREWS 8:1–2

This replica of the Tabernacle exemplifies how temporary the original one from Aaron's time was.

MORNING STAR. See *Bright and Morning Star.*

MOST HOLY. See *Holy One/Holy One of God.*

MY SON, THE BELOVED. See *Beloved Son.*

MY SON, WHOM I LOVE. See *Beloved Son.*

NAZARENE. See *Jesus of Galilee/Jesus of Nazareth.*

OFFSPRING OF DAVID. See *Root and Offspring of David.*

OFFSPRING OF THE WOMAN. See *Seed of the Woman.*

OMEGA. See *Alpha and Omega.*

ONE AND ONLY SON. See *Only Begotten Son.*

ONE CHOSEN OUT OF THE PEOPLE

Then thou spakest in vision to thy holy one, and saidst, I have laid help [NIV: bestowed strength] upon one that is mighty; I have exalted **one chosen out of the people**.
PSALM 89:19
[NIV: **a young man from among the people**]

Psalm 89 focuses on God's promise to King David that one of David's descendants would always occupy the throne of Israel (see 2 Samuel 7:8–17). Thus the "one chosen out of the people" in this verse refers to David, because he was chosen by the Lord from among the sons of Jesse to replace Saul as king (see 1 Samuel 16:10–13).

But this psalm also looks beyond David's time to its ultimate fulfillment in the Messiah, Jesus Christ. The angel Gabriel made this clear when he appeared to the virgin Mary to tell her that she would give birth to the Messiah, God's Chosen One. "He shall be great, and shall be called the Son of the Highest," Gabriel declared, "and the Lord God shall give unto him the throne of his father David" (Luke 1:32).

As the One Chosen out of the People, Jesus was not a king in the same sense as David. He did not seek political or military power. His kingship was spiritual in nature. He ushered in the kingdom of God, the dominion over which He reigns with all those who have accepted Him as Lord and Savior.

Sarcophagus frieze from the fourth century depicts the adoration of the shepherds over David's descendent—the infant Jesus—as the One Chosen Out of the People

ONE WHO SPEAKS TO THE FATHER IN OUR DEFENSE. See *Advocate*.

ONLY BEGOTTEN OF THE FATHER. See *Only Begotten Son*.

ONLY BEGOTTEN SON

Jesus used this name for Himself in His long discussion with Nicodemus about the meaning of the new birth (see John 3:1–21). This verse from that discussion is probably the best known passage in the entire Bible. Most Christians can quote it from memory. It has been called "the gospel in a nutshell" because its twenty-five words tell us so clearly and simply why Jesus came into the world.

The name Only Begotten Son describes Jesus' special relationship with the Father. He is unique—the one and only of His kind who has ever existed. The fact that He was God's one and only Son makes His role as our Savior all the more significant. God the Father sent the very best when He sent Jesus to die on the cross for our sins.

For God so loved the world, that he gave his **only begotten Son**, that whosoever believeth in him should not perish, but have everlasting life.
JOHN 3:16
[NIV: **one and only Son**; NRSV: **only Son**]

This name of Jesus appears only in the writings of the apostle John (see John 1:18; 3:18; 1 John 4:9). John in his Gospel also referred to Jesus as the Only Begotten of the Father (John 1:14).

John 3:16: All the Greatest

An unknown author has explained in memorable terms why John 3:16 is a passage that appeals to all Christians.

God: The greatest lover.

So loved: The greatest degree.

The world: The greatest company.

That He gave: The greatest act.

His only begotten Son: The greatest gift.

That whosoever: The greatest opportunity.

Believeth: The greatest simplicity.

In him: The greatest attraction.

Should not perish: The greatest promise.

But: The greatest difference.

Have: The greatest certainty.

Everlasting life: The greatest possession.

ONLY POTENTATE. See *Blessed and Only Potentate.*

ONLY SON. See *Only Begotten Son.*

ONLY WISE GOD

These final two verses of the epistle of Jude form one of the most inspiring benedictions in the New Testament. Jude wanted his readers to experience the joy of their salvation and to continue to be faithful in their witness to their Only Wise God, whom he clearly identified as Jesus their Savior.

This is the only place in the Bible where Jesus is called by this name. The New King James Version translates this phrase as "God our Savior, who alone is wise." Only Jesus Christ has divine wisdom. Worldly wisdom is a poor substitute for the wisdom that God promises to those who follow Him as Savior and Lord.

Jesus the Son, and God the Father, impart wisdom to

Now unto him that is able to keep you from falling, and to present you faultless before the presence of his glory with exceeding joy, to the **only wise God** our Saviour, be glory and majesty, dominion and power, both now and for ever. Amen.
JUDE 1:24–25

believers by several methods—through the Holy Spirit, through the counsel of fellow Christians, and through the scriptures, the written Word of God. We will never be as wise as God, who is the fount of all wisdom. But we should be growing in this gift of grace as we walk with Him during our earthly journey. James advised the readers of his epistle: "If any of you lacks wisdom, he should ask God, who gives generously to all without finding fault, and it will be given to him" (James 1:5 NIV).

Another name of Jesus similar in meaning to Only Wise God is Wisdom of God (1 Corinthians 1:24).

Seeking Godly Wisdom

- "The wisdom of this world is foolishness with God. For it is written, He taketh the wise in their own craftiness" (1 Corinthians 3:19).
- "Be very careful, then, how you live—not as unwise but as wise, making the most of every opportunity, because the days are evil" (Ephesians 5:15–16 NIV).
- "Let the word of Christ dwell in you richly in all wisdom; teaching and admonishing one another in psalms and hymns and spiritual songs" (Colossians 3:16).

ORIGIN OF GOD'S CREATION. See *Beginning of the Creation of God.*

OUR PASCHAL LAMB. See *Our Passover.*

OUR PASSOVER

In this verse from his first letter to the believers at Corinth, the apostle Paul refers to the Jewish festival known as the Passover. This was the most important religious celebration among the Jews.

Passover commemorated the "passing over" of the houses of the Israelites when God destroyed all the firstborn of the land of Egypt. This occurred as God's final plague against Egypt to convince the pharaoh to release the nation of Israel from slavery. The Jews escaped God's judgment by following His command to mark their houses with the blood of sacrificial lambs (see *Lamb of God* above).

Jesus is Our Passover, Paul declares, because He shed His

Purge out therefore the old leaven, that ye may be a new lump, as ye are unleavened. For even Christ **our passover** is sacrificed for us.
1 CORINTHIANS 5:7
[NIV: **our Passover lamb**; NRSV: **our paschal lamb**]

blood to bring deliverance for God's people, just as the first sacrificial lambs inaugurated the first Passover. We remember His sacrifice with reverence every time we partake of Communion, the Lord's Supper.

The imagery of leaven in connection with Passover also appears in this verse. *Leaven* is another word for yeast, an ingredient used to cause bread to rise. But the Israelites left Egypt in such a hurry on the first Passover that they didn't have time to add leaven to their bread dough and wait for it to rise (see Exodus 12:34). Thus, whenever they observed this holiday from that day on, they were to eat unleavened bread. This part of Passover was known as the Feast of Unleavened Bread.

Paul refers to Christians in this verse as a "new lump," because they were "unleavened." Just as unleavened bread symbolizes the Israelites' freedom from Egyptian slavery, so Christians are unleavened, or separated from sin and death, by the perfect Passover Lamb, Jesus Christ.

Jesus celebrated the Passover meal with his disciples while reclining at the table. For centuries, the symbolism of this meal has pointed to Jesus as "Our Passover."

OUR PASSOVER LAMB. See *Our Passover.*

OUR PEACE. See *Lord of Peace.*

OVERSEER OF YOUR SOULS. See *Bishop of Your Souls.*

PERFECTER OF OUR FAITH. See *Author and Finisher of Our Faith.*

PHYSICIAN

These verses are part of the account of Jesus' calling of the tax collector, Matthew (also known as Levi), as His disciple. To celebrate the occasion, Matthew invited his tax collector associates and other friends to a "great feast" (Luke 5:29) for Jesus and His disciples.

The scribes and Pharisees were horrified that Jesus and His disciples would associate with such sinful people. But Jesus made it clear that He had been sent to people such as these. They needed a Savior and Deliverer. He was the Physician who could heal them of their desperate sickness known as sin.

Jesus' role as Physician is one of the more prominent in the Gospels. Most of His miracles were performed for people who were suffering from various physical problems—blindness, deafness, leprosy, and possession by evil spirits. But in many of these miracles, He went beyond healing the body to healing the soul and the spirit through forgiveness of sin. For example, after healing a paralyzed man, He told him, "Be of good cheer; thy sins be forgiven thee" (Matthew 9:2).

Jesus the Physician is still in the healing business. He

But their scribes and Pharisees murmured against his disciples, saying, Why do ye eat and drink with publicans [NIV: tax collectors] and sinners? And Jesus answering said unto them, They that are whole [NIV: healthy] need not a **physician**; but they that are sick.
LUKE 5:30–31
[NIV: **doctor**]

Jesus touches a blind man's eyes to restore his sight in this relief from the eighteenth century.

offers hope to the discouraged, His abiding presence to the lonely, comfort to the grieving, and peace to the conflicted. But most of all, He brings deliverance from the most serious problems of the human race—sin and death. The apostle Paul expresses it like this: "The wages of sin is death; but the gift of God is eternal life through Jesus Christ our Lord" (Romans 6:23).

No Appointment Necessary

We as Christians don't need an appointment to see Jesus. He is always near, according to an old hymn by William Hunter titled "The Great Physician."

The great Physician now is near,
The sympathizing Jesus;
He speaks the drooping heart to cheer,
Oh, hear the voice of Jesus.
Sweetest note in seraph song,
Sweetest name on mortal tongue;
Sweetest carol ever sung,
Jesus, blessed Jesus.

PIONEER AND PERFECTER OF OUR FAITH. See *Author and Finisher of Our Faith.*

PIONEER OF SALVATION. See *Captain of Salvation.*

PLANT OF RENOWN

And I will raise up for them a **plant of renown**, and they shall be no more consumed with hunger in the land, neither bear the shame of the heathen [NIV: scorn of the nations] any more.
EZEKIEL 34:29
[NASB: **renowned planting place**; NIV: **land renowned for its crops**; NRSV: **splendid vegetation**]

Is this verse from the prophet Ezekiel a description of the coming Messiah or a reference to the fertility of the renewed land of Israel? The KJV and NRSV translations treat the verse messianically, while the NASB and NIV render it as a reference to Israel.

The context of this verse provides support for the messianic interpretation. The entire thirty-fourth chapter of Ezekiel describes how God the Father will send a shepherd, His servant David, to feed His flock (see Ezekiel 34:23). As the Plant of Renown, this servant from David's line will provide God's people with all the food they need so "they shall be no more consumed with hunger."

This name of God the Son is similar in meaning to His description of Himself as *Bread* (see above). Jesus is the spiritual sustenance that Christians need to keep their faith healthy and in tune with His will for their lives.

POTENTATE. See *Blessed and Only Potentate.*

POWER OF GOD

In this verse, the apostle Paul admits that many people were skeptical of a crucified Savior. If Jesus was such a great person, they reasoned, why did He wind up being executed on a Roman cross like a common criminal? To them His crucifixion was a sign of weakness, not a demonstration of strength.

On the contrary, Paul points out, Christ showed great power in His crucifixion. He was the very Power of God whom the Father sent to atone for the sins of the world through His death. The death of One on behalf of the many showed the extent of this divine power.

Jesus' power was demonstrated many times during His earthly ministry. He stilled a storm and calmed the waters on the Sea of Galilee (see Mark 4:37–39). He cast demons out of a demented man (see Luke 4:31–35). He raised His friend Lazarus from the dead (see John 11:43–44). But He refused to come down from the cross and save Himself, although the crowd taunted Him to do so (see Matthew 27:39–43).

This is a good example of power under control. Jesus could have called legions of angels to come to His rescue (see Matthew 26:53). But this would have nullified the purpose for which God the Father had sent Him into the world. His divine power was never greater than when He refused to use it.

> We preach Christ crucified, unto the Jews a stumblingblock, and unto the Greeks foolishness; but unto them which are called, both Jews and Greeks, Christ the **power of God**, and the wisdom of God.
> 1 CORINTHIANS 1:23–24

Christ as the Power of God in Paul's Writings

- "Your faith should not stand in the wisdom of men, but in the power of God" (1 Corinthians 2:5).
- "Though he was crucified through weakness, yet he liveth by the power of God" (2 Corinthians 13:4).
- "Be strong in the Lord, and in the power of his might" (Ephesians 6:10).
- "Be thou partaker of the afflictions of the gospel according to the power of God" (2 Timothy 1:8).

PRECIOUS CORNER STONE. See *Chief Cornerstone.*

PRIEST FOREVER. See *Great High Priest.*

PRINCE

The apostle Peter used this title for Jesus in his sermon before the Jewish Sanhedrin. He and the other apostles had just been released miraculously from prison by an angel after they were arrested for preaching about Jesus. Peter declared in his sermon that the Jewish religious leaders were guilty of crucifying Jesus, the Prince whom God the Father had sent into the world.

Prince is a title with at least three different meanings in the Bible. Peter could have had any one or all of these in mind when he referred to Jesus as a Prince.

1. A prince was the son of a king. If a king had several sons, his oldest was generally the one who succeeded his father on the throne. Perhaps Peter had Jesus as God's Son in mind when he called him a Prince.

2. *Prince* is a generic term often used in the Bible for a leader or ruler. For example, when Moses tried to stop a fight between two Israelites, one of them asked him, "Who made thee a prince and a judge over us?" (Exodus 2:14). When Peter called Jesus a Prince, he may have been saying that Jesus had been exalted by God to serve as a ruler over His people.

3. Sometimes the word *prince* is used as a synonym for *king* (see 1 Kings 11:34). By saying that Jesus was a Prince, Peter could have implied that He was the one and only sovereign ruler over God's people.

What Peter said about Jesus as a Prince boils down to this: He is the one and only Son of God appointed by the Father to rule over His people like a good king, administering justice and righteousness in His name.

> The God of our fathers raised up Jesus, whom ye slew [NIV: killed] and hanged on a tree. Him hath God exalted with his right hand to be a **Prince** and a Saviour, for to give [NIV: that he might give] repentance to Israel, and forgiveness of sins.
> ACTS 5:30–31
> [NRSV: **Leader**]

Another Prince

Jesus is the Prince over God's kingdom. But He recognized there is another prince—Satan—who tries to undermine His work. He referred to Satan several times as "the prince of this world" (see John 12:31; 14:30; 16:11). The apostle Paul called Satan "the prince of the power of the air" (Ephesians 2:2).

PRINCE OF LIFE. See *Life*.

PRINCE OF PEACE. See *Lord of Peace*.

PRINCE OF PRINCES

This verse from the book of Daniel was fulfilled in Jewish history, but it also awaits its ultimate fulfillment in the end time. If refers to Antiochus IV, Epiphanes, an evil Greek ruler who persecuted the Jews, as well as the Antichrist of the last days, who is described in the book of Revelation.

Antiochus tried to force the Jewish people to adopt Greek culture, even going so far as to erect an altar to the pagan Greek god Zeus in the temple. His atrocities led to rebellion by the Jews under the leadership of the Maccabees during the period between the Old and New Testaments. Antiochus died in disgrace following his defeat by these Jewish zealots.

The ultimate earthly evil force will be the Antichrist, who stands against Christ, His church, and their influence for good in the world. But this evil person will be overcome by Christ (see Revelation 14:9–11; 19:20), just as Antiochus met defeat in his time. No earthly power is able to stand against the Prince of Princes.

> And through his policy also he shall cause craft [NIV: deceit] to prosper in his hand; and he shall magnify himself in his heart, and by peace shall destroy many: he shall also stand up against the **Prince of princes**; but he shall be broken without hand [NIV: yet he will be destroyed, but not by human power].
> DANIEL 8:25

PRINCE OF THE KINGS OF THE EARTH

The apostle John addressed the book of Revelation to seven churches of Asia Minor, whose members were undergoing persecution by the Roman authorities. John wanted these believers to understand that he was not writing under his own authority but under the command and direction of Jesus Christ, the Prince of the Kings of the Earth.

Earthly rulers, such as the emperors of the Roman Empire, come and go. But Jesus is an eternal King, not a temporary monarch who rules for a few years and then is replaced by another. Jesus stands above and beyond all the kings of the earth.

Other titles of Jesus that are similar in meaning to this title are King of Kings (Revelation 19:16) and King over All the Earth (Zechariah 14:9). If Jesus is the world's supreme King, there is no doubt that He has the right to reign over His church and in the lives of those who claim Him as their Savior and Lord.

> Grace be unto you, and peace. . .from Jesus Christ, who is the faithful witness, and the first begotten of the dead, and the **prince of the kings of the earth**.
> REVELATION 1:4–5
> [NASB, NIV, NRSV: **ruler of the kings of the earth**]

PROPHET. See *Great Prophet.*

PROPHET MIGHTY IN DEED AND WORD. See *Great Prophet.*

PROPHET OF NAZARETH OF GALILEE. See *Great Prophet.*

PROPHET OF NAZARETH OF GALILEE. See *Great Prophet.*

PROPITIATION FOR OUR SINS

Herein is love, not that we loved God, but that he loved us, and sent his Son to be the **propitiation for our sins**. 1 JOHN 4:10 [NIV, NRSV: **atoning sacrifice for our sins**]

The word *propitiation* comes from an old English word, *propitiate*, meaning "to appease" or "to satisfy." Thus, the apostle John declares in this verse that God the Father sent His Son Jesus to serve as the satisfaction for our sins. This word is the key to one of the classical theories of the Atonement, or the sacrificial death of Jesus.

According to this view, God is a holy God who cannot tolerate sin. This puts us as humans in a dilemma, because we are not capable of living sinless lives, no matter how hard we try. To make matters worse, God is also a just God, who—in order to be true to His nature—must punish sin wherever He finds it. So our sin separates us from God and makes us liable to His punishment. *Hopeless* is the only word that adequately describes this situation.

But, according to John, God loved us too much to allow us to continue in this dilemma. He sent His Son, Jesus, to die to pay the penalty that He demanded from us because of our sin. Jesus was the sacrifice that covered over, or atoned, for our sin and restored the broken relationship between a holy God and sinful humanity.

Propitiation is not a word that most of us drop into casual conversation. Most people would not understand it. But aren't you glad that God knows the term and that Jesus lived out its meaning through His life and death? We as Christians can *celebrate* because Jesus came into the world to *propitiate.*

Jesus as Our Propitiation/Ransom

Ransom is another New Testament term that means basically the same thing as *propitiation.* In the Old Testament, *ransom* describes the price that was paid to purchase a person's freedom from slavery or from deserved punishment. In the New Testament, Jesus applies this word to Himself when he declares, "The Son of man came not to be ministered unto, but to minister, and to give his life a ransom for many" (Mark 10:45).

QUICKENING SPIRIT

This name of God the Son appears in connection with His name as the *Last Adam* (see above). Adam's act of disobedience of God brought sin and death into the world. But Jesus' perfect obedience nullified the divine curse against Adam and brought the possibility of eternal life to humankind.

As the Quickening Spirit, Jesus offers eternal life to all who accept Him as Savior and Lord.

RABBI/RABBONI

In modern society, *rabbi* is the official title of the leader of a Jewish congregation. It is similar to the title of *reverend* for a Protestant minister or *father* for a Catholic priest.

But in Jesus' time, *rabbi* was a term of respect meaning "teacher" or "master" (see *Good Master*; *Master* above). In John 3:2, Nicodemus's reference to Jesus as "rabbi" probably means "teacher." Nicodemus wanted to learn more about this Jewish teacher and miracle worker who was impressing the crowds in the region of Galilee.

In John 20:16, Mary Magdalene's recognition of Jesus as "Rabboni" pays homage to Him as her Master. After His resurrection, she recognized Him as such when He called her by name. *Rabboni* is the Aramaic form of *Rabbi*. Aramaic was the common language spoken in Israel during New Testament times.

Whether we call Jesus Rabbi or Rabboni, the meaning is the same: He is our Master Teacher and Guide, who deserves our utmost respect and loyalty.

> And so it is written, The first man Adam was made a living soul; the last Adam was made a **quickening spirit**.
> 1 CORINTHIANS 15:45
> [NASB, NIV, NRSV: **life-giving spirit**]

> The same came to Jesus by night, and said unto him, **Rabbi**, we know that thou art a teacher come from God: for no man can do these miracles that thou doest, except God be with him.
> JOHN 3:2

> Jesus saith unto her, Mary. She turned herself, and saith unto him, **Rabboni**; which is to say, Master.
> JOHN 20:16
> [NRSV: **Rabbouni**]

A rabbi preaches from a scroll in a synagogue.

RABBOUNI. See *Rabbi/Rabboni.*

RADIANCE OF GOD'S GLORY. See *Brightness of God's Glory.*

RANSOM. See *Propitiation for Our Sins.*

REDEEMER

And the **Redeemer** shall come to Zion, and unto them that turn from transgression in Jacob, saith the LORD.
ISAIAH 59:20

This verse from the prophet Isaiah refers to the coming Messiah, who will serve as a Redeemer for God's people.

In the Old Testament, God is often referred to by this name (see *Redeemer* in part 1, Names of God the Father). A kinsman redeemer in ancient Israel was a blood relative who assumed responsibility for members of his clan who were in trouble. For example, the redeemer would buy back the property of a family member who had lost it through indebtedness. Or he would purchase the freedom of an impoverished relative who had been forced to sell himself into slavery.

But Isaiah's prophecy looked toward the coming of a Redeemer of a different type. Jesus Christ the Redeemer would free God's people from their bondage to sin and death. He would do so by dying on the cross for our benefit. The purchase price that He would pay for our salvation was none other than His own precious blood.

The patriarch Job, like Isaiah, also received a glimpse of this Redeemer of the future. Out of his suffering and despair he declared, "I know that my redeemer liveth, and that he shall stand at the latter day upon the earth" (Job 19:25).

What Isaiah and Job only hoped for has now come to pass. We can rejoice with the apostle John because "the blood of Jesus Christ [God's] Son cleanseth us from all sin" (1 John 1:7).

"Blessed Redeemer," a hymn by Avis Burgeson Christiansen, expresses the praise of all believers for Jesus' work as our Redeemer.

Up Calvary's mountain, one dreadful morn,
Walked Christ my Saviour, weary and worn;
Facing for sinners death on the cross,
That He might save them from endless loss.
Blessed Redeemer! Precious Redeemer!
Seems now I see Him on Calvary's tree;
Wounded and bleeding, for sinners pleading,
Blind and unheeding—dying for me!

REFINER'S FIRE

This name of Jesus appears in the one of the final chapters of the Old Testament, in which the prophet Malachi describes the coming Messiah as a Refiner's Fire, or the hot fire that metalworkers of Bible times used to purify ore such as silver. The ore was heated in a pot until it turned to liquid and the dross or waste material rose to the surface. Then the metalworker used a ladle to skim off the dross, leaving the pure and uncontaminated silver.

This image of the Messiah must have been a surprise to the Jewish people of Malachi's time. They expected the Messiah to come as a conquering hero who would restore Israel to its glory days as a political kingdom. But the prophet informed them that the Messiah would come in judgment against Israel because of its sin and rebellion.

The name Refiner's Fire emphasizes Jesus' role as Judge. His second coming will bring judgment against all who have refused to accept Him as Savior and Lord (see 2 Peter 2:9).

REFLECTION OF GOD'S GLORY. See *Brightness of God's Glory*.

RESURRECTION AND THE LIFE

Jesus used this name for Himself in His conversation with Martha, the sister of Lazarus, after Lazarus had died. She was disappointed that Jesus had not arrived at her home in Bethany in time to save her brother's life. She knew that Jesus could perform miracles of healing, so she scolded Him, "Lord. . . if you had been here, my brother would not have died" (John 11:21 NIV).

Jesus' double-edged reply to Martha made it clear that He was the master of the living and the dead. He was capable at any time of raising Lazarus, as well as any others who had died. At the same time, He could guarantee eternal life for the living. In this sense, those who believed in Him would

> But who may abide [NIV: endure] the day of his coming? and who shall stand when he appeareth? for he is like a **refiner's fire**, and like fullers' soap.
> MALACHI 3:2

An Egyptian figurine of a metalworker working a blowpipe to increase the heat in a crucible.

never die. This included Martha, as well as all believers of the future.

Jesus then proceeded to deliver on His promise. He stood before the burial chamber where the body of Lazarus had been placed, and just as God the Father had created the world with the words of His mouth (Genesis 1:1–31), Jesus the Son brought His friend back to life with a simple verbal command: "Lazarus, come forth" (John 11:43).

Note the things that are missing from this account: no incantations over the body, no lightning flash from heaven, no magical tricks to dazzle the crowd. Just three simple words from Jesus—and Lazarus walked out of the tomb. You don't have to be a genius to figure out that a person of such sensitivity and power is worthy of our loyalty and devotion. Jesus alone has the keys to life and death.

> Jesus said unto her, I am the **resurrection, and the life**: he that believeth in me, though he were dead, yet shall he live. And whosoever liveth and believeth in me shall never die.
> JOHN 11:25–26

RIGHTEOUS

The word *righteous* is used in combination with other words in the Bible to express several different names for Jesus—for example, Righteous Branch (Jeremiah 23:5), Righteous Judge (2 Timothy 4:8), and Righteous Servant (Isaiah 53:11). But this is the only place in the King James Version where Jesus is simply called the Righteous. (Note that the NIV renders this name as the Righteous One.)

Jesus can be called the Righteous or the Righteous One, because He is the only person who has ever lived who achieved perfect righteousness. Although He was *capable* of doing wrong, because of the human side of His nature (see *Flesh* above), He never gave in to temptation or stumbled into sin.

At the beginning of His ministry, Jesus was tempted by Satan to establish an earthly kingdom and to use His powers for His own self-interest. But Jesus resisted all of these temptations (see Luke 4:1–13). In the garden of Gethsemane on the night before His crucifixion, He admitted that "the flesh is weak" (Matthew 26:41). In an agonizing prayer, He asked God to deliver Him from the suffering of the cross, if possible. But He finally yielded His will to His Father's purpose and plan (see Matthew 26:37–42).

Because Jesus is the Righteous One, He calls us, His followers, to a life of righteousness. We will never achieve perfection and a sinless existence in this life, but we ought to be

> My little children, these things write I unto you, that ye sin not. And if any man sin, we have an advocate with the Father [NIV: one who speaks to the Father in our defense], Jesus Christ the **righteous**.
> 1 John 2:1
> [NIV: **Righteous One**]

growing in that direction. He has promised to guide us along this journey. "The eyes of the Lord are over the righteous," the apostle Peter declares, "and his ears are open unto their prayers" (1 Peter 3:12).

RIGHTEOUS BRANCH. See *Branch of Righteousness*.

RIGHTEOUS BRANCH OF DAVID.
See *Branch of Righteousness*.

RIGHTEOUS JUDGE. See *Judge of Quick and Dead*.

RIGHTEOUS MAN. See *Just Man*.

RIGHTEOUS ONE. See *Righteous*.

RIGHTEOUS ONE, MY SERVANT.
See *Righteous Servant*.

RIGHTEOUS SERVANT

The theme of service and servanthood runs throughout the scriptures. For example, several people in the Bible are referred to as "servant of God" or "God's servant" because of the loyal service they rendered for the Lord (see sidebar). But Jesus is the only person who deserves to be called God's Righteous Servant. He was the Holy and Righteous One whom the Father sent on a mission of redemption for the entire world.

This name of Jesus appears in one of the famous servant songs of the prophet Isaiah (see Isaiah 42:1–4; 49:1–6; 52:13–53:12). This Servant, the Messiah, would undergo great suffering while carrying

Jesus washes Peter's feet to teach His disciples true servanthood.

He shall see of the travail [NIV: suffering] of his soul, and shall be satisfied: by his knowledge shall my **righteous servant** justify many; for he shall bear their iniquities.
ISAIAH 53:11
[NASB, NRSV:
righteous one, my servant]

out His mission. But it would be for a divine purpose. His suffering and death would provide a means of deliverance for a human race trapped in sin.

Jesus identified Himself specifically as the Suffering Servant from God the Father, whom Isaiah had predicted. At the beginning of His public ministry, Jesus quoted Isaiah's first servant song (see Isaiah 42:1–4; Matthew 12:18–21). The implication of His words was that the mission of God's Suffering Servant was being fulfilled through His teaching and healing ministry.

Jesus saw His work as that of a humble servant. On one occasion, His disciples began to argue over who would occupy the places of honor at His side in His future glory. He gently reminded them: "Whoever wants to be first must be slave of all. For even the Son of Man did not come to be served, but to serve, and to give his life as a ransom for many" (Mark 10:44–45 NIV).

Today, the servant work of Jesus continues through His church. We who belong to Him are automatically in the serving business. The apostle Paul declares that we as Christians should think of ourselves as "a living sacrifice, holy, acceptable unto God, which is your reasonable service" (Romans 12:1).

Others Called Servants of God

The two people in the Bible who are most often called "servant of God" are Moses (see Exodus 14:31; Numbers 12:7–8; Deuteronomy 34:5; Psalm 105:26; Revelation 15:3) and David (see 2 Samuel 3:18; 1 Kings 3:6; Psalm 89:3; Luke 1:69). But the title is also applied to several other famous and not-so-famous Bible personalities, including the following:

- Abraham (Genesis 26:24)
- Ahijah (1 Kings 14:18)
- Caleb (Numbers 14:24)
- Daniel (Daniel 9:17)
- Elijah (2 Kings 9:36)
- Isaiah (Isaiah 20:3)
- Job (Job 1:8)
- Joshua (Joshua 24:29)
- Samuel (1 Samuel 3:9–10)
- Solomon (1 Kings 1:26)
- Zerubbabel (Haggai 2:23)

RISING SUN. See *Dayspring from on High.*

ROCK. See *Spiritual Rock.*

ROCK OF OFFENCE. See *Head of the Corner.*

ROD OUT OF THE STEM OF JESSE

This verse from the prophet Isaiah is a reference to the coming Messiah. We are accustomed to associations of the Messiah with King David, but Isaiah in this passage traces the Messiah back one more generation—to David's father, Jesse.

Two passages in the Bible tell us all we know about Jesse. His father was Obed, the son of Boaz and Ruth. Thus, Jesse was of mixed blood, because Ruth was a Moabite and Boaz was a Jew (see Ruth 1:4; 4:13–22). Jesse had eight sons, including David. One of the more beautiful stories in the Bible is how God, through the prophet Samuel, turned down all of Jesse's older sons for the kingship of Israel in favor of David, Jesse's youngest son. David had to be summoned from the fields, where he was watching his father's sheep, to be presented for Samuel's review (see 1 Samuel 16:1–13).

Why did Isaiah compare the coming Messiah to a Rod, or shoot, from the Stem, or stump, of Jesse? Perhaps to remind us that the Messiah sprang from a family of mixed Jewish and Gentile blood, signifying that He would be a deliverer for all people, not just the Jews. Isaiah also predicted that the nation of Judah would fall to a foreign power, thus bringing to an end the dynasty of David. But from the stump of this fallen tree, God would bring new life—the Messiah, who would reign in a spiritual sense over God's people.

Isaiah also spoke of the coming Messiah as a Root of Jesse (Isaiah 11:10). This name expresses the same idea as Rod out of the Stem of Jesse.

ROOT AND DESCENDANT OF DAVID. See *Root and Offspring of David.*

ROOT AND OFFSPRING OF DAVID

Jesus used this name for Himself in the closing verses of the final chapter of the last book of the Bible. It's as if He used His last opportunity to tell the world who He is and what His life and ministry are all about.

And there shall come forth a **rod out of the stem of Jesse**, and a Branch shall grow out of his roots. ISAIAH 11:1 [NASB: **Shoot from the stem of Jesse**; NIV, NRSV: **shoot from the stump of Jesse**]

Notice the dual focus of this name—the Root of David and the Offspring of David. It summarizes His existence as the God-man, the One who is both fully human and fully divine.

Because Jesus is the divine Son, who served as the agent of creation (see *Beginning of the Creation of God* above), He is David's creator, or Root. But because he came to earth in human form, He is also David's descendant, or Offspring—the Messiah from the line of David, who reigns over the spiritual kingdom that He came to establish. Thus, Jesus is both superior to David and the rightful heir to his throne.

> I Jesus have sent mine angel to testify unto you these things in the churches. I am the **root and the offspring of David**, and the bright and morning star.
> REVELATION 22:16
> [NASB, NRSV: **root and descendant of David**]

ROOT OF JESSE. See *Rod out of the Stem of Jesse.*

RULER IN ISRAEL. See *Governor.*

RULER OF GOD'S CREATION. See *Beginning of the Creation of God.*

RULER OF THE KINGS OF THE EARTH. See *Prince of the Kings of the Earth.*

SALVATION OF GOD. See *Horn of Salvation*; *Saviour.*

SAVIOUR

An angel spoke these words to shepherds in the fields outside Bethlehem on the day Jesus was born. The shepherds were awestruck and excited by the news that this newborn baby was to be a Savior for God's people (see Luke 2:8–15).

In Bible times, any person who rescued others from danger was called a savior or deliverer. For example, the judges of Israel whom God raised up to deliver His people from oppression by their enemies were called "saviours" (Nehemiah 9:27). But the only true Saviors in a spiritual sense are God the Father and God the Son, both of whom are called by this name many times throughout the Bible (see *Saviour* in part 1, Names of God the Father, and part 2, Names of God the Son).

The name that Mary and Joseph gave their firstborn Son expresses His work as Savior. *Jesus* means "God Is Salvation." From the very beginning it was clear that His purpose was to do for us what we could not do for ourselves—deliver us

> I bring you good tidings [NIV: good news] of great joy, which shall be to all people. For unto you is born this day in the city of David a **Saviour**, which is Christ the Lord.
> LUKE 2:10–11

from bondage to sin and death.

The phrase "all people," in the message of the angels to the shepherds, shows that Jesus was God's gift to the entire world. The universal nature of Christ's redemptive work is expressed by two other "Savior" titles in the New Testament— Saviour of All Men (1 Timothy 4:10) and Saviour of the World (1 John 4:14).

A memorial beneath the Church of the Nativity in Bethlehem, the "city of David," marks the traditional location where the "Saviour, which is Christ the Lord" was born.

Hallelujah Says It All

Philip P. Bliss wrote the hymn "Hallelujah! What a Saviour" to express his joy at the saving work of Jesus Christ.

Bearing shame and scoffing rude,
In my place condemned He stood,
Seal'd my pardon with His blood;
Hallelujah! what a Saviour!

SAVIOUR OF ALL MEN. See *Saviour.*

SAVIOUR OF THE BODY

The context of this verse from the apostle Paul makes it clear that he is not referring to a human body, but to the church as the body of Christ. Paul goes on to say, in verse 25, "Husbands, love your wives, even as Christ also loved the church, and gave himself for it."

Christ is the head of the church, and the church that He founded is so closely related to Him that it is referred to as His body several times in the New Testament (see 1 Corinthians 12:27; Ephesians 1:22–23; Colossians 1:18). Thus, the church is not a building or a lifeless institution but a living organism, dedicated to advancing the cause of the kingdom

For the husband is the head of the wife, even as Christ is the head of the church: and he is the **saviour of the body**.
EPHESIANS 5:23

of God in the world.

Christ not only died for us as individuals, but He also sacrificed Himself for His church. We bring honor and glory to Him when we work through His church to serve as witnesses to others of His love and grace.

Founded on His Life

"The Church's One Foundation," a hymn by Samuel J. Stone, describes the ultimate sacrifice that Jesus made for His church.

The church's one foundation
Is Jesus Christ her Lord;
She is His new creation,
By water and the Word:
From heaven He came and sought her
To be His holy bride,
With His own blood He bought her,
And for her life He died.

SAVIOUR OF THE WORLD. See *Saviour.*

SCEPTRE OUT OF ISRAEL

Scepters like this one held by a stauette of the Pharaoh Senusret III were used by royalty to signify power and authority. Jesus is the supreme authority—the "Scepter Out of Israel."

These words were spoken by Balaam, a pagan magician, who was hired by the king of Moab to pronounce a curse against the Israelites. But Balaam was led by the Lord to bless the Israelites instead. In this verse, Balaam even prophesied that a Sceptre out of Israel, or a strong leader, would rise up to crush the Moabites.

This verse is also considered a prophecy with a long-range fulfillment, referring to Jesus as the Savior-

Messiah, whom God would send to deliver His people.

A scepter is a short staff, similar to a walking stick, that symbolizes the power and authority of a king. In the book of Esther, King Ahasuerus of Persia extends his royal scepter for Queen Esther to touch (see Esther 5:2–3). This gives her permission to come into his presence and present her request to the king.

The imagery of a royal scepter, as applied to Jesus, symbolizes His power, authority, and universal dominion. In the book of Hebrews, God the Father declares to Jesus the Son, "Thy throne. . .is for ever and ever: a sceptre of righteousness is the sceptre of thy kingdom" (Hebrews 1:8).

SECOND MAN. See *Last Adam*.

SEED OF DAVID. See *Son of David*.

SEED OF THE WOMAN

God the Father spoke these words to the serpent, Satan, in the garden of Eden. This conversation occurred after Satan had persuaded Adam and Eve to eat the forbidden fruit in direct disobedience of God's command. This verse is known as the *protoevangelium*, a Latin word meaning "the first gospel."

It is called the first gospel because it contains the first

prediction in the Bible of the coming of Christ into the world. Jesus is depicted as the Seed of the Woman, Eve. He will wage war against Satan's forces. Satan will manage to bruise His heel—a reference to the forces that executed Jesus

> There shall come a Star out of Jacob, and a **Sceptre** shall rise **out of Israel**, and shall smite [NIV: crush] the corners of Moab, and destroy all the children of Sheth.
> NUMBERS 24:17

> And I will put enmity between thee and **the woman**, and between thy seed and **her seed**; it shall bruise [NIV: crush] thy head, and thou shalt bruise [NIV: strike] his heel.
> GENESIS 3:15
> [NIV, NRSV: **offspring of the woman**]

This bronze relief from the Church of the Annunciation in Nazareth is a reminder of how after Adam and Eve's sin in the Garden of Eden, God had a plan to redeem the world through Eve—the "Seed of the Woman."

on the cross—but Jesus will rise triumphantly from the dead and deal a crushing blow to Satan's head. In the end time, Jesus will win the final and ultimate victory over Satan and cast him into the lake of fire (see Revelation 20:10).

The name Seed of the Woman may be a subtle reference to the virgin birth of Jesus. He was conceived in Mary's womb by the Holy Spirit, not by a human father. She was told by the angel Gabriel, "The Holy Ghost shall come upon thee, and the power of the Highest shall overshadow thee: therefore also that holy thing which shall be born of thee shall be called the Son of God" (Luke 1:35).

SERVANT. See *Righteous Servant.*

SHEPHERD. See *Good Shepherd.*

SHEPHERD OF YOUR SOULS. See *Good Shepherd.*

SHILOH

Genesis 49 contains the aging Jacob's blessings on his twelve sons, whose descendants would become the twelve tribes of Israel. This verse is part of his blessing of Judah, the tribe destined to produce the rulers of Israel.

Shiloh is a Hebrew word meaning "the one to whom it belongs." Thus, Jacob was saying that Judah would wield the royal scepter of leadership in Israel (see *Sceptre out of Israel* above) until the one to whom the scepter belonged arrived on the scene. This is a veiled reference to the coming Messiah.

Jesus is the One to whom all authority and power belong, because God has delegated jurisdiction over His people to His Son. Jesus is also deserving of all power, because He rules in justice and righteousness. Just a little power can go to an earthly ruler's head, but Jesus will never use His power for anything but the good of His church—those who devote their lives to Him and His service.

No matter what happens to us in this life, we can rest safe and secure in the arms of Shiloh—the One who holds the whole world in His hands.

> The sceptre shall not depart from Judah, nor a lawgiver [NIV: ruler's staff] from between his feet, until **Shiloh** come; and unto him shall the gathering of the people be.
> GENESIS 49:10

SHOOT FROM THE STEM/STUMP OF JESSE. See *Rod out of the Stem of Jesse.*

SIGNAL FOR THE NATIONS. See *Ensign for the Nations*.

SOMEONE TO ARBITRATE. See *Daysman*.

SON OF ABRAHAM

This is one of two names of God the Son cited in the very first verse of the New Testament (see *Son of David* below). Abraham was the father of the Jewish people. Many centuries before Jesus' time, God the Father called Abraham to leave his home and family in Mesopotamia and move to the land of Canaan. Here, God would begin to build a nation that would be His exclusive possession. He promised Abraham, "I will bless them that bless thee, and curse him that curseth thee: and in thee shall all families of the earth be blessed" (Genesis 12:3).

As the Son of Abraham, Jesus is the fulfillment of this promise, or covenant, that God made with Abraham. In His human lineage and by His nationality, Jesus was a Jew—the people whom God promised to bless above all the nations of the earth.

But God never intended for His promise of blessing to apply only to the Jewish people. He wanted "all families of the earth" to be brought to Him through the influence of Abraham's offspring. When the Jews forgot this part of the covenant, God sent His Son, Jesus, to remind them that He had placed no limits on His love and grace. Jesus as the Son of Abraham fulfilled God's redemptive plan by coming as a Savior for the entire world.

The book of the generation of Jesus Christ, the son of David, the **son of Abraham**.
MATTHEW 1:1

SON OF DAVID

Perhaps it is not accidental that the very first verse of the New Testament refers to Jesus by this name. As the Son of David, He ties together the Old and New Testaments. The genealogies of Jesus in the Gospels of Matthew and Luke make the point that Jesus, in His human lineage, was descended from David (see Matthew 1:6; Luke 3:31). Thus, Jesus fulfilled God's promise to David that one of David's descendants would always reign over His people (see 2 Samuel 7:1–16; Psalm 132:11–12).

During Jesus' earthly ministry, the crowds and individuals whom He healed often called Him the "son of David" (Matthew 9:27; 12:23; Mark 10:47; Luke 18:38). But Jesus

The book of the generation of Jesus Christ, the **son of David**, the son of Abraham.
MATTHEW 1:1

never used this name of Himself. He may have avoided it because it tended to feed the expectation of the Jewish people that the Messiah would come as a political conqueror, not a spiritual Savior (see *Messiah* above).

Another name of God the Son similar in meaning to Son of David is Seed (or Offspring) of David (2 Timothy 2:8).

SON OF GOD

The centurion mentioned in this verse from Matthew's Gospel refers to the Roman military officer who presided over the execution of Jesus. He was so impressed with the miraculous signs that accompanied Jesus' death (see Matthew 27:50–53) that he declared that Jesus was none other than the Son of God. Ironically, this pagan soldier affirmed what the Jewish religious leaders refused to believe.

Son of God, as a name or title for Jesus, appears many times throughout the New Testament (see, for example, Matthew 14:33; Acts 9:20; Romans 1:4). It emphasizes His divine nature and shows that He came to earth under the authority of God the Father on a mission of redemption.

This name also highlights Jesus' close, personal relationship with God. He knew God like no other person has ever known Him, and He addressed Him often in His prayers as "Father" (John 17:1–26). He taught His disciples in a model prayer to approach God in the same way: "Our Father which art in heaven" (Matthew 6:9).

In Bible times, a son was expected to honor and obey his parents (see Exodus 20:12; Ephesians 6:1). Jesus, as God's Son, was perfectly obedient to the Father. He refused to be sidetracked from the mission on which He was sent into the world. His last words from the cross were "it is finished" (John 19:30). This was not the whimper of a dying man, but

> Now when the centurion, and they that were with him, watching Jesus, saw the earthquake, and those things that were done, they feared greatly [NIV: were terrified], saying, Truly [NIV: Surely] this was the **Son of God**.
> MATTHEW 27:54

Other Divine Sonship Titles of Jesus
- Beloved Son (Matthew 3:17)
- Only Begotten Son (John 3:16)
- Son of the Blessed (Mark 14:61)
- Son of the Father (2 John 3)
- Son of the Highest (Luke 1:32)
- Son of the Living God (Matthew 16:16)
- Son of the Most High God (Mark 5:7)

a declaration of victory over the forces of sin and death. He had accomplished the work that His Father had commissioned Him to do.

SON OF JOSEPH

After Jesus miraculously fed the five thousand (see John 6:2–11), He claimed to be the spiritual bread that had come down from heaven (see John 6:32–33). But the Jewish religious leaders rejected this claim. Instead, they attempted to discredit Jesus in the eyes of the crowd by pointing out that they knew His parents. To them, He was only the Son of Joseph, not a special messenger from God.

Jesus was the Son of Joseph, but not in the sense that these religious leaders had in mind. Jesus had no human father; He was conceived in his mother's womb by the Holy Spirit (see Luke 1:35). Technically, He was Joseph's stepson or his adopted son.

The Gospel records tell us very little about Joseph. But the few facts we do have make it clear that he was a person of sterling character. At the time that Joseph learned that Mary was pregnant, they were already engaged to be married. He prepared to break the engagement (see Matthew 1:19), but an angel assured him that Mary had not been unfaithful to him and that her baby was of divine origin (see Matthew 1:20). To Joseph's credit, he believed this explanation—one that must have seemed like a fairy tale—and married Mary (see Matthew 1:24).

Jesus grew up like any normal Jewish boy. Apparently, he learned the trade of carpentry and woodworking from Joseph (see *Carpenter* above). Mark 6:3 refers to an event, soon after Jesus launched His public ministry, in which Jesus is called a carpenter. In this verse, Mary and Jesus' four half-brothers are mentioned, but nothing is said about Joseph. This has led to speculation that Joseph may have died during Jesus' youth. If this is true, Jesus, as Mary's firstborn son, may have assumed responsibility for His family's welfare from an early age.

SON OF MAN

Jesus used this name for Himself when He responded to a man who promised to become His disciple. He wanted this would-be follower to know that serving Him as the Son of Man would require sacrifice.

And they said, Is not this Jesus, the **son of Joseph**, whose father and mother we know? how is it then that he saith [NIV: how can he now say], I came down from heaven?
JOHN 6:42

And Jesus said unto him, Foxes have holes, and birds of the air have nests; but the **Son of man** hath not where [NIV: no place] to lay his head.
LUKE 9:58

Son of Man is the name that Jesus used most often when referring to Himself. It appears in the New Testament almost one hundred times, most of these in the Gospel narratives, on the lips of Jesus. A careful study of these occurrences reveals that He used the name in three different ways.

1. Sometimes He used Son of Man in a general way, almost as a substitute for the first-person pronoun "I." A good example of this usage is Jesus' response to the person in the verse above.

2. When Jesus predicted His suffering and death, He often spoke of Himself as the Son of Man. For example, He warned His disciples, "The Son of man must suffer many things, and be rejected of the elders and chief priests and scribes, and be slain, and be raised the third day" (Luke 9:22).

3. With this name or title, Jesus often referred to Himself as a person of exceptional authority and power. He made it clear that He was not acting on His own, but under the authority of God the Father. When the Pharisees criticized Him for healing on the Sabbath, He told them, "The Son of man is Lord also of the sabbath" (Mark 2:28).

Now we know *how* Jesus used the title; but the *why* is not as easy to explain. Perhaps He wanted to show His total identification with humankind. The Son of Man came to earth as a man—our brother and fellow sufferer—to deliver us from our bondage to sin.

SON OF MARY

This is the only place in the New Testament where this name of Jesus appears. It was spoken by the citizens of Nazareth, Jesus' hometown. They could not believe that the boy who had grown up in their midst could be the Messiah and Great Prophet sent from God. They knew Him only as a carpenter and the son of Mary.

Son of Mary as a title for Jesus is unusual, because a man in Bible times was usually identified by His father's name (for example, "Isaiah the son of Amoz," Isaiah 1:1). Jesus' designation as the Son of Mary in this verse lends support to the view that His father Joseph had died while Jesus was a boy (see *Son of Joseph* above).

Mary knew from the very beginning that Jesus, who was conceived in her womb by the Holy Spirit, was God's special

Is not this the carpenter, the **son of Mary**, the brother of James, and Joses, and of Juda, and Simon? and are not his sisters here with us? And they were offended [NIV: took offense] at him.
MARK 6:3

gift to the world (see Luke 1:26–38). But she apparently brought Him up like any normal boy (see Luke 2:52). Mark 6:3 shows that she had other sons and daughters, who were born by natural means after Jesus' miraculous conception. But Jesus, as her firstborn son, must have had a special place in her heart.

Mary knew about Jesus' special powers, because she told the servants at a wedding feast where the wine had run out, "Do whatever he tells you" (John 2:5 NIV). Jesus responded to her confidence in Him by turning plain water into wine—His first miracle, as reported in John's Gospel.

Did Mary realize that her firstborn was destined to be executed like a common criminal? We don't know. But the Bible does tell us that she was at the execution site when Jesus was nailed to the cross. One of the last things Jesus did before He died was to make arrangements for Mary's welfare. With the words, "Behold thy mother," He instructed His disciple John to take care of her. John reports in his own Gospel, "From that hour that disciple took her unto his own home" (John 19:27).

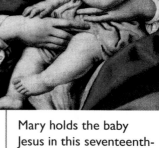

Mary holds the baby Jesus in this seventeenth-century painting by Sassoferrato.

Mary and the Manger

The Christmas hymn "Gentle Mary Laid Her Child," by Joseph Simpson Cook, reminds us that the Savior of mankind came into the world like an ordinary baby with a human mother.

Gentle Mary laid her Child
Lowly in a manger;
There He lay, the undefiled,
To the world a stranger:
Such a Babe in such a place,
Can He be the Saviour?
Ask the saved of all the race
Who have found His favor.

SON OF THE BLESSED. See *Son of God.*

SON OF THE FATHER. See *Son of God.*

SON OF THE HIGHEST. See *Son of God.*

SON OF THE LIVING GOD. See *Son of God.*

SON OF THE MOST HIGH GOD. See *Son of God.*

SON OVER GOD'S HOUSE. See *Son over His Own House.*

SON OVER HIS OWN HOUSE

One purpose of the book of Hebrews is to show that Jesus Christ is superior to the religious laws and regulations and the sacrificial system of the Old Testament. These verses are part of an argument by the writer of the book that Jesus is superior to Moses, the great deliverer and lawgiver of God's people in Old Testament times.

Moses was faithful in his house, or the household of God's people of faith. But he was nothing more than a servant in this house. But Jesus was a Son over His Own House, or the church that He founded by His sacrificial death. Because a son who rules *over* a household is superior to a servant *in* that house, this means that Jesus is superior to Moses.

These verses refer to a time in the wilderness when Moses' brother and sister, Aaron and Miriam, questioned his leadership over the people of Israel. God put an end to their rebellion by pointing out that Moses was His true prophet, "who is faithful in all mine house" (Numbers 12:7).

But no matter how faithful Moses had been to God, Jesus was even more so. He was God's own Son, who gave His life to set people free from their bondage to sin. All Christians are blessed by the faithfulness that Jesus demonstrated to God's redemptive plan.

And Moses verily was faithful in all his house, as a servant, for a testimony of those things which were to be spoken after [NIV: testifying to what would be said in the future]; but Christ as a **son over his own house**; whose house are we, if we hold fast the confidence [NIV: hold on to our courage] and the rejoicing of the hope firm unto the end [NIV: the hope of which we boast].
HEBREWS 3:5–6
[NIV: **son over God's house**]

SPIRITUAL ROCK

These verses from the apostle Paul reminded the Jewish people of their wilderness wandering years after their deliverance from slavery in Egypt. God guided them with a cloud, signifying His presence (see Exodus 13:21), and He gave them safe passage through the Red Sea with the Egyptian army in hot pursuit (see Exodus 14:21–27).

In the dry and barren wilderness, God also provided water for His people. It gushed from a rock when Moses struck it with his staff at God's command (see Numbers 20:8–11). Paul picked up on this rock imagery and described Jesus as the Spiritual Rock who meets the needs of God's people. Just as the rock in the desert was the source of water for the Israelites, so also Christ guides and protects those who place their trust in Him.

Was Jesus actually present with the Israelites in the wilderness? Paul declares that Christ their Spiritual Rock "followed them." Or was Paul speaking metaphorically? We can't say for sure. We know that Jesus existed with God the Father from eternity, before the world was created (see John 1:1–3). He came to earth in human form many centuries after the Israelites left Egypt. But He had the power to assume any form He desired at any time.

Maybe it's best to leave this argument to the theologians and scholars. But one thing we can say for sure is that Jesus is a modern day Spiritual Rock, who quenches our thirst and provides strength and stability for daily living. That's all we as Christians really need to know.

All our fathers were under the cloud, and all passed through the sea. . .and did all drink the same spiritual drink: for they drank of that **spiritual Rock** that followed them: and that Rock was Christ.
1 CORINTHIANS 10:1–4

En Avdat in the Wilderness of Zin. It was in the Wilderness of Zin where Moses, in his anger at the quarreling of the Israelites, struck the rock and water gushed forth and God "showed himself Holy among the people."

STANDARD FOR THE NATIONS.
See *Ensign for the Nations*.

STAR OUT OF JACOB

This is another name assigned to the coming Messiah by Balaam, a pagan magician who blessed the Israelites (see *Sceptre out of Israel* above). The Messiah would be a Star out of Jacob, who would rule over His people with great power and authority.

The nation of Israel is sometimes referred to in the Bible as "Jacob" because it sprang from the twelve sons, or tribes, of the patriarch Jacob. A star was considered the symbol of an exceptional king. For example, Joseph had a dream in which the sun and moon and eleven stars bowed down to him (see Genesis 37:9). The eleven stars symbolized his brothers, who did eventually fall on their faces before him. This happened several years after this dream, when Joseph became a high official in Egypt (see Genesis 43:26; 44:14).

When Jesus was born in Bethlehem, a bright star appeared in the eastern sky to mark the occasion. This star guided the wise men from the east to the place in Bethlehem where He was born (Matthew 2:2–9).

The word *star* is tossed around loosely in our time. We have rock stars, movie stars, and superstars in every sport from badminton to wrestling. But the name of Jesus will live on long after all these pseudo-stars have disappeared. His eternal reign as the Star out of Jacob is assured by none other than God the Father: "And the seventh angel sounded; and there were great voices in heaven, saying, The kingdoms of this world are become the kingdoms of our Lord, and of his Christ; and he shall reign for ever and ever" (Revelation 11:15).

STONE; STONE OF STUMBLING.
See *Chief Cornerstone; Head of the Corner*.

SUN OF RIGHTEOUSNESS. See *Dayspring from on High*.

SUNRISE FROM ON HIGH. See *Dayspring from on High*.

I shall see him, but not now: I shall behold him, but not nigh [NIV: near]: there shall come a **Star out of Jacob**, and a Sceptre shall rise out of Israel, and shall smite [NIV: crush] the corners of Moab, and destroy all the children of Sheth.
NUMBERS 24:17

SURE FOUNDATION. See *Foundation*.

SURETY OF A BETTER TESTAMENT.
See *Mediator of the New Testament*.

TEACHER. See *Master; Teacher Come from God*.

TEACHER COME FROM GOD

This name of Jesus was spoken by Nicodemus, a wealthy and respected Pharisee who wanted to learn more about Jesus and His teachings. He had probably heard about Jesus from others in the region of Galilee. To his credit, Nicodemus did not judge Jesus based on hearsay. He sought to talk with Him face-to-face before deciding what to make of this teacher and miracle worker from Nazareth.

The Gospels contain many references to Jesus' ministry as a teacher. In this role, He communicated God's message to individuals, such as Nicodemus, as well as to large groups of people (see Mark 4:1). He was also a patient teacher with His disciples, who were slow to understand His mission of redemptive suffering (see Luke 24:45–47).

Jesus was an effective Teacher Come from God because of His teaching style. He did not focus on abstract theories, but on down-to-earth truths that the common people could understand. He used familiar objects from everyday life— birds, flowers, sheep, salt, bread, water, light—to connect with the life experiences of His audience. He told stories, or parables, to illustrate divine truths He wanted the people to understand and act upon.

> The same came to Jesus by night, and said unto him, Rabbi, we know that thou art a **teacher come from God**: for no man can do these miracles that thou doest, except God be with him.
> JOHN 3:2

Some Subjects on Which Jesus Taught
- Eternal life (Matthew 22:9–10; John 7:37–38)
- Faith (Matthew 14:27, 31; Luke 17:6, 19)
- Forgiveness (Mark 11:25–26; Luke 17:3–4)
- Holiness (Matthew 5:8; Luke 1:74–75)
- Kingdom of God (Matthew 13:11–50; Luke 22:29–30)
- Love (Matthew 18:15; John 13:34–35)
- Money (Mark 12:43–44; John 6:27)
- Prayer (Matthew 6:9–13; John 14:13–14)
- Service (Matthew 20:28; Luke 22:27)
- Wisdom (Mark 4:12; John 6:45)

But the most impressive thing about Jesus' teaching is that it was stamped with the power of God the Father. Jesus did not quote learned rabbis from the past to authenticate His words, as was the custom among the religious teachers of His day. He made it clear that He spoke under direct commission from God Himself. The people were "amazed at his teaching, because his message had authority" (Luke 4:32 NIV).

Good teachers work with their students to be sure they understand what they've learned.

TREASURE OF ALL NATIONS. See *Desire of All Nations.*

TRIED STONE. See *Chief Cornerstone.*

TRUE. See *Faithful and True.*

TRUE BREAD FROM HEAVEN. See *Bread.*

TRUE GOD. See *God.*

TRUE LIGHT. See *Light.*

TRUE VINE. See *Vine.*

TRUE WITNESS. See *Faithful and True Witness.*

TRUTH

Jesus used this name for Himself in a conversation with His disciple Thomas. This is the only place in the New Testament where Jesus is referred to as the Truth.

We usually use the word *truth* in referring to words or speech. For example, we might pay a compliment to a friend by saying, "She always tells the truth." This use of the word certainly applies to Jesus. He always spoke the truth to His disciples and to others, even when they had a hard time accepting it. This was especially the case with His statements about His coming death (see Matthew 16:21–22).

But beyond speaking the truth, Jesus *acted out* the truth in His life and ministry. And even more importantly, He *was* and *is* the Truth, because He is the ultimate reality in the universe. This is the sense in which Jesus referred to Himself as the Truth in His conversation with Thomas.

We live in a world in which it is sometimes hard to nail down the truth. Our materialistic society tries to convince us that money and possessions are the essence of truth and the way to the good life. Some people say that learning or knowledge is the ticket to the truth. Others believe that each person has to find truth for himself by constructing it from his own life experiences. What is truth for one person may not be truth for another, these people say, because there is no such thing as absolute truth.

These modern theories remind us of Pilate, the Roman governor who pronounced the death sentence against Jesus. When Jesus told him that He had come into the world to "bear witness unto the truth" (John 18:37), Pilate asked sarcastically, "What is truth?" (John 18:38). The Truth stood so close to Pilate that he could touch it, but he missed it because of his unbelief.

What a tragedy! And what an accurate picture of a sinful and unbelieving world—the arena into which we as Christians are sent to bear witness of the Truth (see Mark 16:15).

> Jesus saith unto him, I am the way, the **truth**, and the life: no man cometh unto the Father, but by me.
> JOHN 14:6

Jesus as the Truth
- "Then they that were in the ship came and worshipped him, saying, Of a truth thou art the Son of God" (Matthew 14:33).
- "Ye shall know the truth, and the truth shall make you free" (John 8:32).
- "And if I say the truth, why do ye not believe me?" (John 8:46).
- "When he, the Spirit of truth, is come, he will guide you into all truth" (John 16:13).

UMPIRE. See *Daysman*.

UNSPEAKABLE GIFT. See *Gift of God*.

VINE

I am the **vine**, ye are the branches: He that abideth [NIV: remains] in me, and I in him, the same bringeth forth much fruit: for without me [NIV: apart from me] ye can do nothing.
JOHN 15:5.

Vineyards of antiquity were common at the time of Christ. The image of the vine stretching out across the ground with multiple branches bearing fruit was something the disciples could easily relate to.

Jesus spoke these words to His disciples during the Last Supper, which He ate with them on the night of His arrest. He knew they would need to be firmly attached to Him as the Vine in order to weather the crisis of His forthcoming execution and death.

The imagery that Jesus used was that of a grapevine. This domestic vine has one main stem with several smaller shoots or runners branching off in all directions. These smaller branches owe their lives to the main stem. They could not live apart from the big vine that is rooted in the ground. In the same way, Jesus' disciples were to stay attached to Him as their Lord and Savior. He as the Vine would sustain and nourish them so they would bear "much fruit" in the days ahead.

The fruit that Jesus mentions probably refers to the witness that they would bear for Him after His resurrection and ascension to God the Father. Most of these disciples, His "branches," abandoned Jesus when He was arrested and executed on the cross (see Matthew 26:56). But after His

resurrection, they regained their courage and continued the work that Jesus had trained them to do (see Acts 1:13–14; 2:42–43).

In the Old Testament, the nation of Israel was often referred to as a vine (see Psalm 80:8; Isaiah 5:2). But the people fell into sin and idolatry, becoming an empty vine that bore no fruit for the Lord (see Hosea 10:1). Jesus, therefore, has become the True Vine (see John 15:1) whom God has sent to bring salvation to His people.

WAY

This is one of only three places in the Gospels where Thomas is mentioned apart from a mere listing of the twelve disciples (see John 11:16; 20:24–29). The context of these two verses shows that Thomas was puzzled by Jesus' statement that He would leave His disciples soon after His death, resurrection, and ascension (see John 14:1–4).

Thomas wanted to know how he and the other disciples could find their way to Jesus after He left. Jesus replied in spiritual terms, assuring him that He was the only Way to their eternal reward, and that Thomas didn't need to know all the details about this destination or how to get there.

This conversation between Jesus and Thomas provides a valuable lesson for modern Christians. Sometimes our curiosity about heaven takes our eyes off the One who has promised to take us there. We wonder where heaven will be. What will our resurrected bodies look like? Will we know our family members and friends? Will heaven's streets be paved with literal gold?

The truth is that we don't know the answers to any of these questions. But we do have a grasp of the most important thing: Jesus is the only Way to that wonderful place. He knows the way there, and we know Him as the Way. So we can relax, put away our road maps, and leave the driving to Him.

> Thomas saith unto him, Lord, we know not whither thou goest [NIV: we don't know where you are going]; and how can we know the way? Jesus saith unto him, I am the **way**, the truth, and the life: no man cometh unto the Father, but by me.
> JOHN 14:5–6

WEALTH OF ALL NATIONS. See *Desire of All Nations*.

WISDOM OF GOD. See *Only Wise God*.

WITNESS. See *Faithful and True Witness*.

WONDERFUL COUNSELOR. See *Counsellor.*

WORD

The prologue of John's Gospel (John 1:1–18), of which this verse is a part, focuses on Jesus as the eternal Son, who existed with God the Father before the creation of the world.

> In the beginning was the **Word**, and the **Word** was with God, and the **Word** was God.
> JOHN 1:1

This verse is an obvious reference to the first three words of the book of Genesis. Just as God was "in the beginning" (Genesis 1:1), so Jesus existed "in the beginning" (John 1:1) as the eternal Word. This Word, who assumed human form to make His dwelling among human beings on earth (see John 1:14), is comparable to the words that God used to speak the universe into being (see Genesis 1:3).

Words are the primary units of language that enable humans to communicate with one another. In the same way, Jesus reveals the will and mind of God the Father to earthbound mortals.

The description of Jesus as the Word is unique to the apostle John's writings. In his first epistle, John declares, "There are three that bear record in heaven, the Father, the Word, and the Holy Ghost: and these three are one" (1 John 5:7). This leaves little doubt that John thought of Jesus as the Word who was the second person of the Trinity.

John continues this imagery in the book of Revelation. He describes Jesus as victorious over all His enemies in the end time: "He is dressed in a robe dipped in blood, and his name is the Word of God" (Revelation 19:13 NIV).

The German monk, Martin Luther, translated the Bible into his native German so others could understand Jesus as "the Word" in their own language.

WORD OF GOD. See *Word.*

WORD OF LIFE. See *Life.*

YOUNG MAN EXALTED FROM AMONG THE PEOPLE. See *One Chosen out of the People.*

PART 3
Names of God the Holy Spirit

The Holy Spirit has fewer names than God the Father and God the Son in the Bible. You will find twenty-six names assigned to the Spirit in this section. But this does not mean that He is less important than the first two Persons of the Trinity.

The Holy Spirit is God's agent who convicts people of sin and leads them to the Father in repentance and confession. He empowers God's people for the task of witnessing, leads them to recognize the truth, and brings honor and glory to Jesus the Son. The Spirit inspired biblical writers to record God's revelation of the scriptures, and He also illuminates our minds to understand the message of the Bible.

ADVOCATE. See *Comforter*.

BREATH OF THE ALMIGHTY

> The Spirit of God hath made me, and the **breath of the Almighty** hath given me life.
> JOB 33:4

This name of the Holy Spirit comes from the long speech that the young man Elihu addressed to Job. He spoke after Job's three friends—Eliphaz, Bildad, and Zophar (see Job 2:11)—had ended their speeches.

Elihu stated that he owed his life to the Breath of God. This is a reference to God's creation of the first man in the Garden of Eden. The Lord "breathed into his nostrils the breath of life; and man became a living soul" (Genesis 2:7). It was God's own breath that brought Adam to life. Even today, our ability to breathe life-giving oxygen into the lungs is evidence of God's care of the physical world through the agency of His Spirit.

The Holy Spirit, or the Breath of God, also energizes Christians in a spiritual sense. Just before His ascension to His Father, Jesus empowered His followers for the task of carrying on His work by breathing on them and charging them to "receive the Holy Spirit" (John 20:22 NIV). This is the same life-giving Spirit that enables Christians in our time to witness to others about God's transforming power.

The Breath of the Spirit

In his hymn "Breathe on Me," Edwin Hatch expresses the prayer of every believer for divine power from the Father through His Spirit.

Holy Spirit, breathe on me,
Fill me with power divine;
Kindle a flame of love and zeal
Within this heart of mine.
Breathe on me, breathe on me,
Holy Spirit, breathe on me;
Take thou my heart, cleanse every part,
Holy Spirit, breathe on me.

COMFORTER

Jesus spoke these words to His disciples after He told them that His death was drawing near (see John 13:33). He would no longer be with them in a physical sense, but He was not leaving them alone. He would send a Comforter, the Holy

Spirit, to fill the void caused by His own return to the Father in heaven after His resurrection.

Notice that Jesus referred to the Holy Spirit as "another" Comforter. The Greek word He used means "another of the same kind." This implies that Jesus Himself was the other or first Comforter of His disciples and He was sending another like Himself to serve as His stand-in. So close and personal would be the presence of the Holy Spirit that it would seem as if Jesus had never left.

The Greek word behind Comforter is *parakletos*, meaning "one called alongside." This is the same word translated as "Advocate," one of the names of God the Son (see 1 John 2:1; see also, *Advocate* in part 2, Names of God the Son). In addition to "Comforter" and "Advocate" as rendered by the King James Version, this word is translated as "Counselor," "Companion," "Guide," "Helper," "Instructor," or "Teacher" by other English versions of the Bible.

When Jesus promised that the Comforter will come "alongside" us, He meant that the Holy Spirit would help us in our times of need. If we are lost and stumbling, He will serve as our Guide. If we are discouraged, He will lift us up. If we are confused, He will bring wisdom and understanding. If we are mired in grief, He will sustain us with His presence. The Comforter will be there for us when we need Him most.

COUNSELOR. See *Comforter.*

ETERNAL SPIRIT

The Gospels make it clear that the Holy Spirit guided and empowered Jesus throughout His public ministry. For example, Jesus was led by the Spirit into the region of Galilee, where He began to teach and heal (see Luke 4:14). He cast demons out of people "by the spirit of God" (Matthew 12:28). And this verse from the book of Hebrews shows that the Holy Spirit—described here as the Eternal Spirit—gave Jesus the determination and strength to offer His life as a sacrifice to atone for our sins.

This is the only place in the Bible where the phrase "Eternal Spirit" appears. It clearly identifies the Holy Spirit as a divine being. Only the three persons of the Trinity—Father, Son, and Holy Spirit—are eternal. Everything else is created matter.

And I will pray the Father, and he shall give you another **Comforter**, that he may abide with you for ever.
JOHN 14:16
[NASB: **Helper**; NIV: **Counselor**; NRSV: **Advocate**]

How much more shall the blood of Christ, who through the **eternal Spirit** offered himself without spot to God, purge [NIV: cleanse] your conscience from dead works [NIV: from acts that lead to death] to serve [NIV: so that we may serve] the living God?
HEBREWS 9:14

The eternality of the Holy Spirit is evident in the very first book of the Bible. As God began to mold and shape the universe, "the Spirit of God moved upon the face of the waters" (Genesis 1:2). Thus, the Spirit of God existed with God before time began and participated with Him in the creation of the world. The Bible makes it clear that Jesus was also involved with His Father in the Creation (see John 1:1–3). So Creation was an activity in which all three Persons of the Godhead played an active role.

The Creative Work of God's Spirit

- "The spirit of God hath made me, and the breath of the Almighty hath given me life" (Job 33:4).
- "By the word of the LORD were the heavens made; and all the host of them by the breath of his mouth" (Psalm 33:6).
- "Thou sendest forth thy spirit, they are created: and thou renewest the face of the earth" (Psalm 104:30).

FREE SPIRIT

> Create in me a clean heart, O God, and renew a right spirit within me. . . . Restore unto me the joy of thy salvation; and uphold me with thy **free spirit**.
> PSALM 51:10, 12
> [NASB, NIV, NRSV: **willing spirit**]

David's prayer for forgiveness in Psalm 51 is one of the most eloquent prayers in the Bible. He had plotted the murder of Uriah, the husband of Bathsheba, to cover up his sin of adultery, which had resulted in her pregnancy (see 2 Samuel 11:1–17). David's great sin had separated him from God. He prayed for the restoration of this relationship ("a right spirit") through a movement of God's Spirit, which he described as God's Free Spirit.

The Holy Spirit of God might be described as "free" in two distinct senses.

He is free because His presence is offered freely by God the Father to those who accept His Son Jesus as Savior and Lord. We can't buy God's grace and forgiveness (see Acts 8:18–20; Ephesians 2:8). But He offers it willingly to those who repent of their sins and commit themselves to His lordship over their lives.

The Holy Spirit is also free in the sense that He is not bound by our expectations. God is sovereign; He does not have to wait for our permission before He acts in His world. Sometimes, His actions take us by surprise. For example, it took a while for the early church to realize that the gospel was meant for all people, not just the Jews. The famous vision of the apostle Peter on the roof of Simon the tanner convinced him that he "should not call any man common or unclean" (Acts 10:28).

This insight came to Peter from the Holy Spirit, who brought many Gentiles to saving faith in Jesus Christ. The work of God's Free Spirit is evident throughout the book of Acts. So powerful is the Spirit's work in this New Testament book that it is often called "The Acts of the Holy Spirit" rather than "The Acts of the Apostles."

We should be grateful that God's Free Spirit is not limited by time or circumstances. He kept on working until He convicted us of our sin, drove us to our knees in repentance, and brought us into God's kingdom.

Peter encountered the Free Spirit that is not bound by expectations when he was told to eat the "unclean" animals at Simon the Tanner's house, as shown in this painting from the St. Peter's Monastery in Jaffa.

Free as the Wind

This is how Jesus described the work of the Holy Spirit as God's Free Spirit to Nicodemus: "The wind bloweth where it listeth, and thou hearest the sound thereof, but canst not tell whence it cometh, and whither it goeth: so is every one that is born of the Spirit" (John 3:8).

GOOD SPIRIT

This verse describes the provision of God for the Israelites in the wilderness after their release from slavery in Egypt. These words were spoken by Levites in Nehemiah's time who led the people to renew the covenant with God the Father. They described the Holy Spirit as God's Good Spirit.

Because the very essence of God is goodness, He showered His people with goodness during the perilous years of their wandering in the wilderness. He led them by His presence in a cloud and fire, encouraged them with His promise of a land of their own, and instructed them in how to live,

> Thou gavest also thy **good spirit** to instruct them, and withheldest not [NIV: did not withhold] thy manna from their mouth, and gavest them water for their thirst.
> NEHEMIAH 9:20

through the laws that He delivered to Moses. Through His Good Spirit, God provided many good things for His people.

God is still the God of goodness who provides abundantly for us through His Spirit. He expects us to exemplify this spirit of goodness to others. The apostle Paul told the believers at Rome: "I. . .am persuaded of you, my brethren, that ye also are full of goodness, filled with all knowledge, able also to admonish one another" (Romans 15:14).

HELPER. See *Comforter.*

HOLY GHOST

This farewell speech of the apostle Paul to the elders of the church at Ephesus is one of many places in the King James Version of the Bible where the Holy Spirit is referred to as the Holy Ghost.

> Take heed therefore unto yourselves, and to all the flock, over the which the **Holy Ghost** hath made you overseers, to feed the church of God, which he hath purchased with his own blood.
> ACTS 20:28
> [NASB, NIV, NRSV: **Holy Spirit**]

When the KJV was first published in England in 1611, *ghost* was a word that meant the spirit, or immaterial part of a person, in contrast to the physical or visible body. In modern times, the word *ghost* refers to the shadowy, supernatural appearance of a dead person. All modern translations render the KJV's "Holy Ghost" as "Holy Spirit."

HOLY ONE

The name Holy One is applied to God the Father and Jesus the Son (see *Holy One* in part 1, Names of God the Father; and part 2, Names of God the Son). In this verse, the apostle John also refers to the Holy Spirit by this name.

> But ye have an unction [NIV: anointing] from the **Holy One**, and ye know all things [NIV: all of you know the truth].
> 1 JOHN 2:20

John makes it clear in this verse that the specific role of the Holy Spirit as the Holy One is to safeguard Christians from erroneous thinking about the nature of Jesus. Some false teachers in John's time were attesting that Jesus was the divine Son of God, but denying that He had come to earth in human form. To them, He only *seemed* to be human. In his second epistle, the apostle John also declares that Jesus was both fully human and fully divine (see 2 John 7) .

The word *unction* in this verse from 1 John means "anointing." Thus, John declares that the Holy One anoints or fills believers with the truth about Jesus. We know "all things"—or the only thing we really need to know—about Jesus and His nature as the God-man who came into the world as the Mediator between God and man.

HOLY SPIRIT OF GOD

These words from the apostle Paul to the believers at Ephesus emphasize several important truths about the Holy Spirit.

It is clear from this verse that the Holy Spirit can be grieved or pained by the sinful actions of Christians. This shows that the Holy Spirit is not a vague, ethereal force, but a person. Only a person can experience emotions such as grief and sorrow. Thus, we should speak of the Spirit not as "it" but as "He." He is as much a person as God the Father and Jesus the Son.

This verse also emphasizes the *sealing* work of the Holy Spirit. A seal symbolizes ownership and security. The seal of the Holy Spirit upon us as Christians marks us as God's property until the day of our total and final redemption in the end time (see Romans 8:23).

If some actions by Christians grieve the Holy Spirit, it follows that certain acts and attitudes bring Him joy and pleasure. These include the fruit of the Spirit in the apostle Paul's famous list in Galatians 5:22–23 (see sidebar). Paul contrasts these positive attributes with works of the flesh that he lists in Galatians 5:19–21. The fruit that we bear as Christians should issue from the influence of the divine Spirit in our lives rather than from our fleshly human nature.

> Let no corrupt communication [NIV: unwholesome talk] proceed out of your mouth, but that which is good. . .that it may minister grace unto the hearers. And grieve not the **holy Spirit of God**, whereby ye are sealed unto the day of redemption. EPHESIANS 4:29–30

Paul's List of the Fruits of the Spirit (Galatians 5:22–23)

- Love
- Joy
- Peace
- Longsuffering
- Gentleness
- Goodness
- Faith
- Meekness
- Temperance

HOLY SPIRIT OF PROMISE

This is the only place in the Bible where the Holy Spirit is called by this name. The apostle Paul used it in his long greeting to the church at Ephesus—the congregation that he founded and where he spent more than two years (see Acts 19:1–12). Paul wanted these Ephesian Christians to

In whom ye also trusted, after that ye heard the word of truth, the gospel of your salvation: in whom also after that ye believed, ye were sealed with that **holy Spirit of promise**.
EPHESIANS 1:13
[NIV, NRSV: **promised Holy Spirit**]

realize what a treasure they had received in the Holy Spirit of Promise.

This is an appropriate name for the Spirit, because of the revelation given to the prophet Joel about six hundred years before Paul's time. God promised through Joel that He would pour out His Spirit "upon all flesh. . .and also upon the servants and upon the handmaids in those days will I pour out my spirit" (Joel 2:28–29).

God's Spirit was active among God's people in Old Testament times, but the Spirit seemed to be given only to select leaders for accomplishing specific tasks (see *Spirit that Was upon Moses* below). God's promise through Joel was that in the future He would place His Spirit as a constant presence in all His people.

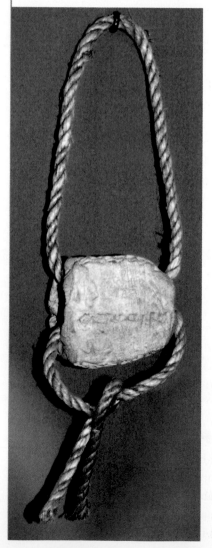

Seals, like this ancient Sumerian seal, were used to authenticate the authority of the one who used it. Today, God uses the Holy Spirit as His seal, authenticating that we belong to Him.

During Jesus' earthly ministry, He renewed this promise of God the Father. Jesus told His disciples that He would send the Spirit as a *Comforter* (see above) to them after He had ascended to the Father. His Spirit would fill them with power so they could continue His work through the church after He was gone (see John 14:16, 26; Acts 1:8).

Both these promises of the coming of the Spirit—from Joel and Jesus—were fulfilled on the Day of Pentecost. The sound of a "rushing mighty wind" and the settling of "cloven tongues as of fire" on each of the apostles left no doubt that they had been filled with the Holy Spirit (see Acts 2:2–3). This gave them confidence and power and turned them into bold witnesses for Jesus Christ.

The Holy Spirit is also the Spirit of Promise because of what He provides for Christians of all generations. Paul declares in this verse that all believers are sealed by the Spirit.

This "sealing" is a reference to the process by which documents were authenticated in Bible times. A king would stamp a decree or official proclamation with his royal seal to show that it had been issued under his authority. This order was to be obeyed because it came from the highest authority in the land.

Our sealing by the Holy Spirit at our conversion shows that we belong to Jesus Christ. We have His irrevocable promise that He will abide with us forever—in this life and the life beyond. When the Spirit stamps us with His seal, we are safe and secure in God's love.

NEW SPIRIT

Just as Jeremiah is known as the prophet of the new covenant (see Jeremiah 31:31–34; see also, *Husband* in part 1, Names of God the Father; and *Mediator of the New Testament* in part 2, Names of God the Son), so, too, Ezekiel might be called the prophet of the New Spirit. This name of the Holy Spirit is unique to him, and he uses it three times in his book (see also Ezekiel 11:19; 18:31).

The word *new* does not mean that God would give His people the Holy Spirit for the first time at some time in the future. The Holy Spirit was active with God the Father in the Creation and among selected people in Old Testament times. *New Spirit* refers to the spiritual redemption that God would provide for His people through His love and grace. God's Spirit would bind believers to Him in a new covenant sealed with the blood of Jesus Christ.

> A new heart also will I give you, and a **new spirit** will I put within you: and I will take away the stony heart out of your flesh, and I will give you an heart of flesh.
> EZEKIEL 36:26

POWER OF THE HIGHEST

These words of assurance were spoken to Mary, the mother of Jesus, by the angel Gabriel. Although Mary was a virgin, she would give birth to the Son of God. His conception would occur through the action of the Holy Spirit, whom Gabriel described as the Power of the Highest.

No other word describes the work of God's Spirit as well as *power*. Throughout the Bible, this is the dominant feature of His miraculous work.

For example, Saul, as the first king of Israel, learned

> And the angel answered and said unto her, The Holy Ghost shall come upon thee, and the **power of the Highest** shall overshadow thee: therefore also that holy thing which shall be born of thee shall be called the Son of God.
> LUKE 1:35
> [NASB, NIV, NRSV: **power of the Most High**]

firsthand about the overwhelming power of the Holy Spirit. Insanely jealous of David, he sent several assassins to kill him. But the Spirit of God came upon them, causing them to utter prophecies instead of carrying out the king's orders.

Finally, Saul himself went to murder David, but the same thing happened to him (see 1 Samuel 19:19–24). He fell into a prophetic trance, and the people asked, "Is Saul also among the prophets?" (1 Samuel 19:24). King Saul was the most powerful man in Israel, but he was no match for the Holy Spirit and His power. God's Spirit protected David, who had been selected by the Lord to succeed Saul as king.

In the New Testament, when Jesus prepared to ascend to His Father, He told His disciples, "Ye shall receive power, after that the Holy Ghost is come upon you: and ye shall be witnesses unto me both in Jerusalem, and in all Judea, and in

Painting from the Church of the Annunciation in Nazareth depicting the angel Gabriel informing Mary that the Power of the Highest will overshadow her.

Samaria, and unto the uttermost part of the earth" (Acts 1:8).

As Jesus promised, the Holy Spirit empowered His disciples and other early Christians to carry out the Great Commission. The initial outpouring of the Holy Spirit occurred on the Day of Pentecost (see sidebar), transforming the followers of Jesus into bold witnesses for Him. Their zeal in preaching the gospel is described throughout the book of Acts. From the Jews to the Samaritans to the Gentiles, the good news about Jesus spread like a roaring forest fire until it reached the very center of the Roman Empire, the capital city of Rome (see Acts 28:14–31).

But the Holy Spirit has not restricted His work to that long-ago time. He is still at work in our day and age through those who follow Jesus as Lord and Savior. God the Father will do His work through us as Christians: "Not by might, not by power, but by my spirit, saith the LORD of hosts" (Zechariah 4:6).

Holy Spirit Power at Pentecost (Acts 2:1–4)

"And when the day of Pentecost was fully come, they were all with one accord in one place. And suddenly there came a sound from heaven as of a rushing mighty wind, and it filled all the house where they were sitting.

"And there appeared unto them cloven tongues like as of fire, and it sat upon each of them. And they were all filled with the Holy Ghost, and began to speak with other tongues, as the Spirit gave them utterance."

POWER OF THE MOST HIGH. See *Power of the Highest*.

PROMISED HOLY SPIRIT. See *Holy Spirit of Promise*.

SEVEN SPIRITS

This reference to the Holy Spirit as Seven Spirits is puzzling to many Bible students. We know from the apostle Paul's writings that the Holy Spirit is one. He declared to the believers at Corinth, "By one Spirit are we all baptized into one body" (1 Corinthians 12:13). So how could the apostle John

> John to the seven churches which are in Asia: Grace be unto you, and peace, from him which is, and which was, and which is to come; and from the **seven Spirits** which are before his throne; and from Jesus Christ, who is the faithful witness.
> REVELATION 1:4–5

in these verses from Revelation claim that the Holy Spirit is seven in number?

The best explanation is that John used the number seven to emphasize the fullness and completeness of the Holy Spirit. Seven was considered the perfect number in Bible times, and it appears often throughout the Bible to symbolize wholeness and perfection (see Deuteronomy 16:15; Matthew 18:21–22). John uses the number in this sense many times throughout Revelation: seven candlesticks (1:12), seven stars (1:16), seven seals (5:1), seven horns (5:6), and seven eyes (5:6).

SPIRIT OF ADOPTION

In this verse, the apostle Paul compares our situation before we become believers to the new status we enjoy after our conversion. The old life is comparable to that of a slave in bondage, with no rights or privileges. But after coming to new life in Christ, we have all the advantages of sonship as children of God the Father.

> For ye have not received the spirit of bondage again to fear; but ye have received the **Spirit of adoption**, whereby we cry, Abba, Father.
> ROMANS 8:15
> [NIV: **Spirit of sonship**]

Paul uses the concept of adoption to emphasize our new status with God. We were once children of sin, but God delivered us from our bondage and adopted us as His own. So close is our relationship to God as our adoptive Father that we can call Him "Abba," an Aramaic word equivalent to our modern "Daddy" or "Papa" (see *Abba, Father* in part 1, Names of God the Father).

The Holy Spirit has a vital role in this adoption process. His presence in our lives assures us that we belong to God.

Adoption brings diverse people together into a unified family.

The Spirit will never let us forget that we enjoy a position of dignity and honor with Him in the family of God the Father and Jesus the Son.

SPIRIT OF BURNING.

See *Spirit of Judgment/Spirit of Burning.*

SPIRIT OF CHRIST

This is one of those verses in the King James Version that is made even more impressive by a modern translation. The New International Version renders it like this: "You, however, are controlled not by the sinful nature but by the Spirit, if the Spirit of God lives in you. And if anyone does not have the Spirit of Christ, he does not belong to Christ."

The first dramatic truth emphasized by this verse is that the Holy Spirit is both the Spirit of God and the Spirit of Christ. This is a bold affirmation that Jesus was one with the Father, yet distinct from Him at the same time. Our minds have a hard time taking in this concept, but this is the clear teaching of the Bible.

The apostle Paul also declares in this verse that the Holy Spirit is a gift of God's grace that transforms us when we accept Jesus as Savior and Lord. Paul even goes so far as to say that the presence of the Holy Spirit in our lives is proof of our salvation, showing that we "belong to Christ."

This name for the Holy Spirit—Spirit of Christ—also shows that He was closely connected with Jesus' earthly ministry and that He continues to empower the church to continue Jesus' work in our time. The Holy Spirit enabled the prophets to foresee the coming of Jesus into the world (see 1 Peter 1:10–11). The Spirit unites the church, Jesus' body, to Him as the head of the church (see 1 Corinthians 12:12–13). The Holy Spirit causes us as Christians to grow more and more like the Lord whom we serve (see 2 Corinthians 3:18).

Two similar names that Paul uses for the Holy Spirit are Spirit of God's Son (Galatians 4:6) and Spirit of Jesus Christ (Philippians 1:19).

> But ye are not in the flesh, but in the Spirit, if so be that the Spirit of God dwell in you. Now if any man have not the **Spirit of Christ**, he is none of his.
> ROMANS 8:9

SPIRIT OF COMPASSION. See *Spirit of Grace and Supplications.*

SPIRIT OF COUNSEL AND MIGHT

The prophet Isaiah in this passage looks more than six hundred years into the future and predicts the coming of the Messiah. This great leader among God's people would be filled with God's Spirit, to whom the prophet refers as the Spirit of Counsel and Might.

All of us have known people who love to give us their

And the spirit of the LORD shall rest upon him, the spirit of wisdom and understanding, the **spirit of counsel and might**, the spirit of knowledge and of the fear of the LORD.
ISAIAH 11:2
[NASB: **spirit of counsel and strength**; NIV: **Spirit of counsel and of power**]

Sixth-century fresco of the Apostle Paul discovered in a cave in the hills overlooking the harbor of Ephesus. The early Church recognized that Paul's life exemplified someone who lived by the Spirit of Faith.

advice and counsel—at no charge! And we know others who are people of action. But how many people do you know who can tell you what to do and then fill you with the strength to accomplish their advice? People like this are a rarity, but Isaiah declares that work like this is just a routine "day at the office" for the Holy Spirit.

The Holy Spirit knows what we should do to bring our lives into line with God's will. He warns us about the dangers of temptation. But He also gives us the strength to resist temptation. When we do stumble and fall, He assures us of our restored relationship with God, when we confess our sins before God the Father and Jesus the Son.

Counsel *and* might. This unusual combination of skills is just one more proof of God's love for His people.

SPIRIT OF FAITH

This is the only place in the New Testament where the Holy Spirit is called the Spirit of Faith. It is no accident that it appears in the writings of the apostle Paul, who has more to say about faith than any other New Testament writer (see sidebar).

To understand this verse from 2 Corinthians, we need to consider Paul's famous statement in the book of Ephesians about the centrality of faith: "For by grace are ye saved through faith; and that not of yourselves: it is the gift of God: not of works, lest any man should boast" (Ephesians 2:8–9).

Notice that Paul does not say that we are saved *by* faith, but *through* faith. It is Christ's sacrifice on the cross that saves us; we claim this sacrifice for ourselves by placing our faith in Him as our Savior and Lord. Faith is our human response to His sacrifice, which we must exercise before we can experience forgiveness for our sins and find new life in Jesus Christ.

If human faith is an essential element of the salvation process, how do we have such faith? Paul's answer is that saving faith is a work of the Holy Spirit—the Spirit of Faith. He alone can convict us of sin and lead us to declare our faith in Jesus Christ as our Savior. Without the movement of the Holy Spirit to kindle faith in our hearts and minds, we would remain hopelessly lost in our sin.

> We having the same **spirit of faith**, according as it is written, I believed, and therefore have I spoken; we also believe, and therefore speak.
> 2 CORINTHIANS 4:13

Paul: The Apostle of Faith

- "Therefore being justified by faith, we have peace with God through our Lord Jesus Christ" (Romans 5:1).
- "I am crucified with Christ: nevertheless I live; yet not I, but Christ liveth in me: and the life which I now live in the flesh I live by the faith of the Son of God, who loved me, and gave himself for me" (Galatians 2:20).
- "I have fought a good fight, I have finished my course, I have kept the faith" (2 Timothy 4:7).

SPIRIT OF FIRE. See *Spirit of Judgment/Spirit of Burning.*

SPIRIT OF GLORY

The apostle Peter may have been thinking back to the time when Jesus told His disciples what to do when they were persecuted for following Him. They were to "take no thought how or what ye shall speak: for it shall be given you in that same hour what ye shall speak. For it is not ye that speak, but the Spirit of your Father which speaketh in you" (Matthew 10:19–20).

In effect, Jesus told them not to retaliate against or resist their persecutors, but to trust the Holy Spirit—the Spirit of

> If ye be reproached [NIV: insulted] for the name of Christ, happy [NIV: blessed] are ye; for the **spirit of glory** and of God resteth upon you: on their part he is evil spoken of, but on your part he is glorified.
> 1 PETER 4:14

Glory—to take care of them and give them the words to say in rebuttal. The same Spirit that guided Jesus throughout His ministry would also abide with the disciples, strengthening them to serve as Jesus' bold witnesses.

The Spirit of Glory does not desert us during our times of persecution. He honors us for our sacrificial suffering in God's service, just as He gloried Jesus by raising Him from the dead (see 1 Peter 3:18).

SPIRIT OF GOD

These verses describe Jesus' baptism by John the Baptist at the beginning of His public ministry—an event reported by all three Synoptic Gospels (see also Mark 1:9–11; Luke 3:21–22).

But Matthew's Gospel is the only one of the three that calls the Holy Spirit who descended upon Jesus the Spirit of God. This is a common name for the Spirit in the Old Testament (see 1 Samuel 11:6; Job 33:4), but it appears only a few times in the New Testament (see Romans 8:9; 1 Corinthians 2:11).

Perhaps Matthew used this name for the Holy Spirit because he wanted to emphasize that Jesus was empowered directly by God Himself when God sent His Spirit upon His Son. Matthew's Gospel is also known for its portrayal of Jesus as the fulfillment of Old Testament prophecy. And the coming of the Spirit upon Jesus at His baptism fulfilled Isaiah's prophecy about the Messiah that "the spirit of the LORD shall rest upon him" (Isaiah 11:2).

One of the most interesting things about this passage is Matthew's description of God's Holy Spirit "descending like a dove" and alighting on Jesus. As a spirit being, the Holy Spirit is invisible. The only other time in the Bible when the Spirit appeared in visible form was on the Day of Pentecost, when He appeared to the apostles as "cloven tongues like as of fire" and settled on "each of them" (Acts 2:3).

Was the visible appearance of the Holy Spirit on this occasion God's way of assuring Jesus of His power and presence? Possibly. But Jesus had been conscious of His unique mission from an early age (see Luke 2:48–50).

Did the Holy Spirit actually look like a dove, or was Matthew using symbolic language? Matthew says the Spirit descended "like a dove," but Luke's account says the

And Jesus, when he was baptized, went up straightway out of the water: and, lo, the heavens were opened unto him, and he saw the **Spirit of God** descending like a dove, and lighting upon him. And lo a voice from heaven, saying, This is my beloved Son, in whom I am well pleased.
MATTHEW 3:16–17

Spirit came down "in a bodily shape like a dove upon him" (Luke 3:22).

Maybe we're trying a little too hard to make sense of the details in this passage and missing the real message that Matthew was trying to get across. Here's the double-edge bottom line: (1) God was pleased to send His Son into the world as His personal representative on a mission of redemption. (2) This mission was so important that God empowered Jesus with His own Spirit for the task.

Relief from the Church of the Annunciation in Nazareth depicting the Spirit of God descending on Jesus in the form of a dove after His baptism by John the Baptizer.

Names that Associate the Spirit with God

- "For it is not ye that speak, but the **Spirit of your Father** which speaketh in you" (Matthew 10:20).
- "Forasmuch as ye are manifestly declared to be the epistle of Christ ministered by us, written not with ink, but with the **Spirit of the living God**" (2 Corinthians 3:3).
- "And when they were come up out of the water, the **Spirit of the Lord** caught away Philip, that the eunuch saw him no more: and he went on his way rejoicing" (Acts 8:39).
- "The **Spirit of the Lord God** is upon me; because the Lord hath anointed me to preach good tidings unto the meek; he hath sent me to bind up the brokenhearted, to proclaim liberty to the captives, and the opening of the prison to them that are bound" (Isaiah 61:1).

SPIRIT OF GOD'S SON. See *Spirit of Christ.*

SPIRIT OF GRACE. See *Spirit of Grace and Supplications.*

SPIRIT OF GRACE AND SUPPLICATIONS

The prophet Zechariah in this verse looks into the future to the coming of the Messiah, the one "whom they pierced"—

> And I will pour upon the house of David, and upon the inhabitants of Jerusalem, the **spirit of grace and of supplications**: and they shall look upon me whom they have pierced, and they shall mourn for him, as one mourneth for his only son.
> ZECHARIAH 12:10
> [NRSV: **spirit of compassion and supplication**]

a clear reference to the crucifixion of Jesus. Along with the Messiah, God the Father would also send the Holy Spirit, whom Zechariah describes as the Spirit of Grace and Supplications.

The Holy Spirit is the Spirit of Grace because He convicts people of their sin and leads them to place their faith in Jesus Christ (see John 16:8–11). No one can earn God's grace or purchase His indwelling Spirit. He gives His grace and His Spirit generously to those who confess His Son Jesus as Savior and Lord.

Supplication is a distinct form of prayer in which a person is keenly aware of his sin and he cries out to God for forgiveness. Jesus commended the unrighteous publican or tax collector because he prayed, "God be merciful to me a sinner" (Luke 18:13). The Holy Spirit is the Spirit of Supplications because He leads us to drop our self-righteous pride and throw ourselves on the mercy and grace of God for forgiveness and restoration.

SPIRIT OF HIS SON. See *Spirit of Christ.*

SPIRIT OF HOLINESS. See *Holy Spirit of God.*

SPIRIT OF JESUS CHRIST. See *Spirit of Christ.*

SPIRIT OF JUDGMENT/SPIRIT OF BURNING

This verse from the prophet Isaiah emphasizes the Holy Spirit's work as Judge. His twin titles—Spirit of Judgment and Spirit of Burning—show that He is active with God the Father and Jesus the Son in exercising divine judgment against sin and rebellion.

> When the Lord shall have washed away the filth of the daughters of Zion, and shall have purged the blood of Jerusalem from the midst thereof by the **spirit of judgment**, and by the **spirit of burning**.
> ISAIAH 4:4
> [NIV: **spirit of judgment and spirit of fire**]

Isaiah speaks in this verse about the Spirit's judgment against the sinful nation of Judah, but the three Persons of the Trinity have the authority to exercise judgment against sin wherever it is found.

The name Spirit of Burning depicts divine judgment as a fire. Most of us think of fire in negative terms because of the destruction it can cause. But fire can also purify, as it does when ore is heated to separate useless dross from a precious metal such as silver. We as Christians should pray for the Spirit of Burning to convict us of our sin, refine our lives, and shape us into instruments of usefulness in God's service.

These names of God the Holy Spirit are similar to names by which God the Father and God the Son are known. God is called a Consuming Fire (Hebrews 12:29), and Jesus is described as a Refiner's Fire (Malachi 3:2).

Judgment throne at the ancient site of Dan in northern Israel.

SPIRIT OF KNOWLEDGE AND THE FEAR OF THE LORD

These two names of God the Holy Spirit are among six that the prophet Isaiah uses in this one verse. This in itself is unusual, but another striking feature of the verse is that the prophet groups these names together into three sets of two names each. Perhaps he thought of these sets of two as names that were closely related to each other.

So how do the Spirit of Knowledge and the Spirit of

And the spirit of the LORD shall rest upon him, the spirit of wisdom and understanding, the spirit of counsel and might, the **spirit of knowledge and of the fear of the LORD**.
ISAIAH 11:2

the Fear of the Lord relate? Isaiah may have had in mind a well-known verse from the book of Proverbs: "The fear of the LORD is the beginning of knowledge" (Proverbs 1:7 NIV). In the Bible "fear of the Lord" means respect or reverence for God. Thus, this proverb declares that a healthy respect for God is the most important attitude for a person to have as he accumulates the knowledge he needs in order to be happy and successful in life.

Through His Spirit, God plants in our hearts a reverence for Him that leads us to honor God in our lives. This is the foundation on which we build knowledge and understanding through the continuing influence of His Spirit.

This is what happened with the prophet Daniel in the Old Testament. When he was a young man, He was taken into captivity after his native Judah fell to the Babylonian army. Trained for service as an administrator in the Babylonian government, he managed to remain faithful to God while rendering service to a pagan king. Even his captors recognized that "an excellent spirit, and knowledge, and understanding. . .were found in the same Daniel" (Daniel 5:12).

SPIRIT OF LIFE

For the law of the **Spirit of life** in Christ Jesus hath made me free from the law of sin and death.
ROMANS 8:2

This statement of the apostle Paul reminds us of another of his famous declarations about the Holy Spirit in 2 Corinthians 3:17: "Where the Spirit of the Lord is, there is liberty." By the "law of the Spirit of life" in Romans, Paul means the principle by which the Holy Spirit operates.

Life in the Spirit gives us the power to live free from the law, or principle, of sin and death. This does not mean that Christians will never experience death, because physical death is the lot of every human being. Paul means that those who have accepted Jesus Christ as Savior and Lord are no longer in bondage to sin and death. Just as Jesus defeated death, He has promised that all believers will enjoy eternal life with Him.

As the Spirit of Life, the Holy Spirit shares this name with Jesus (see *Life* and *Resurrection and the Life* in part 2, Names of God the Son). Those who have Jesus and the Holy Spirit in their lives are not held hostage by the threat of death.

Tapestry from the school of Raphael in Brussels illustrating the Spirit of Life culminating in the resurrection of Jesus.

Life for the Church

In his hymn "O Spirit of the Living God," Henry H. Tweedy prays that the Holy Spirit would continue to empower the church for its work in the world.

> *O Spirit of the living God,*
> *Thou light and fire divine,*
> *Descend upon thy church once more,*
> *And make it truly thine.*
> *Fill it with love and joy and power,*
> *With righteousness and peace;*
> *Till Christ shall dwell in human hearts,*
> *And sin and sorrow cease.*

SPIRIT OF MIGHT. See *Spirit of Counsel and Might.*

SPIRIT OF POWER. See *Spirit of Counsel and Might.*

SPIRIT OF PROPHECY

The apostle John, author of the book of Revelation, fell in awe before an angel at the throne of God. The angel told John not to worship him but to worship God and His Son, Jesus Christ. The angel went on to identify the Holy Spirit, who bore witness of Jesus as the Spirit of Prophecy.

The coming Messiah was often spoken of by the prophets of the Old Testament. This insight did not come to them

Mosaic above the chapel entrance of the Cave of the Apocalypse on the island of Patmos depicting John's dictation of his vision recorded in the book of Revelation.

through the power of their intellect but by direct revelation of God through the agency of His Holy Spirit.

These inspired prophecies were not restricted to the Old Testament. When Simeon saw the infant Jesus in the temple, He declared that He was the long-awaited Messiah whom God had finally sent to His people. This truth was revealed to Simeon by the Holy Spirit (see Luke 2:25–27).

SPIRIT OF REVELATION. See *Spirit of Wisdom and Revelation.*

SPIRIT OF SONSHIP. See *Spirit of Adoption.*

SPIRIT OF STRENGTH. See *Spirit of Counsel and Might.*

SPIRIT OF SUPPLICATION. See *Spirit of Grace and Supplications.*

SPIRIT OF THE FATHER. See *Spirit of God.*

SPIRIT OF THE FEAR OF THE LORD. See *Spirit of Knowledge and the Fear of the Lord.*

SPIRIT OF THE LIVING GOD. See *Spirit of God.*

SPIRIT OF THE LORD. See *Spirit of God.*

SPIRIT OF THE LORD GOD. See *Spirit of God.*

SPIRIT OF TRUTH

This is one of three places in the Gospel of John where Jesus refers to the Holy Spirit by this name (see also John 14:16–17; 15:26–27). In all three cases, He was explaining to His disciples that He would soon be leaving them to return to the Father. But they would continue to feel His presence through the operation of the Spirit of Truth in their lives.

One dimension of truth is "accordance with fact." In other words, do the facts support a specific statement or claim, proving it to be true? But the word *truth* can also refer

> And I fell at his feet to worship him. And he said unto me, See thou do it not: I am thy fellowservant, and of thy brethren that have the testimony of Jesus: worship God: for the testimony of Jesus is the **spirit of prophecy**.
> REVELATION 19:10

> Howbeit when he, the **Spirit of truth**, is come, he will guide you into all truth: for he shall not speak of himself; but whatsoever he shall hear, that shall he speak: and he will shew you things to come.
> JOHN 16:13

to something that is enduring or authentic, in contrast to something that does not last or is artificial or of little value.

The second meaning of *truth* is what Jesus had in mind when He spoke of the Holy Spirit as the Spirit of Truth. His disciples would discover that the Spirit was enduring and dependable. He would never leave them or forsake them. When all else crumbled and faded away, the Spirit would continue to empower their lives.

In John 15, Jesus tells His disciples that the Spirit of Truth would also help them bear witness of Him "because ye have been with me from the beginning" (John 15:27). The memory of Jesus' physical presence would eventually grow dim in their minds. But the Holy Spirit would help them recall His life and teachings and pass these truths on to others. This is exactly what happened in the book of Acts as the apostles bore witness about Jesus to people who had not seen Him in the flesh.

But even the disciples would not live forever. To preserve a record of Jesus' life, they recorded, under the inspiration of the Holy Spirit, what they remembered about Jesus. They also repeated these stories to other early Christians, who faithfully wrote down these eyewitness accounts. These records were passed on to future generations through the written Gospels of the New Testament. All believers are beneficiaries of their faithful witness.

Jesus was right. The Spirit of Truth is eternal. He is still revealing the truth about Jesus almost two thousand years after His death, resurrection, and ascension. Though we have not seen Jesus in the physical sense, we feel His presence through the work of His Spirit.

SPIRIT OF UNDERSTANDING. See *Spirit of Wisdom and Revelation.*

SPIRIT OF WISDOM AND REVELATION

This name of the Holy Spirit—Spirit of Wisdom and Revelation—from the apostle Paul is striking because of its combination of three important ingredients of the spiritual life: wisdom, revelation, and knowledge.

Revelation is the process by which God makes Himself known to man. Our human minds would know nothing about God unless He had chosen to reveal Himself to us. He has done this supremely through the written scriptures.

The writings that make up the Bible were revealed by God. But He inspired human beings through the activity of His Spirit to understand these divine messages and to write them down. "No prophecy of Scripture came about by the prophet's own interpretation," the apostle Peter declares. "For prophecy never had its origin in the will of man, but men spoke from God as they were carried along by the Holy Spirit" (2 Peter 1:20–21 NIV).

Through the inspired scriptures, we gain knowledge about God—His nature as Creator, Sustainer, and Redeemer. But the Spirit teaches us more than factual information about God. We come to know Him in a personal sense as the God who loved us enough to send His own Son, Jesus Christ, to save us from our sins.

Finally, wisdom is one of the ministries of the Holy Spirit in our lives. Wisdom is the ability to apply the facts to practical situations. Knowing the truth, and applying and living the truth, are two different things. The Holy Spirit gives us the wisdom to honor God in the way we live out our faith in the real world.

Another name of the Holy Spirit that is similar to Spirit of Wisdom and Revelation is Spirit of Wisdom and Understanding (Isaiah 11:2). In addition to inspiring human beings to write down God's revelation in the Bible, the Holy Spirit works with us as we read these writings. He opens our understanding so we can comprehend and apply God's message to our lives. With the Holy Spirit as our Helper and Guide, the Bible is always as fresh and meaningful as the nightly television newscast.

SPIRIT THAT WAS UPON MOSES

During the exodus from Egypt, the Israelites often frustrated Moses, their leader who had been selected by the Lord. Finally, Moses grew tired of their constant bickering and the burden of solo leadership. He needed others to help him with the task of hearing complaints and settling disputes. "I am not able to bear all this people alone," he told the Lord, "because it is too heavy for me" (Numbers 11:14).

God responded by instructing Moses to select seventy elders with leadership skills from among the tribal leaders of

> That the God of our Lord Jesus Christ, the Father of glory, may give unto you the **spirit of wisdom and revelation** in the knowledge of him.
> EPHESIANS 1:17

And the LORD came down in a cloud, and spake unto him, and took of the **spirit that was upon him [Moses]**, and gave it unto the seventy elders: and it came to pass, that, when the spirit rested upon them, they prophesied, and did not cease.
NUMBERS 11:25

the people. Then He empowered them for their assignment as Moses' assistants by filling them with the Spirit that was upon Moses. The same Spirit of God that enabled Moses to bear the responsibility of leadership among God's people would strengthen the elders for their work under Moses' supervision.

This account shows that leadership and the Holy Spirit go together like a portrait in a picture frame. God never selects a person for a job without giving him the power through His Spirit to accomplish the task He has called him to do. The Bible is filled with examples of people whom God filled with His Spirit after calling them to serve as leaders of His people (see sidebar).

If God has called you to some important leadership task, you can rest assured that His Spirit will make you equal to the challenge.

Biblical Leaders Who Were Empowered by God's Spirit

- Balaam (Numbers 24:2)
- Joshua (Numbers 27:18; Deuteronomy 34:9)
- Othniel (Judges 3:9–10)
- Gideon (Judges 6:34–35)
- Jephthah (Judges 11:29)
- Samson (Judges 13:24–25; 14:6, 19; 15:14)
- Saul, king of Israel (1 Samuel 10:10; 11:6–7)
- David (1 Samuel 16:13; 2 Samuel 23:1–2)
- Amasai (1 Chronicles 12:18)
- Azariah (2 Chronicles 15:1)
- Zechariah (2 Chronicles 24:20)
- Ezekiel (Ezekiel 2:2; 8:3)
- Micah (Micah 3:8)
- Jesus (Luke 4:14)
- Philip (Acts 8:29)
- Paul and Barnabas (Acts 13:2, 4)

WILLING SPIRIT. See *Free Spirit.*

Scripture references in **bold** indicate the background passages for major articles on divine names included in the book. For example, Genesis 3:15 contains a prophecy about Jesus the Messiah as the *Seed of the Woman*. See the article on this name of Jesus on p. 185. Numbers in *italics* indicate book page numbers.

Collection of the Israel Museum, Jerusalem and Courtesy of the Israel Antiquities Authority, Exhibited at the Israel Museum, Jerusalem: Page 21

Corbis/Alinari Archives: Page 179

Corbis/Araldo de Luca: Page 169

Corbis/Benjamin Lowy: Page 111

Corbis/Bettmann: Pages 85, 126, 159

Corbis/Leonard de Selva: Page 128

Corbis/Pascal Deloche/Godong: Page 139

Corbis/Paul Almasy: Page 148

Corbis/Ron Nickel/Design Pics: Page 104

Corbis/Stefano Bianchetti: Pages 107, 157

Corbis/The Corcoran Gallery of Art: Page 67

Corbis/The Gallery Collection: Pages 191, 200

Design Direct: Pages 24, 37, 62, 108, 141, 153

Dr. James C. Martin: Pages 22, 23, 27, 29, 34, 35, 38, 40, 42, 45, 47, 50, 51, 56, 57, 59, 60, 61, 63, 64, 72, 76, 79, 118, 121, 129, 133, 137, 163, 165, 177, 183, 184, 185, 193, 198, 205, 208, 210, 214, 217, 219, 221, 222

Dr. James C. Martin/Illustrated by Timothy Ladwig: Page 168

Dr. James C. Martin/Photographed with permission from The British Museum: Pages 31, 33, 54

iStockphoto: Pages 5, 7, 11, 15, 16, 52, 66, 74, 81, 90, 93, 94, 99, 103, 115, 124, 149, 175, 196, 201, 212

NASA/Hubble Space Telescope/NGC 2207 & IC 2163: Page 19

The British Museum: Page 18